Invisible Privilege

❖　　❖　　❖　　❖　　❖　　❖　　❖　　❖　　❖　　❖　　❖　　❖　　❖

Invisible
Privilege

A MEMOIR ABOUT RACE, CLASS, AND GENDER

Paula Rothenberg

UNIVERSITY PRESS OF KANSAS

In a number of cases, the names of people mentioned in this work have been changed in order to respect their privacy.

Portions of the text previously appeared in *Creating an Inclusive College Curriculum: A Teaching Sourcebook from the New Jersey Project*, ed. Ellen Friedman, Wendy Kolmar, Charley Flint, and Paula Rothenberg (New York: Teachers College Press, 1996), and "Integrating the Study of Race, Gender, and Class: Some Preliminary Observations," *Feminist Teacher* 3, no. 3 (fall/winter 1998); 37–42.

Published by the University Press of Kansas (Lawrence, Kansas 66049), which was organized by the Kansas Board of Regents and is operated and funded by Emporia State University, Fort Hays State University, Kansas State University, Pittsburg State University, the University of Kansas, and Wichita State University

Library of Congress Cataloging-in-Publication Data

Rothenberg, Paula S., 1943–
Invisible privilege : a memoir about race, class, and gender / Paula S. Rothenberg.
p. cm.— (Feminist ethics)
ISBN 0-7006-1004-9 (alk. paper)
1. United States—Race relations—Case studies. 2. Racism—United States—Case studies. 3. Social classes—United States—Case studies. 4. Sex role—United States—Case studies. 5. Rothenberg, Paula S., 1943– —Children and youth. 6. Jewish women—United States—Biography. I. Title. II. Series.
E185.615 .R68 2000
305.8'00973—dc21   99-046333

Printed in the United States of America

10 9 8 7 6 5 4 3 2 1

The paper used in this publication meets the minimum requirements of the American National Standard for Permanence of Paper for Printed Library Materials Z39.48–1984.

For my mother

CONTENTS

ACKNOWLEDGMENTS

❖   ❖   ❖

Thanks to the many teachers, friends, acquaintances, colleagues, neighbors, students, and incidental travelers who have contributed to this book in ways that they and perhaps I cannot even imagine. At the risk of leaving some people out, I offer love and thanks to some dear friends who nourished me both literally and figuratively over the years, sharing good food, strong coffee, moderately good wine, stories and conversation, newspapers, magazines, and themselves: Dorothy and Bob Greenwald, Evelyn and Steve Shalom, Barbara and Daniel Pope. Additional thanks to Barbara for help with the French translations and to Steve for a miscellany of information and technical support.

Thanks to Marcia Treffman for always being there—throughout everything.

Particular thanks to my editor Nancy Scott Jackson for being so supportive of this project, and to Melinda Wirkus and Susan Schott and the other professionals at the University Press of Kansas who made turning the manuscript into printed text an unexpectedly pleasant and professional experience. Thanks to both Claudia Card and Tom Digby for their careful and constructive readings.

Thanks to Karen Jackson Petersen and Gina Lo Saura, my student assistants, who left no stone unturned in the course of their enthusiastic and energetic researching, and to Brandeis University, the New York City Board of Education, and Peter Kriendler of 21 Club, for their time and help tracking down stray pieces of information.

Special thanks to my friend Lois Tigay, who read and commented on a portion of the manuscript when I was feeling very discouraged and who was always willing to talk things through with me; to Jane

Lazarre, who was kind enough to read the manuscript during another tough time; to Judy Baker, for her years of support and friendship; to my brother, Stu Rothenberg, who put his doubts aside—at least long enough to help me reconstruct a few pieces of family history. I hope he will have no regrets. And to Naomi Miller for her friendship, good sense, punctuation, and everything else.

My daughter Andrea has been my unfailing, unflagging cheerleader and sounding board throughout the lengthy process of bringing this manuscript into print—she has cheered my successes and refused to accept my setbacks—and has never stopped believing that this book would come to be. Her boundless energy and zest for living have kept a smile on my face. My son Alexi has underwritten the entire process with his deep and abiding love, his steady presence, his unfailing example of personal integrity, and his unshakable belief in me. He refused to let me become discouraged, and he was always there when I needed him. Both of them bring joy and meaning to my life and give me hope for the future. My partner Greg Mantsios has done all those things you might expect—and more. He makes forever seem too short.

PROLOGUE

A major East Coast bank provides some of its customers with a service called "privileged checking." Those who qualify are allowed to write checks in amounts that exceed their balance with the assurance that they will not bounce. In many ways, this service stands as a metaphor for the kinds of invisible privilege some people in our society enjoy because of their class position, their race or ethnicity, their gender, or some combination of all three. The beneficiaries of a history of privilege, they are able to draw on a seemingly inexhaustible supply of credit to bankroll whatever initiatives they undertake. This provides them with advantages that most other people do not enjoy and provides their children with a head start in the race of life.

This book uses incidents in my own life to examine some of the ways in which privilege is constructed in our society and to uncover the forces that often render it invisible to those who benefit from it most. In this respect, it follows the work of Peggy McIntosh, Jane Lazarre, Maureen Reddy, and others who have sought to come to terms with the ways in which white skin privilege colors every aspect of a person's life, and it responds to the challenge implicitly offered by bell hooks in *Teaching to Transgress* when she writes: "Curiously, most white women writing feminist theory that looks at 'difference' and 'diversity' do not make white women's lives, works, and experiences the subject of their analysis of 'race.'"* Instead of limiting myself to an examination of race, I have chosen to attempt a kind of anatomy of privilege in all its complexity. As in my anthology *Race,*

---

*bell hooks, *Teaching to Transgress* (New York: Routledge, 1994), p. 103.

Class, and Gender in the United States, I have tried to capture the subtle and complex ways in which issues of race, class, and gender intersect to weave a fabric of knots, tangles, and webs that each of us must negotiate every day. While the anthology is the result of many years of thinking and teaching about these issues, this book grows out of a deeply felt need to reflect in a more personal way on what it means to be a privileged white woman coming to terms with that privilege and acquiring some deeper understanding of the ways in which race, class, and gender difference is constructed in contemporary U.S. society.

When I announced my intention to edit an anthology on "racism and sexism" in 1984 (the first edition of the text was marketed under the title "Racism and Sexism in a Changing America"), my partner, Greg Mantsios, counseled against it. He worried that as a white feminist, I would be leaving myself open to all sorts of criticism by claiming "expertise" on issues of race. But I believe that racism is a white problem and that white people have a special responsibility for undoing the damage that has been done in our name and to our advantage. This means that white people *must* talk about race. The real issue for us is not *whether* but *how* to do so. (This is similar to the problem men face when they choose to address "women's issues.") In my own case, I see my primary audience as other white people, and I see my task as using the privilege I am able to draw upon to get a hearing for things that are not always said. I believe it is essential that white people ask hard questions about the distribution of privilege and power in this society and acknowledge the ways in which we benefit from racism. I try to use my public place and space to do this whenever possible. I have both a responsibility to do this because of my whiteness

_____

*Peggy McIntosh, "White Privilege and Male Privilege: A Personal Account of Coming to See Correspondences Through Work in Women's Studies" (Working Paper 189, Wellesley College Center for Research on Women, Wellesley, MA, 1988), and "White Privilege: Unpacking the Invisible Knapsack," *Peace and Freedom*, July/August 1989, pp. 10–12; Jane Lazarre, *Beyond the Whiteness of Whiteness: Memoir of a White Mother of Black Sons* (Durham, NC: Duke University Press, 1996); Maureen T. Reddy, *Crossing the Color Line: Race, Parenting, and Culture* (New Brunswick, NJ: Rutgers University Press), 1994; Paula Rothenberg, *Race, Class, and Gender in the United States* (New York, St. Martin's Press, 1998).

and my privilege, and I have a need to do this in order to make sense of the immediate world in which I live. Surrounded by well-intentioned white liberals, I need to understand why those who continually draw on their privileges (at the expense of others) so often fail to recognize them—consistently confusing what they have come to expect with what they have a right to demand.

The first five chapters of this book examine the particular ways in which race, class, and gender privilege have shaped my own life. These chapters are not meant to serve as an autobiography in the traditional sense. No attempt is made to detail all the events of my life during this period. Instead, through a selective reporting of experience, I try to provide a picture of the ways in which these factors shape and focus an individual life—providing privileges in some respects while creating obstacles and erecting barriers in others. For example, while my parents' wealth and connections could gain me entrance to a New York City private school, they could not protect me from the consequences of the sexism that was rampant in education during the 1940s and 1950s. And while that wealth might buy me a private school education, the fact that I was only a girl in a family with money but not unlimited means, ensured that I would attend a relatively mediocre private school designed to service children of the middle class, in contrast to the more expensive and more rigorous boys' country day school that catered to children of the upper class selected by my parents for my brother, their only son.

The first two chapters are about growing up in New York City during the 1940s and 1950s as the girl child in an upper-middle-class, white, Orthodox Jewish family. This was a family trying to negotiate the contradictions that arose from being "Orthodox," "modern," and reasonably well off in cosmopolitan New York during the middle of the twentieth century. Although I did not understand it at the time, throughout my childhood, my parents were struggling to reconcile their desire for upward mobility with their commitment to retaining their Jewish heritage. We worshiped at a strictly Orthodox synagogue (no "temples" for us), but other parts of our life took place in other venues entirely.

Committed to observing the strict dietary laws of kashruth at home—which forbid eating pork and shellfish and require separate sets of dishes, silverware, and pots and pans to avoid mixing dairy and meat products—our family nonetheless enjoyed dinners out at some of New York's most fashionable restaurants, including the 21 Club, the Oak Room at the Plaza Hotel, and the (newly opened) Four Seasons. My fashionably dressed mother wore suits by Mollie Parness and Christian Dior, two of the better known designers of the day, but she still rendered her own chicken fat several times a year for use in the chopped liver and the matzoh ball soup that, along with calf's-foot jelly, were childhood staples. Each year, in preparation for the Jewish High Holy Day of Yom Kippur, we carefully prepared stacks of toilet paper so that after sundown we would not violate the injunction against performing any kind of physical labor by tearing sheets from the roll—a practice typical of only the most observant Jews—and yet my brother and I attended secular private schools, not yeshivas. Growing up fairly insulated in New York's Upper West Side Jewish community during the 1940s and 1950s, I rarely had to face anti-Semitism directly, but growing up Orthodox in a community of Conservative and Reform Jews, I often felt different and inferior.

The third chapter focuses on my years as a female undergraduate and graduate student, beginning in September 1960 when I entered the University of Chicago and ending in 1966 at the time I received my master's degree in philosophy from New York University. Reflecting on my college and university days—after years of reading and teaching about racism and sexism in education, and thinking about the ways in which education reproduces rather than subverts class stratification—provides me with an opportunity to interrogate that experience. Having recently gone through the process of choosing colleges with both my son, Alexi, and my daughter, Andrea, I am horrified when I reflect on the selection process that resulted in my attending the University of Chicago—probably the singularly worst school in the country I could have chosen for myself. No wonder I dropped out after four quarters, narrowly avoiding being asked to leave.

Throughout these first chapters, I frequently look back at the way privilege and lack of privilege shaped the lives of each of my parents, with special emphasis on my mother's early and very privileged, but very narrow, upbringing. My parents came from different worlds. She grew up in relative luxury on New York's Riverside Drive, surrounded by polished woods and servants. He was the youngest of four children raised in relative poverty on the Lower East Side. By the time my mother and her parents had begun to despair of making a good match for her, my parents were introduced by mutual friends at a Jewish resort hotel. They married six months later—without ever really having gotten acquainted.

My mother was raised to live in a world of wealth and grace: a world she inhabited briefly as a child, a world that has never existed for most people, and a world that did not exist for her adult self. My father probably exceeded his own expectations of financial success when he rose to the position of vice president in his brother's textile firm. But what looked like a lot to him never came close to what she once had, and the Orthodox Judaism that both filled and circumscribed my father's life merely circumscribed hers once she married into it.

In the course of telling these stories, particularly in the early chapters, I have deliberately chosen to move back and forth in time and awareness—sometimes using the voice of one who fails to understand that the world she takes for granted as "everyday life" is in fact already riddled with "privilege," and sometimes using the voice of the narrator years later, when she is capable of making this distinction and commenting on it. At times, that early voice may sound prideful, insensitive, cruel—even racist to some people. This is no accident. It is necessary to hear, see, touch, taste, and smell the way the world looks to people who are blind to their own privilege. We see "others" everywhere but never see ourselves. Because we "mean well," it never occurs to us that the choices we make may have devastating consequences for others. In fact, it is this failure or refusal on the part of so many white liberals of my own generation to identify themselves and their children as the current beneficiaries of privilege that fascinates me today. Here are people who once marched, sang, and chanted for social justice and who now fight with equal passion to preserve the institutions that replicate racism and class divisions—thereby guaranteeing that their own children will continue to benefit from race, class, and gender privilege. They refuse to acknowledge that the unfair advantages they jealously guard for their own children ensure that other peoples' children will have less. I have tried to capture this myopia at various moments in the story, in the hope that some reader might recognize her/himself in these pages and be moved to engage in similar reflection.

The fourth chapter begins in the summer of 1965 when I taught my first college classes at the now defunct University Heights campus of New York University. It includes these early teaching experiences, my years as a Ph.D. candidate at NYU, and my relationship with American philosopher Sidney Hook—a disciple of John Dewey and one of my mentors. It ends during the early 1970s. These were the years during which the Vietnam War, the black power movement, and soon after, the women's liberation movement, called into question fundamental assumptions and practices in virtually every area of individual and collective life for many of us. Things we had taken as fundamental truths about gender roles, relations between the races, citizenship, sexuality, and the nature of the family were exploding around us. The war and these movements form the background against which I tell the story of my personal journey, a journey in the course of which I came to redefine what it meant to me to be a teacher, scholar, educator, and activist. In addition to being my story, it is also the story of thousands of others who came to embrace feminist practice and liberatory pedagogy during that period.

The fifth chapter focuses on events surrounding the publication of my college text, *Race, Class, and Gender in the United States,* one of the first diversity texts published during the contemporary period. Shortly after it appeared, the book was attacked by a string of conservative journalists and public figures, including syndicated columnist George Will; Lynn Cheney, chair of the National Endowment for the Humanities; and right-wing educators who were often members of the National Association of Scholars, a group committed to "defending" the traditional curriculum against multicultural and gender curriculum reform. The attention these attacks brought to the book turned me, for a brief period, into a public figure who was often called on to give on- and off-screen interviews and commentary on events of the day. In this chapter, I reflect on the reaction to the book's publication and some of the questions that were raised for me as a white woman and a feminist by the public role into which I found myself propelled.

In the sixth chapter, I turn my attention to the dynamics of race, class, and gender privilege as they have played themselves out in the lives of my own children and their classmates and friends in Montclair, New Jersey, the town in which we live. In particular, I look at the way people in our town reacted to a modest proposal to detrack a single course in the high school during the early 1990s. Montclair, an affluent, integrated, northern New Jersey suburb located a half-hour bus ride from midtown Manhattan, has long been touted as a model of how to achieve racial balance in public schools by using voluntary busing and a magnet school system. In the early 1990s, it became clear that while the schools in Montclair are integrated, the classrooms are not. A long-standing, often invisible, practice of tracking by race and class perpetuates the privileges of some and virtually ensures the failure of others. This chapter is an attempt to understand opposition to a plan to detrack the high school and to a related proposal to implement a multicultural curriculum in the ninth-grade English program. In it, I explore the anger and confusion of opponents of the plan, a group of self-defined white liberals of good intentions who consciously choose to live in an integrated community but who are unable to identify or compromise their own privilege in the interest of fairness or justice. These are the people we once would have counted on to make integrated public schools work. They are the first to be appalled by blatant expressions of racism or other forms of hatred. They consistently vote for the progressive candidate (Montclair was one of a very few towns that voted for George McGovern in 1972), worry about the ozone layer and about child labor in the Third World, turn out to raise funds for every sort of liberal cause—but are blind to the ways in which their personal life choices consistently reinforce their own privilege and perpetuate institutionalized racism in the town's public schools. Because I am white and I understand that I could so easily have been one of them, I am compelled to understand how privilege gets constructed in ways that render it invisible to basically decent people who should know better.

An epilogue brings the story full circle as it briefly chronicles the death of each of my parents as a victim and beneficiary, simultaneously, of the various forms of privilege that have been examined throughout this book. My father spent the last ten years of his life in an expensive nursing home, where the long-term effects of Parkinson's disease left him increasingly helpless and disoriented. My mother, a lifelong smoker, died of lung cancer, in her bed at home, determined to avoid the depersonalized care that hospitals offered. In the end, each of them was entirely dependent on the care and kindness of women of color, working as nurse's aides, who fed, washed, changed, and soothed them. But in the end, their dollars bought them only the kind of care that one might expect from people who are forced to work long hours for low pay, at jobs that our society holds in contempt. My parents exercised their privilege right up to the end, but, ironically, in the end, it didn't buy them very much.

1

A Jewish Girlhood

❖ ❖ ❖ ❖ ❖ ❖ ❖ ❖ ❖ ❖ ❖ ❖ ❖ ❖ ❖

As the first and, for a while, only child of upper-middle-class, Orthodox Jewish parents growing up in New York City, race and class privilege came easily to me, but it was gender that was always problematic. I understood in some vague way that it would have been preferable had I been born a boy, but my parents were well off and certainly wanted to do well by their children. Because my brother was not born until six years after me, the privileges that ordinarily would have accrued to him as the *male* child in a *Jewish* home went to me as the *only* child in an *upper-middle-class* home—a case of class winning out over gender, and clearly to my advantage. But what about race?

Certainly I knew many people who were not white, and I felt sorry for them—just as I pitied those born poor or with physical disabilities. On the other hand, it never occurred to me that I was white because my whiteness was coextensive with my membership in the human race. In the world in which I lived, human beings had no race—which is to say—they were white, just as they had no class—which is to say, they were all materially well off. The only caveat was, of course, that human beings had no gender either—which is to say, they were all men. I have spent much of my adult life trying to make sense of the paradoxes that arise from the intersections of race, class, and gender privilege as they have shaped my life and the lives of others.

Far from being absolute and unmalleable, privilege is a quixotic thing—hard to pin down. It ebbs and flows, depending on a host of variables. At another time and in another place, perhaps, my parents would have found the birth of a *girl* child so burdensome that they would have simply abandoned me or sold me into marriage as an infant. While infanticide is no longer an acceptable way of dealing with girl children in most countries, in many places it has been replaced with the systematic neglect of daughters, a neglect so severe that in some countries girls between the ages of two and four die at nearly twice the rate of boys.* Even in the United States, white women who bear children out of wedlock are twice as likely to keep the child if it is a boy. But I was fortunate; I was born into a family that did not have to choose which of its children to feed and clothe, or which would receive medical treatment and which would die from neglect. In this respect, a potential fate for others of my gender was mitigated by my class.

While we were far from "wealthy," my family certainly would have been considered well off by most people. My brother and I attended private schools, and even in my parents' years of declining income, when I mentioned to my mother that I was having trouble with the carburetor in my year-old car, she wondered out loud whether it was worth repairing or whether I should simply get a new one—car, that is. We had an apartment in the city and a house in the country as well as a Buick or an Oldsmobile to take us back and forth between them. Our apartment, especially on the weekends, was filled with fresh flowers—bouquets of white or salmon gladiolas and vases of huge, yellow, pom-pom mums around the Jewish holidays in addition to bowls of rhododendron leaves, pussy willows, forsythia, or lilacs to mark each of the seasons. We lived well and looked "rich," but from the inside, things often felt tentative. Unlike that of those who are truly "wealthy," our family's lifestyle was entirely dependent on my father's salary, which could fluctuate dramatically from year to

---

*This statistic appears in Lori Heise, "The Global War Against Women," in *Feminist Frameworks*, ed. Paula S. Rothenberg (New York: McGraw-Hill, 1993, p. 63).

year and which was not supplemented by inherited wealth or significant income from investments. In good times, there was a lot; in bad times, there was less.

My family's fluctuating prosperity could be inferred throughout my childhood by the size and color of the women who worked for us. My earliest memories are of Odessa, a very dark, heavy-set Black woman who had grown up in the South and who came to work for my family when I was quite young. If pressed to remember her, I would say that she was warm and loving and kind to me. But such descriptions of Black mammies by little white girls are so common as to be trite, almost insulting. And after all, what did I really know of her? She worked for us until I was eight, and I accepted her presence in my world without question, just as I took for granted the furniture in my room and the food on my plate. Years later, when I went through my mother's papers after she died, I found a note from Odessa written in pencil on a piece of torn brown household paper. It offered congratulations on the occasion of my brother's birth, and it was signed "With Respect. Your Maid, Odessa." Mother had kept it for thirty-seven years.

Odessa was followed by a steady stream of "Ethels" and "Eunices," ever lighter, ever thinner Black women who had been born in the United States and who were themselves replaced by women from the Caribbean who carried themselves with considerable dignity and spoke, quite literally, "the King's English." Day workers who left before dinner were replaced by women who stayed to serve the meal and wash up, and they, in turn, were replaced, if only briefly, by a young, white, Canadian woman who wore crisp uniforms, lived in, and spoke French.

Her name was Renée, and she couldn't have been older than twenty-two or twenty-three. She worked for us for three or four months one spring before getting pregnant by a member of a visiting Canadian hockey team that had come to play the Rangers at Madison Square Garden. She lived, of course, in the maid's room off the kitchen—a tiny room with a small window that never saw a bead of sunlight. The window looked out onto a rear courtyard, far from the street, and each morning the garbage cans hobbled their way across the cement as the building's janitor dragged them to the curb. Pigeons made their nests in the dark recesses of a broad ledge outside the window. They made loud nesting sounds early in the morning, and the ledge was always thick with bird droppings that looked to me, when I was a child, like slightly soiled wedding cake frosting.

Until Renée was hired, the room had been used for storage, but in preparation for Renée's arrival, my mother set out to make the room as comfortable as she could. This was not easy. It was a room so tiny that after fitting it with a bed and a dresser, there was no space for a chair. My mother hung a few shelves on the wall above the bed and bought a cheerful bedspread, curtains, and a few brightly colored towels. Always considerate, she replaced the adjoining bathroom's toilet seat with a new one and bought a new rubber mat for the tub. She placed an alarm clock, a small lamp, and a plastic radio on a tiny table that just managed to fit at the head of the bed, and she bought a small TV that was positioned on the bureau at the foot of the bed. I remember being amazed that someone would actually live in that room and being confused by the pleasure my mother seemed to get from furnishing it. Did she really believe that this room could be someone's home?

As it turned out, Renée was found wanting from the start. My mother considered her "slow" and was constantly frustrated by her unwillingness or inability to learn the way my mother wanted things done. I was in my early teens and slightly embarrassed by having to relate to someone so young—and so white—as a servant. As a result, I often tried to pretend that she wasn't there so that I could avoid having to talk to her. Sometimes I felt sorry for her, consigned to that awful room, with only a TV for company—her real life, or so I imagined, limited to Thursday afternoons and all day Sunday. But other times, I resented her for her willingness to live that way and blamed her for it.

Now when I think back to her, I see a young girl from rural Canada with little formal education. Perhaps she wasn't sorry or homesick at all. Perhaps coming to New York to work as a domestic seemed to her the opportunity of a lifetime, or perhaps it represented the end of all her hopes and dreams—after all these years, who can really say? An easy prey for the visiting hockey players, after a few months in my parents' employ, Renée took to spending more and more time in her room, crying. That's how my mother discovered that she was pregnant. And, having made this discovery, she had no choice but to turn her out—or so she said. For months, I tried to imagine what might have happened to Renée after she left our home.

Unlike her treatment of the countless Black women who worked for us before and after Renée, my mother made no attempt to treat Renée as one of the family. I suspect that that was because being white and young, Renée easily could have been. It was unnecessary for my mother to keep her distance from the Black women who worked for us because that distance was already built into their relationship. Within the socially constructed context of white superiority and Negro inferiority of the time, it was convenient for many white people to believe that "Beulah" or "Matilda" was part of the family. In addition to allowing whites to feel good about themselves by dissociating them from the heartless inhumanity of slavery and racism, it rationalized the long hours, low pay, and limitless demands made on Black women servants on the grounds that they were more like family than paid labor. This is not entirely dissimilar from the rationale that has been used for so many years to deny fair pay to all working women—that in contrast to men, women work for pin money, for "extras." In both cases, questions of fair and equitable compensation and treatment don't arise because the assumption is that women work not out of need but in one case out of devotion and in the other, in pursuit of frivolous luxuries. In addition, the pretense that Black women were part of the white family helped render their own families invisible. This made it unnecessary for white women to ask who was caring for their servants' children or to feel guilty about keeping them from their homes. Whites enjoyed the illusion that Black women servants acted out of love for their white families because only love could have justified the unequal nature of the relationship from which whites benefited so greatly. The same might be said of the relationship between women and men within traditional marriages.

In spite of my family's history of privilege, the reality that we were well off but not wealthy meant that over the years, as my father's earning capacity diminished, the live-in maids were replaced once again by weekly help and, finally, by an elderly part-time cleaning woman, Black and U.S. born, who made the trip from Harlem on Tuesdays and Fridays. Verlene became my mother's friend and confidante, and long after she had stopped making the trip and my mother had been forced to move into a studio apartment, the two of them talked on the phone regularly to commiserate over their mutually declining standards of living. By then, my mother said "Negroes" instead of "shwartzas," and she and Verlene, who preferred to speak of "colored people," spent long hours on the phone irate over the Black power movement and the linguistic alterations it recommended.

In each of their communities, my mother and Verlene would have been recognized as genteel women who had suffered a diminution in their social and economic position as a result of their husbands' losses. Verlene was married to a musician; after he became too old and sick to work any longer, her part-time cleaning job made a significant contribution to the family income. In earlier years, her husband had performed with some of the well-known Black bands of the day, and Verlene had had an opportunity to travel with him and see something of the world. (Ironically, something my mother longed to do but had never done.) Like my mother, she was a cultured woman who had seen her position in life decline through no fault of her own. You could almost say their friendship was inevitable. How could my mother ever have asked Verlene to wash her floors?

My parents were registered Republicans with democratic tendencies. They taught me that all people were equal and reacted with horror to the violence they witnessed in the televised coverage of the attempts to integrate the schools in Little Rock in 1957. My mother, who had voted for Eisenhower, faulted him loudly for failing to take early and decisive action to end the conflict and deplored the behavior of southern whites who would attack children just because of their race. At the same time, my parents spent considerable money to send me to private school so that I could avoid going to school with children who were not white.

Unlike my brother's country day school, which boasted a rigorous curriculum, including classes in Latin and Greek for which I yearned, my own school had no redeeming academic virtues. It simply ensured that middle-class Jewish girls and boys would grow up surrounded by one another. This choice of schools, of course, reflected my parents' gender-based assumption that a son was educated to earn a good living and a daughter, to be a good wife and mother.

Ironically, my brother's elite private school was a veritable mini-United Nations that enrolled the sons (but not the daughters) of various U.S. and foreign political and economic leaders. My own school did have a few "Oriental" kids, as we called them, who had been admitted to several of the younger grades. But although I passed them in the halls and in the lunchroom, I do not remember speaking to any of them at any time during my entire high-school career, and I don't remember any other white kids speaking to them either. If I thought about it at all, I would have told you it was fine that they were in the school but, to be perfectly honest, I can't recall that I ever thought about it—that's how irrelevant they were to me. I think I believed that by failing to challenge their presence, I had done as much as could be expected. I see their faces now in my memory and can hardly begin to imagine the cruelty of that awful isolation in which they were confined and the part I played in it.

Although allowed to occupy the margins of the classroom, these Asian children never studied anyone who looked or lived like them, and, of course, neither did most of us. The curriculum was firmly rooted in the white, male, European experience, which was offered up as reality. Girls were forced to see their own adolescence through the eyes of J. D. Salinger, Samuel Butler, Theodore Dreiser, and Samuel Richardson—always object, never subject.

The literature and culture of Latin America, Africa, Asia, even Jewish writers, was virtually absent from our syllabi and bibliographies, although in the early grades we spent one class period each filling in first a map of Africa and then one of South America using bits of cotton, pieces of foil, and other scraps to identify the natural resources of each country. Having completed this survey of resources to exploit, we evidently had learned all that was necessary to know about our neighbors near and far.

Although almost all the children and teachers at the school were Jewish, we celebrated all the Christian holidays with great enthusiasm but always included "Dreidel, Dreidel, Dreidel" as part of the annual holiday sing. The rest of the time, we made paper chains to decorate the Christmas tree and sang "O Tannenbaum." Oddly enough, I don't remember my parents ever objecting. I think that all of us accepted the fact that we lived in a Christian society that legislated a school calendar around Christmas, Easter, and Good Friday rather than Chanukah, Passover, and Succos. Besides, all of us wanted to believe in the illusion of "brotherhood" (*sic*), which was so prevalent then, and that required singing Christmas carols, along with an occasional Negro spiritual, a traditional Spanish folk song, and a token Chanukah melody. Those of us who were not at the center of the curriculum or the culture were simply grateful to be there at all—ever anxious to claim a piece of the core by fitting in. There was nothing to be gained by calling attention to being left out.

Although the streets between Columbus and Amsterdam Avenues on New York's Upper West Side were beginning to be home to a number of Puerto Rican families, there was no danger of any Latin music at my school or any danger of Puerto Ricans either. They went to school several blocks from my apartment house, a world away, in the public school that my father's dollars saved me from attending. After a while, a "Spanish" man was hired as a maintenance worker at our apartment building, but his primary responsibility was to collect the trash and take it down on the rear elevator. He rarely ran the passenger elevator or stood guard at the front door. Lobby duty was reserved for Irish Pat and German Henry.

I began my elementary education, at the age of five, at the local public school on West End Avenue. After four days, for reasons best known to them, my parents became convinced that this was not the right school for their first and only child, and they set out to enroll me in private school. But even in the late 1940s, getting into private school in Manhattan wasn't easy, and doing so on very short notice at the start of the term was almost impossible. Although the school my parents chose for me was hardly prestigious, even it had a long waiting list. To circumvent this unfortunate impediment to my education, my parents, in the first of a series of efforts on behalf of their children's future, called on their privilege to ensure my own. Determined that I would not return to the public school for even one more day, they made calls to their contacts—friends, friends of friends, and business acquaintances—whose children already attended the private school and who were generous in their support of it. Within a matter of days, I found myself standing on the front steps of our apartment building and waiting for the yellow school bus that would transport me across Central Park each morning to the handsome building on the Upper East Side that was to become my school for the next six years.

Throughout my life, my parents would call on these and other contacts as a matter of course to help my brother and me navigate a cumbersome bureaucracy or to provide us with the margin of safety that would guarantee our success. In this way, they were able to secure my brother's admission to his country day school, place each of us in summer jobs that would add to our résumés and enhance our college applications, if not our bank accounts, make sure that each of us got into college, and, finally, circumvent yet another long waiting list to obtain a bed for my father in the nursing home where he would die. Like all people of privilege, my family has always benefited from a special kind of affirmative action that results from a network of well-placed friends, relatives, acquaintances, and business contacts. Because the beneficiaries of this kind of affirmative action believe that they are simply getting what is due them, it remains largely invisible.

Although immersed in my Jewish roots at home and surrounded by Jews everywhere, being Jewish was complicated for me. On the one hand, most of the people I knew as equals were Jewish, so being Jewish was just part of being alive; on the other hand, my family was Orthodox in a world of Conservative and Reform Jews, which meant that we were different in a way that I found uncomfortable and embarrassing. When my classmates, whose parents were Conservative or Reform Jews, missed school for one day because of a Jewish holiday such as Rosh Hashanah or Passover, I was likely to be out for two or four, as required by Orthodox observance. While my classmates might eat matzoh at their Passover seders as a symbolic gesture, I was doomed to an entire week of cardboard box lunches consisting of buttered matzoh and hard-boiled eggs eaten in shame. For one week each year, the glutinous and unappealing food served in my school's cafeteria took on an allure that has rarely been rivaled since.

Like those "Oriental" children to whom I never spoke, I understood what it felt like to be an outsider. The Orthodox practices in our family separated me from my classmates who had learned how to be *American* Jews. Walking the twelve blocks from our apartment house to the synagogue dressed in our High Holy Days best—because we were prohibited from riding in any kind of motor vehicle on the Sabbath—made me feel like a recent immigrant to these shores, even though my suit was from Hattie Carnegie. And my Jewish friends regarded the old-world practices of my family with the same mixture of contempt and morbid fascination that we otherwise reserved for children who were neither white nor well to do. Even those of my friends' parents who must have known better acted as though the rules of kashruth—which prohibit eating pork and shellfish and mixing dairy products with meat—were an incomprehensible embarrassment instead of part of their own recent family history.

My first trip to a Chinese restaurant with Barbara Kurtz and her parents left me literally ill with embarrassment when my friend and her parents discovered that I had never eaten wonton soup, egg rolls, or spare ribs. My eight-year-old self ate them that night, trying hard to enjoy their forbidden delights, caught between shame at my own ignorance and revulsion at the new tastes and textures on my tongue. I liked the feeling of the egg roll's crisp wrapper between my fingers and was mildly aroused by its musky aroma, but it was difficult not to gag on its suspicious mixture of ingredients, which even the sticky sweet duck sauce could not make palatable. I longed to participate in the Chinese restaurant world of Upper West Side normalcy that was denied me by my parents' Orthodox Judaism, but its prohibitions were so deeply etched that even the fortune cookies brought little joy.

Repeated trips to synagogue taught me firsthand that separate most certainly was not equal—even before the Supreme Court handed down *Brown v. Board of Education.* Our family attended the Jewish Center on West Eighty-sixth Street, an orthodox synagogue for Jews with old money. The rabbi was a well-respected scholar named Leo Jung, who always looked to me as though he had just stepped out of a painting by El Greco. And for a time, the assistant rabbi was a young man named Norman Lamm, who would go on to become president of Yeshiva University. Men sat in the central portion of the sanctuary, with women seated behind a wooden partition in elevated rows on either side and tucked away in a balcony at the rear of the *schull.*

From an early age, it was clear to me that my mother was ambivalent about this seating arrangement and about other aspects of Orthodox Judaism. When questioned, she offered me the traditional explanation that women and girls were to sit safely beyond the sight of the men, lest the women's presence distract them from their prayers, but made it clear that she found the practice and the reasoning behind it insulting. Although the seating arrangement was largely symbolic, with the women separate from but clearly visible to the men, its implications were clear. Jewish women had standing in the home, but in the synagogue, they were second-class citizens whose participation was carefully circumscribed. I found this somewhat confusing because boys like my brother, sitting with their fathers, often became bored and frequently fidgeted in their seats or whispered to each other to pass the time. It was difficult to understand why sitting with grown women would be more distracting to the men.

While I was confused and offended by the seating arrangement and felt intimidated by the stern demeanor of the rabbi, the cantor, and my own uncle, who served as president of the congregation, a part of me found it difficult to take the gender hierarchy in Judaism very seriously. My own sense of self-worth was partly derived from my own privileged position in the family, guaranteed by my brother's delayed arrival, and partly derived from my mother's class position, with which I identified. While my father had been raised in a relatively poor Orthodox family, the youngest of four children who were raised by their widowed father, a tailor, my mother's family was considerably better off and considerably less Orthodox. My mother, for example, was raised in a kosher home but often ate in restaurants and hotel dining rooms, enjoying shrimp, lobster, and other, to my mind, "upper-class" delicacies. From an early age, I connected my father's Orthodoxy with his inferior class background and identified with my mother's family's elevated class standing. The gender-based hierarchy of privilege and status dictated by Orthodox Judaism was for me mitigated by the hierarchy of status and privilege to which my mother, but not my father, laid claim by virtue of her family's real-estate holdings. My father went to synagogue on Saturday mornings and often took my brother with him, but my mother and I went to Carnegie Hall on Friday nights to hear Arthur Rubinstein play. Although both halls were located in imposing stone buildings and were similarly appointed with red velvet seat cushions, deeply stained mahogany woods, ceiling frescoes, and burnished brass, and both had markedly similar standards of decorum, to my mind, there was no contest.

As a young girl, I attended a Jewish day camp, Nep-O-Rock, located between Neponsit and Far Rockaway on Long Island. It was there that I made my parents proud by being chosen more often than anyone else to light the Sabbath candles at Friday lunch while reciting the Sabbath prayer. It was there, too, that, at the age of eight, I learned to sit still and not tell while a young male counselor sat me on his lap and stroked the inside of my thigh—his fingers playfully skirting the elastic cuffs on my little girl underpants. After a while, I did tell; but my mother was so angry with me that I have regretted telling ever since.

I began taking religious instruction at the age of five or six, studying Hebrew and religious ritual and culture with a young rabbi who came to the house. In spite of this, and although I dutifully said the Shema Yisrael every night before going to sleep, for as long as I can remember I found it difficult to believe in God or understand why anyone else would. By the time I was nine or ten, the idea of divine punishments and rewards and the bizarre lists of injunctions, responsibilities, and prohibitions that defined all religions made both religion and God seem transparently contrived. On a personal level, the degree of human misery that I knew existed in the world, along with the persistent unhappiness in my own family resulting from my parents' ill-conceived marriage, left me convinced either that there was no God or that the one who existed was hardly worth believing in. The fact that my parents believed in him made me pity them. I wished that they were strong enough to take charge of their own lives and perhaps redeem their futures.

At eleven or twelve, convinced that there was no God, I set out to put my belief to the test by deliberately violating one of the most serious prohibitions in our religion. One Yom Kippur, the holiest time of the year for Jews and a fast day as well, I waited until my family was asleep and then ate a piece of bread—ate it not because I was hungry, but simply because I was defiant. I remember sitting cross-legged ("Indian-style," as we then called it) on my bedroom floor in the dark, waiting for something to happen. No thunder erupted from the heavens; no lightning bolts seared my comforter. I didn't even get sick. Later that year, during Passover, I hid a piece of bread in my room so that I could eat it once the holiday had begun and the prohibition against *chometz* was in place. Again I waited in vain for some sign. When none was forthcoming, I ended my empirical investigation into the matter of God's existence. For the rest of the time I lived in my parents' home, I fasted on Yom Kippur and forsook bread during Passover, but I no longer believed in God or said my prayers. It was not until I went away to college that I transgressed those dietary laws one final time. I spent Yom Kippur night in the cafeteria at Billings Hospital with several other students, nonobservant Jews themselves, consuming an assortment of improbable foods in order to assert my now adult personhood. After that, it wasn't necessary—I did as I chose—but there was no longer the possibility of transgression.

While it was clear to me that my father observed the laws of kashruth and the other requirements of his religion out of fear and with an uncritical, blind faith, I was never sure what motivated my mother, and to this day I still am unclear about the extent and nature of her commitment. My father laid tefillin each morning. He bound each of his arms and several of his fingers with strips of black leather as part of the ritual saying of the morning prayers—an obligation that each Jewish man assumes when he comes of age. Attached to these strips of leather, and to one worn round his head, were small leather boxes containing lines from the Torah. Over his head and around his shoulders was draped a white and blue fringed tallis, or prayer shawl. In my eyes, this process, carried out in the gray light of early morning, transformed him from a warm and loving father into a remote and impersonal figure to whom I dared not speak. From the first moment when he began to wrap the tefillin around his arms, his total allegiance was to the God of his fathers. There was no room for a seven-year-old girl in this schema. As I was growing up, I often stood in the doorway watching him, feeling like an intruder. And, of course, this was true. As a girl child, I knew that that ritual was forever forbidden to me. Sometimes I stepped forward in the hope of attracting his attention. Would he raise his eyes from the prayer book and meet mine or, better still, smile and call to me? But, of course, he never did. Later, when I began to debate outright God's existence with the intellectual arrogance and passionate intensity of a high-school and then a college student, my father found my questioning, even at its most respectful and thoughtful, intolerable. His was not the faith of an Aquinas or even an Augustine; he believed in a vengeful God and had so little experience with intellectual inquiry that he found it irrelevant as a basis for living his life.

A 1918 graduate of the High School of Commerce in New York City, my father went to work immediately after graduation. Embarrassed by his failure to go on to higher education, for most of my life he maintained that he had attended City College, even offering this false information to me as fact when I wrote out my college applications. Years later, I remember how proud he was when he was able to help one of his nephews enroll at Rutgers University. He read the *New York Times* each morning and, during my childhood, the *Journal American* each night, but never to my memory read a book.

My mother, on the other hand, was a great and eclectic reader. Her tastes ran the gamut from movie star magazines, bought in hotel smoke shops while we vacationed at Jewish resorts, to contemporary novels and classical literature. I remember her stretched out on her bed or on the chaise lounge in her bedroom reading *Immortal Wife* or *Love Is Eternal,* two of the many Irving Stone historical biographies that were so popular in the 1950s, or perhaps Herman Wouk's *The Caine Mutiny* or *Marjorie Morningstar.* Or she might have been reading Françoise Sagan's *Bonjour Tristesse* or some Jewish humor by Sam Levinson or Leo Rosten. She subscribed to the *Ladies' Home Journal* and *Redbook* but not to the more risqué *Cosmopolitan,* although she sometimes bought that magazine as well. And for many years, she had a subscription to Harry Golden's *The Carolina Israelite.*

Golden, a white, Jewish Northerner who had relocated to the South, was a passionate advocate for civil rights and used his paper during the 1950s and 1960s to publish telling editorials on the evils of racism, often using humor to make his point. My mother admired his courage and read the paper religiously. I think she especially admired Golden because she regarded him as someone who had a strong sense of Jewish identity but refused to be bound by what she considered to be the petty conventions of Jewish society when forced to choose between them and justice. My mother identified with Golden—at times believing herself to be just like him; at others, I think, wishing she were.

My mother's mother, Anna Kashowitz, the only grandmother I ever knew, was also an avid reader, but her tastes defied my understanding. I remember frequent trips to Womrath's, a book store on upper Broadway, where she used the lending library to borrow and return an astonishing number of murder mysteries by Erle Stanley Gardner, Agatha Christie, and others. These books always struck me as improbable choices for her. Gram was a very proper and well-educated lady who had graduated from Washington Irving High School in New York City in 1908 and then gone on to complete a teacher-training course that certified her to teach in the New York City public schools. She taught school for a few months, before marrying my grandfather, Isaac Siegel, eighteen years her senior, in December 1910. I have never been sure whether she left because of her marriage or because, as my mother once told me, she succumbed quickly to an attack of spitballs. A demanding and critical, although loving, taskmaster throughout much of my young life, she despaired of my penmanship, especially the messy way I wrote figures, and had very strict ideas about what constituted appropriate behavior in any situation. I can hardly remember a time when she was not dressed conservatively in black and wearing sturdy burnished gold jewelry, a black hat with a short veil, and long black suede gloves. That such a figure of propriety would actually read books with the unlikely titles *The Body in the Grass* and *The Case of the Blue-eyed Blonde* never ceased to amaze me. How she would have loved today's feminist mystery writers, women like Amanda Cross and Anne Perry, and maybe even Sue Grafton and Sara Paretsky, all writers I frequently turn to in order to get me through the night.

When I think of my grandmother, I imagine her entering our apartment and carrying a treat from Mrs. Herbst's Bakery: a delicious buttery babka made with raisins, chopped walnuts, and a honey glaze, or wonderfully flaky butter cookies that fooled me every time. The cookies looked so humble and unassuming that I always forgot how utterly and indescribably delicious they could be. Or perhaps I remember her taking me to a movie at Loew's and then to Schrafft's on Broadway and Eighty-fourth Street for coffee ice cream smothered in hot butterscotch sauce and sprinkled with slightly salty, still warm, toasted almonds. The price of these treats and cherished excursions was allowing her to hold my hand tightly during the movie or as we walked to it. I hated this prolonged and obviously needy physical contact and tried to avoid it whenever possible. I did not yet understand how lonely some old people could be or how starved for physical contact. I wish I could hold her hand now. I would never let go.

Just after it opened in 1955, I persuaded Gram to take me to see *Love Is a Many Splendored Thing* on one of our afternoons out. Being twelve years old, I was somewhat ambivalent about going to see this film with my grandmother instead of my friends, but it was the movie everyone was waiting for and I wanted to see it right away. We had barely settled into our seats when a boy I knew and coveted from afar appeared a few rows away with a group of other boys. Seeing such a film with your grandmother was embarrassing enough, but having to hold hands with her throughout the movie was more than I could bear. I sat on my hands.

Set in Hong Kong during the Korean War, the film tells the story of a beautiful Eurasian doctor, played by Jennifer Jones, who falls in love with a white, American newspaper correspondent, played by William Holden. I think that my grandmother was a little shocked by the film, not for herself, but because she worried about whether it was entirely appropriate for someone my age. Not only did it portray a passionate romance with some serious kissing, but it also raised the issue of interracial marriage. I remember being both fascinated and, if I am to be honest, mildly disturbed by William Holden's attraction to Jennifer Jones and its implications. Keeping them apart made no sense, since they were clearly destined for each other, and their love was most certainly a many splendored thing. On the other hand, it was apparent that any future for them would transgress carefully drawn boundaries, and I was unsure how I felt about that.

Some years later, my own "liberal" parents and their friends would recast their unqualified condemnation of interracial marriages by saying that while such relationships might be okay for the parties themselves, they were ultimately unacceptable because they weren't fair to the children. In taking this position, they were confident that there was no racism involved. Unlike those greedy and selfish individuals who put their own pleasure or passion first and were willing to condemn their biracial kids to a life of misery as misfits, my parents and their peers were confident of the moral superiority of their position. Why is it that they never thought to ask who would inflict this misery on the children and what role they might play in preventing it?

For some years after I saw the film, my model of a "mixed" couple was Jennifer Jones and William Holden. Although Jones had been born Phylis Isley in Tulsa, Oklahoma, I never questioned my erroneous assumption that Jones herself was "biracial," nor did I think very much about the absence of people of all colors from the silver screen. A serious moviegoer as a child and then a teen, I could not notice the absence of color from film because the occasional appearance of people of color, most often Black women as maids, mirrored my world. In my own life, no leading characters or feature roles were played by anyone who wasn't white, so their absence from the screen wasn't problematic. In this way, as in so many other ways, I could not recognize racism because for me it masqueraded as "reality."

In the summer, Grandma would bring the babkas and butter cookies with her on her visits to our summer home in Connecticut. Several times each summer, she would emerge from my great-grandfather's black Cadillac early on a still cool Saturday morning carrying neatly tied bakery boxes. Chauffeured by Irish Mike, who had worked for the family for years, she would arrive at our house in time for a second cup of breakfast coffee and spend the day visiting, while Mike passed the time sleeping or reading the newspaper in the car.

When my mother was a girl, this same chauffeur had the responsibility of delivering her and a friend to school each morning at Julia Richmond, the public school she attended before switching to the Calhoun School, from which she graduated. In later years, my mother liked to tell the story of how she and her friend Anita had persuaded Mike to let them out a block or two away from school to save them the embarrassment of arriving in a chauffeur-driven car. As far as she knew, he never told their parents. But now I wonder what he made of their request and why he was willing to risk reprimand or termination by agreeing to it. Did he pity them?

I remember Mike as a quiet and unassuming man who never once accepted my mother's invitation to wait in the house during the long hours of my grandmother's visits. Once or twice during the day, someone—perhaps it was me—would bring him a cool drink and perhaps a plate of food as well. Was my mother's invitation merely a courtesy that he was expected to reject, or was it genuine, rejected by Mike because of his own sense of place rather than my mother's assumption of it? Does it matter?

Strange as it may seem, although my mother had grown up surrounded by servants, she had very little confidence in herself and was very intimidated by the nursemaids, cooks, and cleaning ladies she hired. As a result, she often believed herself to be the victim of their slights and subterfuge and felt vulnerable in their presence. Perhaps the only servant far enough down on the chain not to cause her worry was the laundress who came each Monday to pick up a large wicker basket filled with our dirty clothes. She descended with them, a sandwich, and a Hellman's mayonnaise jar filled with milky coffee to the bowels of the building, where she washed and ironed with others like herself. Each Monday afternoon when I returned from school, the apartment was filled with the smell of freshly ironed clothes. The laundress, always a large Black woman, usually quite old, or at least she seemed so to me, received her pay in cash in a clean white envelope. At Christmastime, this was accompanied by a bottle of lily of the valley toilet water and an extra $10 bill.

The other servants seemed to fill my mother with fear and provide a constant source of worry. They answered back, they did not listen, they took money from her handbag and liquor from the cabinet—or so she feared. In her mind, they were wasteful, slovenly, careless, and rude, and her attempts to correct their behavior often met with sullen silence or worse. My father, on the other hand, commanded instant respect. The servants were deferential as they passed the broiled chicken, glazed carrots, and baked potatoes, quietly unobtrusive as they served the canned Elberta peach halves (accompanied by lady fingers if I was lucky); my father could never understand why mother found dealing with them so difficult. He could never understand that, unlike himself, she felt herself to be utterly dependent on their goodwill for her comfort, safety, and peace of mind. And although she frequently felt herself to be the object of some real or imagined slight, threat, or challenge, she could rarely summon the courage needed to make a straightforward request or respond to a well-intentioned question. Feeling powerless in all her privilege, she felt happiest of all, if only briefly, when out to lunch at the Palm Court at the Plaza or perhaps Longchamps.

My father was a blurry figure throughout much of my childhood. When I was very young, certainly no older than four or five, he seemed to love me quite a lot. In those days, he was on the road a great deal, visiting the factories that manufactured shirts for his brother's company and selling those shirts to large discount stores like Montgomery Ward and Sears. Gone for most of the week, he returned home without fail each Friday in time for Shabbos.

His homecoming was always a time of tremendous anticipation for me, perhaps back then for my mother as well. He would open his suitcase and produce one comic book after another: Little Lulu, Katy Keene, Donald Duck, Sylvester and Tweety, Uncle Scrooge—all my favorites. Also, he would bring me candy, and sometimes a small toy. As I got older, an awkwardness seemed to develop between us, and there was never much to say. I guess he simply didn't know what to do after the comics ran out.

Although, as I have said, we were well off by most people's standards, for most of my childhood I felt "poor" in comparison with other people I knew—a feeling I acquired from my mother. We lived in a large and wonderful apartment on Central Park West, but my mother believed that the right place to live was across the park on the east side of Manhattan. In her eyes, and consequently in my own, there was always a sense of "making do." Although our apartment was filled with antiques carefully assembled with the help of an interior decorator, my mother's budget for its periodic refurbishing was more limited than that of many of her acquaintances. In those days, she had a closet full of designer clothes, but she shopped for them at special discount boutiques located in Upper East Side brownstones, not designer showrooms, and she shopped carefully rather than with the careless abandon of her friends. While most women she knew had several furs, she was limited to a single mink coat or mink stole, which, as she never failed to remark, wasn't made from the best skins.

But it was more than a matter of money. My mother carried with her a feeling of her own inferiority throughout her life, as though in her hands it was inevitable that gold would turn to dross. Shortly before she was born, my mother's four-year-old sister, Florence, had died in a tragic accident, having fallen down the elevator shaft in the apartment building where the family lived. As a result, my mother's birth was surrounded by grief and mourning—not celebration. She would always be second best to her dead sister, whose beauty and talents seemed to grow with the passing of time. Whether these constant comparisons with the sister she had never known were real or imagined mattered less than her firm conviction that she would always come up short. Her cousin Hope was considered more beautiful and more talented; her cousin Stanley was considered brilliant. She saw herself as the ugly duckling who would always disappoint her mother in comparison with the daughter she had lost.

A stickler for quality, somehow Mother always ended up with what she considered second rate. At the end of her life, when she knew she was dying of cancer, she gave me several pieces of her jewelry but deliberately decided to pass her engagement ring on to my sister-in-law. Because the original emerald-cut diamond was only a few carats, she long ago had had it remounted and paired with an emerald of similar size and shape and framed by baguettes to create a more dramatic affect. Because it was so much a part of my childhood, I would have liked to have had that ring for remembrance, but my mother's feelings about the ring precluded her giving it to me. She told me that some years after her marriage, she had taken the ring to be appraised for insurance purposes and learned that the diamond was flawed. She never forgave my father. In so many ways, she felt cheated and tricked by her marriage to him; the flawed diamond in her engagement ring came to symbolize what was, for her, the shoddy quality of everything he provided. The lifestyle he was able to buy could never measure up to her childhood memories or to the wealth and comfort enjoyed by her grandparents, aunts, and cousins. In comparison with their charmed and affluent lives, she always felt herself disadvantaged. More than that, she saw my father as someone without ambition of his own who took the easy way out, who wanted to make an impression more than he wanted to make a life, who would always choose what *looked* good over what *was* good. Whether this was actually true, I do not know to this day.

Having said this, I feel compelled to acknowledge that I grew up in an apartment with a foyer larger than most people's living rooms. How is it possible to be surrounded by so much privilege and yet feel like Cinderella at the ball? If my mother were alive today, I would ask her this question—and she would still have no answer. But the fact is that my mother never stopped believing that what she had was second best, and, depending on your frame of reference, it was. While our Central Park West apartment would have been impressive to most people, it was at the rear of the building and had only one or two windows that allowed a partial view of the park. In our world, that made a difference. The best apartments were in the front of the building and had a park view from every window. And while we lived in a handsome building just a few blocks from the American Museum of Natural History, with doormen and elevator men and a wood and gilt paneled elevator, my school friends lived in even larger apartments on the East Side in buildings their fathers owned.

Perhaps in context, my mother's discontent makes perfect sense. Periodic surveys of people from different income brackets indicate that, regardless of income, virtually everyone thinks that they would need roughly double their current income to feel really well off. It should not be surprising to find that even people like my mother, who are extremely well off by most standards, feel this way too. Wealth, like privilege, is relative and has a subjective component to it. I say this less to ask for sympathy for her than to reflect on the futility of composing a life based on the attainment of wealth. As my friend Ros said to me some years ago when most of our neighbors were "moving up" into conspicuously larger suburban homes, there's always someone with a bigger house.

At some point the building we were living in went co-op, allowing current residents to purchase their apartments at a very low price and sell them later, if they chose, reaping a huge profit. My parents bought our three-bedroom apartment in the mid-1950s for somewhere between $6,000 and $7,000. Before the ink was dry on the contract, its value had probably tripled or quadrupled. Today it would sell for over a million dollars. One consequence of "going co-op" was that a monthly maintenance fee replaced the rent previously paid, and it was considerably lower than the rent any of us had paid before the conversion, lower even than what many families in other parts of the city paid to live in cramped apartments in marginal neighborhoods.

Although a firm was hired to manage the building, policy matters were decided by the tenants themselves. My father served on the board of directors, which had responsibility for making them. Each time a family wanted to sell an apartment, it had to go before the board and seek approval for the sale. The board's approval was contingent on the acceptability of the prospective new owners, who were required to provide numerous financial and character references. I remember the time there was considerable debate about whether to allow a well-known actor and his family into the building. Ultimately, the board decided to "blackball" him on the grounds that he would lower the morals of the building. But I never believed that was the real reason. I always believed it was because the board members had recently rejected a prominent Black physician and his wife and wanted to make it clear that they also had high standards for white people.

When I was eleven, my mother took me to Best and Company to buy a bra, just as years earlier she had taken me to have my first haircut. Our shopping trip was the result of months of pleading during which I tried to make her understand that even though I was flat-chested, I couldn't return to summer camp with a trunk full of undershirts. In the end, she agreed to take me, but she made sure that every salesgirl on the third floor knew why we were there and how ludicrous she felt it was, considering my shape—or lack of one. The clerk who was destined to help me make this leap into womanhood kept asking what size bra I wanted. Each time I said that I wasn't sure, she asked the question a little louder, as though she were speaking to someone who was deaf or didn't understand the language. Since I had no idea of the sizes in which bras came, I had no idea of what to say. I kept hoping that my mother would intervene, but I think she believed she had fulfilled her obligation by hailing the cab.

Somehow we managed to leave the store with a 32AA white cotton bra that had a tiny pink rosebud sewn between the cups. How I loved that bra all the way home in the cab, all the way upstairs in the elevator, through the front door, and into my parents' bedroom, where my mother snatched the bag from my hands in a single unexpected movement, pulled the bra from its tissue-paper cocoon, and held it up by one end, like a dead fish, for my father to see. As soon as he realized what it was, he averted his eyes, as embarrassed as I, but it was already too late.

In sharp contrast to her own upbringing, my mother prided herself on being very liberal when it came to discussing sex. That this was not in the least true didn't stop her from congratulating herself for it. It did, however, produce considerable confusion in me, since I was never sure whether to take her at her word or her deed. Her favorite childhood story, shared with me as proof that she was quite liberated, was about getting her period for the first time while away at camp and announcing the news on a postcard by telling her mother that she had just fallen off the roof—slang, in those days, for having begun to menstruate. To my mother's mortification, grandmother called the camp in a great state of agitation and asked whether her daughter had broken any bones in the fall.

My mother's inability to discuss sex comfortably with my Victorian grandmother made her resolve to be different with her children. This decision was reinforced by seeing Rosalind Russell play Auntie Mame, a character my mother loved because she expressed all the sense of joy and spontaneity so absent from my mother's own life. I like to think that if she had lived long enough to see my children in their teenage years, she would have become Auntie Mame in earnest. In my dreams, I picture her carrying them off for wildly indulgent vacations in Europe and offering them their first highballs and, even in these enlightened times, their first cigarettes. All of this not withstanding, after I became engaged during my first year in college and asked my mother about birth control, she was shocked and, to my surprise and confusion, ended the conversation immediately. She told me that she and my father had never discussed birth control in all the years they had been married, and she saw no reason why a nice girl would need to know anything about it. You never knew when my

mother, the product of an enormously confined and confining upbringing, would turn into a woman as proper as her own mother had
been.

Throughout much of my childhood, as part of her obligation to
prepare me to assume my proper place in society, my mother held
Queen Elizabeth up to me as a model of comportment and good breed-
ing. Ever eager to provide me with useful information on my journey
toward womanhood, my mother illustrated what it meant to be well
bred by assuring me that even in the unlikely event that the queen
got a run in her stocking or noticed that her seams were crooked, she
would carry on as though nothing were wrong. Although I could not
be sure how my mother was so certain of this fact, this behavior came
to serve in my mind as a model of how a lady must act. For years, I
was both puzzled and charmed by this piece of seemingly useless
advice, even as I marveled at the self-confidence and equanimity that
such comportment would require. Surprisingly, in later years I have
called on its memory on a number of occasions. It has stood me in good
stead at those occasional luncheons when I have managed to splatter
salad dressing on my silk blouse moments before going to the podium
to address a large audience. In spite of its anomalous nature, it has
turned out to be one of the more useful and realistic pieces of advice
that my mother ever shared with me. In addition, it has created a bond
between the queen and me that, despite her ignorance of it, persists
to this day.

Although I was a Brooklyn Dodger fan, or perhaps because of it,
my brother Stu rooted for the Yankees and the Giants. So in addition
to going to games at Ebbets Field, on occasional spring or fall Sunday
afternoons we got into our gray Buick and drove uptown to the Polo
Grounds or to Yankee Stadium. It amazed me to see how quickly
neighborhoods changed. Before we had gone very far, my mother
would caution us to make sure that the car doors were locked and
instruct us to keep the windows closed. We drove though streets that
might have been in some other country inhabited by people who
seemed more foreign than the tourists who landed at Idlewild, later
Kennedy, Airport. While I lived in a world of pharmacies and foyers,

not drug stores and hallways, these people lived in a world of bodegas and debris. I remember watching in fascination as the streets became increasingly dirty and the buildings began to disintegrate, their windows cracked or missing entirely. It never occurred to me to wonder why the garbage wasn't picked up more frequently or why no one repaired the windows. Like a former mayor of New York City, Ed Koch, I was raised to believe that certain people were simply dirty or preferred to live that way.

On warm days, many of the apartment windows were open, with no more than a scrap of material to impede my view, but I could never catch a real glimpse of life in the dark rooms beyond the scraps no matter how hard I tried. For me it was a forbidden world, remote and romantic even as it was potentially dangerous and explicitly devalued. I remember being vaguely embarrassed as we drove through those streets. I think the rest of my family was too, embarrassed and uncomfortable, but like so much in our lives, we tastefully and carefully avoided talking about it. Before long, we were settled in a box seat on the first-base line, enjoying the game—a typical all-American family at the ball park. Well, not exactly. No matter how good they smelled, we could never eat the hot dogs. They weren't kosher.

The class and political implications implicit in the choice of a baseball team to root for was evident to me even as a child, although I could not have articulated them. The Yankees, of course, represented all that was white and clean and good about America, and Yankee Stadium was reputed to attract a better class of people; the Giants came next; and at the bottom of the social ladder came the Brooklyn Dodgers, the first baseball team to allow a Black man to take the field. My parents cheered Jackie Robinson and Roy Campanella and the "Say-Hey Kid," Willie Mays, and split their allegiance equally among the three New York ball clubs. Later, when Sandy Koufax began to pitch, we were all Dodger fans. That Koufax would insist on a clause in his contract excusing him from mound duty during the Jewish High Holy Days was a source of tremendous pride for my parents, even though it was clear to us all that being a professional athlete was hardly an appropriate career choice for a nice Jewish boy.

Going away on vacation was always a treat, and we did so with considerable frequency when my father was earning good money. When I was very young, my mother and I would spend several weeks each summer at the Grand Hotel in High Mount, New York, to escape the city's heat. My father would join us on the weekends. By the time I was six, our weekend getaways included annual excursions to Atlantic City. Once a year on some fall or spring weekend, we would check into our rooms at the Shelbourne or the Traymore and then walk along the same boardwalk that my grandparents and great-grandparents had walked along years earlier on excursions of their own. We bought cotton candy and salt water taffy, window-shopped, and, when I couldn't wait another minute, stopped to play Okeeno at the concessions that lined the boardwalk. A high point of the trip was always having my photo taken on a pony and then having a ride in the sand, even in winter.

As I got older, we began to make regular visits to Grossingers in the Catskills and to my favorite place of all, the Laurel in the Pines, in Lakewood, New Jersey. The Laurel, like the Grand Hotel, was owned by Al and Sadie Tisch, whose sons Lawrence and Preston would become movers and shakers on the New York scene. My father knew the Tisches, and so we always felt quite at home—an important prerequisite for travel in our family. My brother and I would ice-skate in the mornings and perhaps again after lunch, and then look forward to the "tea dansant," which took place every weekday afternoon in the hotel bar. Tea and cookies were served at four o'clock, and a live band played popular tunes while guests nibbled and danced. If I got bored, I could usually beg change from my parents and head for the smoke shop, where four pinball machines kept the younger guests happy for hours.

A printed schedule distributed each morning at breakfast offered a series of amusements for all ages. They might include group calisthenics or dance lessons, a fashion show, bingo, and, of course, the favorite pastime at all Jewish resorts—an adult version of Simon Sez for fun and prizes. When I entered my teens, I took private fox-trot and cha-cha lessons at a dance studio in the hotel's basement and learned to use make-up at the tiny beauty parlor down the hall. And there was an indoor pool, a game room with several Ping Pong tables, a card room, and even a synagogue where, on Saturday mornings, my father went to help make a minyan, ensuring the presence of the minimum number of adult males required to say Kaddish and certain other prayers.

But to my mind, the high point of each visit was the enormous cocktail party held every Wednesday and Saturday night before dinner. For this event, the Palm Room—a lovely green oasis with potted palms, green carpeting, green floral-print couches, and an indoor fish pool—was transformed into the equivalent of a bar mitzvah reception hall. Long, linen-draped tables were literally covered with enormous bowls of herring, mounds of chopped liver, trays of deviled eggs, cold hors d'oeuvres, celery, radishes, olives, pickles, and an occasional, strategically placed, ice sculpture. Waiters and waitresses circulated through the crowd, passing pigs in blankets, miniature potato and liver knishes, small potato pancakes served with apple sauce, tiny kosher egg rolls, and other delights. Open bars were set up around the periphery of the room. I loved the crowds, the music, the food, the fancy dress, and the feeling of excess that was everywhere. But I always tried to leave before the crowd thinned and the only hors d'oeuvres left on the trays were sad little rectangles of red and white colored fish eggs beginning to bleed into each other.

Looking at jewelry in the hotel store while waiting for the dining room to open each night was a hotel tradition, and we usually joined the other guests in admiring an assortment of gold bracelets, necklaces, rings, and pins, decorated with precious and semiprecious gems. My family continued to patronize this jeweler when he, like the Tisch brothers, became successful enough to expand beyond the limited world of kosher Jewish hotels and open a store in New York City just off Fifth Avenue. On one of my mother's birthdays, my father came home with a velvet jewelry box in each pocket, supplied by this jeweler, and told my mother to pick her gift. My brother and I watched wide-eyed with amazement as these treasures were revealed, but my mother was not pleased. Did she know that we could not afford such an extravagant gesture, or was she simply incapable of allowing herself the pleasure? I'll never be sure.

Family vacations are some of my best memories, probably because my mother was so happy during them and my parents usually got on well. But I know that I caused my parents considerable frustration as I got older because a subtext of these holidays was always the possibility of introducing me to eligible young men. In spite of my parents' hopes and best efforts, the nice Jewish boys I met who were hotel guests along with their parents were never very appealing. By ten o'clock, when the kitchen and dining room staff went off duty, I could usually be found hanging out with one of the waiters or busboys in the staff quarters. The only downside of this proclivity was being served orange juice and pancakes by them the next morning. But I am getting ahead of myself.

2

Negotiating Adolescence

❖ ❖ ❖ ❖ ❖ ❖ ❖ ❖ ❖ ❖ ❖ ❖ ❖ ❖

Once I passed puberty, I dreaded the summer because it meant walking the streets of the city without a coat and having to listen to whistles and cat calls. This attention came not because I was particularly attractive and certainly not because I had large breasts—I didn't—but simply because I was female. Even after the temperature had climbed into the seventies, I wore my trench coat whenever I went out. It was my own personal chador, and I relinquished it only when the heat became intolerable. After that, I had to armor myself against the taunts and invitations shouted or whispered by men in the street. Walking to a friend's house or doing an errand was mortifying, especially at twelve and thirteen when my tiny breasts had begun to bud and I thought the whole world knew my body's secrets. The well-dressed men going to or from their offices didn't even see me, but the construction workers, delivery boys, and utility workers never left me alone. At construction sites, the men made loud clucking and smacking noises with their mouths.

One day when I was no more than fourteen, a man shouted out the invitation that I sit on his face. I had no idea what he meant by this suggestion, but I was filled with shame. The Puerto Rican delivery "boys" and messengers, lowest on the totem pole of menial laborers, were the worst. Perhaps to protect themselves in case another man chose to claim his white skin privilege by protecting a white girl from harassment, they waited until you were almost upon them and then made soft kissing sounds or hissed "Here pussy, pussy, pussy" under their breath.

Throughout these encounters I felt shame, not anger. I was not angry at the men who harassed me, a behavior that had not yet been named. Instead, I was embarrassed that others would hear them and think less of me. It never occurred to me that someone else might hear those comments and fault the men for making them; I simply assumed that others would hear them and take me for a slut. My mother often made it clear to me that people could tell what you were by how you dressed. She considered it inappropriate to wear slacks on the street and certainly would never tolerate a child of hers chewing gum in public. Each time I left the safety of our building's canopy and ventured beyond that portion of sidewalk presided over by our doorman, I prayed that no one would say anything and wished that I could become invisible. Why did they do it? Why did I blame myself? Some of those men must have had daughters.

By the time I was a teenager, I had begun to eat forbidden foods on a regular basis with my less Orthodox Jewish friends and considered myself a nonbeliever. But the religion still had its hold on me, as I found out after attending a party given by a gentile girl who lived in our apartment building and who had become a casual friend. I was shaken to the core the day after the party when I discovered that the boy I had spent all my time with was not Jewish. Memories of slow dancing and warm bodies that moments before had filled my head with giddy fantasies suddenly left me feeling unclean. Although I now loudly and firmly rejected most tenets of Orthodoxy, I had a visceral reaction to the knowledge that I had been physically intimate, which in this case meant nothing more than having danced closely, with a *shagitz*. Intellectually comfortable with the idea of such "mixed" relationships, my body still had not caught up with my mind. Needless to say, I did not see him again.

But the nice Jewish boys my parents encouraged me to date were not the answer either. By the time I was a high-school senior, their favorite was a tall, handsome pre-law student who attended the University of Pennsylvania. Polite and deferential in their presence, this mother's dream became a sexual predator the moment my parents said good night. Trying to keep his tongue out of my mouth and his hands out of my pants took all my energy and cunning. At more than six feet, he was a full foot taller and a great many pounds heavier than me and believed firmly that his future earning power and his current ability to purchase movie tickets and mixed drinks entitled him to whatever he wanted. My parents were bitterly disappointed when we stopped dating after a few months and wondered what I had done to lose such a good prospect.

My first opportunity to relate to African-Americans my own age came at fifteen, the summer I went away to a theater-arts summer program in the Berkshires—by mistake. I spent six weeks being incredulous at my good fortune. How had my parents blundered into sending me to such a place? The actual number of Black boys and girls who were there has long since left my memory, and there were certainly no more than a handful—but still more than I had ever been with in my life. I spent the summer mooning over one of the boys, who was tall and thin and looked a little like pop singer Johnny Mathis. Philip was extremely shy and quiet, very handsome—with a fair complexion. The son of a college president, he played the violin and was society's perfect token. Being fair-skinned with blond hair, I was bitterly disappointed when he started going steady with another white girl, one whose complexion approximated his own and whose hair was curly and jet black. Like my other smitten and slightly jealous friends, I wondered whether I had been the victim of color-based discrimination; he never gave us a chance. Didn't he know it was wrong to judge people by the color of their skin?

The days that summer were filled with rehearsals for *Twelfth Night*—making costumes, painting scenery, and attending early-morning, mandatory chorus rehearsals presided over by Harold Brown of the New York Renaissance Chorus. The nights were filled with a delicious terror. A friend and I sneaked out regularly, first with a trip to the kitchen in search of *anything* to eat to tide us over until breakfast, and then a long talk, while we picnicked lying on the grass under the stars. But there was always the danger of being discovered by Bill. Bill was a large, fierce, Black man who ruled the kitchen and exuded a quality of raw sexuality by his sheer physical presence.* All the white girls lived in terror of him. Unlike Philip and the other Negro teenagers in the program, he had very dark skin and he treated us with derision bordering on contempt. Because of him, we dreaded doing our stint in the kitchen, another mandatory experience at this progressive theater-arts camp/school. Bill was never deferential or even polite. There was no pretense about him. He never allowed us to feel good about who we were. I was simultaneously repelled and attracted by him. Each time we sneaked out on a midnight adventure, I worried—perhaps hoped—that Bill would find us and do something awful.

Back at school, there were no Blacks in the classes, but there were still Blacks in the kitchen. The dietician was a white woman, as was the cook, but the people who did the cleaning and washing up were all Black men. The abysmally low social standing of these men was ensured both by their performing what was essentially women's work and by their being supervised entirely by women. All the men had very dark skin and, of course, rarely, if ever, spoke to us or, from what I could tell, to one another. Unlike the dietician, who dressed in street clothes, they wore fairly crude kitchen uniforms that made them, in my eyes, simultaneously homogeneous and invisible. They seemed to me like another race of creatures entirely.

Years later, while living in an integrated suburb where I thought I was raising my own children differently, I was horrified one day when my four-year-old son identified a stylishly dressed Black man who was jogging by our house as a "garbage man." What to my eyes

---

*Every reviewer of this manuscript was scandalized by my use of the phrase "exuded a quality of raw sexuality," which they took to be very un-PC, and so I feel the need to assure you that it is not used thoughtlessly. Stereotypes exist because they have some basis in reality, even if misguided. Thus it is not surprising that a fifteen-year-old girl's experience, which is what is being conveyed here, would itself reflect the way in which her culture socially constructs both race and sexuality.

clearly was a designer sweatsuit and color-coordinated sweat band, was in his eyes the standard uniform of the Black men who rode the town's trucks picking up our trash twice each week. And he was absolutely right. In those days, virtually all the men who collected the town's garbage were Black, and most of them dressed in sweats and tied rags around their heads. No wonder my son couldn't distinguish between a Black corporate executive jogging in his Calvin Klein warm-up suit and a Black man picking up the trash. By the age of two or three, he already had absorbed the racial hierarchy that had been constructed for him in a thousand small ways, and his eyes could not see past the construct—any more than I could so many years earlier.

How he has fared with gender is still a puzzle to me. I remember taking him to register for summer day camp the year he turned four. As we navigated the large room filled with hundreds of other mothers and children, he slipped his small hand into mine, confident that I could shepherd him through registration. What did he think when in answer to my question about whether to wait in one particular line, the man behind the desk replied, "That's right, all the pretty girls have to see me first." At the time I was thirty-nine or forty, a college professor, the author of several books. When did my son first discover that his mother was just another pretty girl?

While I was in middle school and then high school, we ate lunch in the same cafeteria each day. After lunch, my friends and I would file out of the lunchroom and hand our trays to the silent Black men who scraped the remaining food on our plates into large metal garbage cans. Unlike my brother's school, which had both an art room and a cafeteria, at my school the art room doubled as the cafeteria; unlike my brother's school, which had a science lab *and* a refuse area, at my school the two were one. After lunch, when the dirty trays had been emptied, the garbage cans disappeared and this basement room became our science lab. It was small and dark, and there were bars on the window. Two sinks and four raised wooden tables painted an institutional gray, each with a Bunsen burner, rounded out the equipment. But even after the room had been turned back into a science lab, it still smelled of sour trash.

I liked science a lot and wanted to be a doctor. But when I was sixteen and planning my future, my science teacher, Mr. Cantor, assured me that no medical school would accept me because the admission committees knew that I would get married and have children. Confused by this foreknowledge allegedly possessed by admission committees, I had many conversations with Mr. Cantor about it. Being a reasonable person, I tried hard to see it his way. "After all," he explained, "why waste all those years of education and training on a girl when she'll never end up practicing medicine." But fortunately for me, I was not inclined to take his words too seriously. Why listen to a man who has done no better in life than end up as a science teacher in a mediocre private school? Women who choose to be teachers made sense to me and had probably achieved about as much as they could expect, but, to my mind, only a man who was a loser would settle for such a low-status career. Besides, I knew that his wife had a job and earned a salary, which was virtually unknown in my limited world, where mothers did volunteer work and fathers brought home the bacon. That his wife actually worked at a job for which she got paid lost him considerable respect in my eyes. What kind of a man, I wondered, would let his wife work? More important, I knew that my family had money, had even contributed to the building fund at Brandeis, and I had faith that once again class privilege and my parents' connections would compensate for my having been born a girl.

In my junior year, Mr. Cantor, at my request, nominated me for a special citywide science honors program for high-school students. It was run by Columbia University and coordinated by Dean Donald Barr, an innovative educator who would later serve as headmaster at the Dalton School in New York City. I wanted to be accepted in the worst way.

I left our apartment building early one Saturday morning in the spring and traveled uptown to compete with hundreds of other city school kids for admission to the program. Only there weren't hundreds of other kids; there were hundreds of boys, with an occasional girl thrown in, and virtually all the boys were white. They came from public schools like Stuyvesant and Bronx High School of Science, both of which offered intensive and highly advanced science and mathematics courses, as well as from the most elite private schools, such as Horace Mann and my brother's school, Riverdale. One look at the test, and I knew it was hopeless. I could never answer those questions. I sat in a cavernous lecture hall, surrounded by well-prepared white boys from high-powered schools, and felt sick. All the way uptown, I had dreamed of the opportunities that admission to the program would bring, but, alas, Mr. Cantor's science class and the ersatz science lab/trash room had not prepared me to take this test. Devastated by the prospect of losing my chance, I picked one of the boys nearest me at random and began copying down every one of his answers. Several weeks later, the envelope arrived. I had been accepted to the Columbia University Science Honors program.

I read the letter several times and waited to feel remorse. None came. Although in the abstract I believed that cheating was wrong, I was already less a Kantian than a pragmatist and believed that, in this case, the end justified the means. After all, in the scheme of things, the fact that I had cheated seemed a minor infraction and one undertaken to right a wrong. The real injustice was being consigned by my gender to a third-rate school with a fourth-rate science teacher and a fifth-rate science lab. I burned for the opportunity that the Columbia program offered. Convinced of the justice of my desire, or, rather, the injustice of my position, and armed with the sense of entitlement that came from my class position, I never wavered in my resolve. I had cheated on the test to get something I knew I deserved. After all, I reasoned, my lack of preparation for the test was not a reflection on my ability or my hard work but the result of a quirk of fate. Years later, when our society first began debating the concept of affirmative action, it was difficult for me to understand what all the fuss was about. Affirmative action seemed to me an obvious and appropriate mechanism for achieving social justice. My own experience made it clear to me that affirmative action, like reverse discrimination and reparations, was a way to redress a wrong, not extend a privilege.

Once in the program, I became fast friends with two of the boys and one of the few girls who attended. Unlike many of the participants, boys from fairly elite backgrounds, this particular trio came from a public high school in Brooklyn and got up early each Saturday morning to ride the subway to 116th Street and Broadway. We were heady with our good fortune. Each Saturday morning during the fall semester, we heard a lecturer talk about a different area of science. One week, it was microbiology; another, it was astronomy; and the next, it might be zoology. Unlike the tedium of my high-school science classes, these lectures, which were designed to provide us with engaging introductions to the various branches of science and to specialties within them, gave me a taste of what I hoped was waiting for me after high school. Each afternoon, we worked on our own projects in one of the college's well-equipped laboratories.

In the spring semester, each participant selected an area of specialization and took a semester-long course. I chose to spend my mornings studying population genetics and my afternoons studying fruit flies. Most days we ate lunch in the cafeteria, but on one or two occasions during the year, each of us would be invited to a formal lunch in what must have been a faculty dining room. Seated at linen-draped tables, we were served a hot meal and enjoyed the company of a prominent scientist with whom we could talk, just as though we belonged there. I will never forget eating a chopped-meat patty—no hamburgers here—while sitting next to world-renowned geneticist Theodosius Dobzhansky and talking with him as if I belonged there.

At the end of the semester, each of us had to submit a lengthy treatise in our subject, a kind of cross between a term essay and an elaborate take-home exam. The topic was polymorphism in *Cepaea nemoralis* (land snails). The assignment asked us to assume the role of population geneticists and outline the kinds of observations, experiments, and calculations we would perform in order to explain the observable polymorphism in the population. When the papers were returned, I found out that mine had been awarded "honors."

By this time in my life, when I wasn't studying fruit flies, I was thinking about boys and trying to lose my virginity. In the absence of any serious contenders, I gave my heart to James Dean. He typified the way we liked our men—moody, sullen, and huggable, a cross between a porcupine, a beagle, and a teddy bear. Like so many other girls my age, I was convinced that I was in love with him, and, perhaps unlike them, I identified with him. Like me, he was misunderstood, out of place, impatient with the trivial demands of ordinary life. My room in our summer house in Westport, Connecticut, had two closets. I turned one of them into a shrine for him, papering the walls and the ceiling with photos and news clippings. The closet was just big enough to hold a chair and a small table, and I spent hours in there, hiding from the world and either pouring over or adding to a scrapbook of his life. Growing up female in the 1950s wasn't easy. If you didn't choose to identify with Debbie Reynolds or Doris Day, your choices were few. I wanted to be James Dean or Jack Kerouac or one of the bearded beatnik poets whose words kindled my fire at the Gaslight Café in Greenwich Village. I longed to write like Thomas Wolfe or F. Scott Fitzgerald, but knew I did not want to be Alison Bernstein or Zelda. I looked in vain through the books on my shelves and the images on the screen for a role model, but came up empty-handed. I wanted to be all the boy-men I was in love with, but never for a moment could stomach being one of the women they might love.

From second through tenth grade, my best friend was a boy named Allen Waller, who somehow managed to be popular without ever going out for sports or treating girls badly. His dark good looks made him a favorite among the girls, and the fact that he was both tall and smart and had an older brother who was a mover and shaker at school solidified his class standing. Allen's brother, Ben, who eventually went on to Dartmouth, was two years older and equally serious. Ben passed along the books he read to Allen, and Allen passed them along to me. Under his/their tutelage, I discovered Tolstoy, Dostoyevsky, Proust, Thomas Wolfe, and more. Literature, great literature, unlike the books by Irving Stone and James Michener that my mother read, seemed to me to be the clear prerogative of men, and I was grateful to have Allen to help me gain entry into this special and select world. Until our senior year, all the English teachers at my school were men, and as the class assignments and summer reading lists made clear, all the great books were written by men as well. Although my own father never read books, I understood that as a man, albeit a Jewish man from an impoverished background, he still had a right to claim public space. Unlike my mother and virtually all the other mothers I knew who did volunteer work or stayed home, my father went to work in a suit and a tie and spent his days navigating and even controlling portions of the public world. My mother read a great deal, but in my mind she read "novels," which, according to her own account, she read to "escape." This was very different from reading "literature." As a young girl, I had enjoyed a steady diet of Cherry Ames and Nancy Drew and, before that, Rebecca of Sunnybrook Farm and Anne of Green Gables. But now I considered myself fortunate to have Allen to tell me what to read, and although he was the same age as me, I thought of him as older and wiser. It was my friendship with him that seemed to give me permission to enter the world of great books.

In retrospect, it seems as though I spent my adolescence and early adulthood playing Eliza Doolittle to a succession of Professor Higginses. Each new relationship with a boy brought a new literary or academic interest. There was Bob, who gave me the Modern Library edition of *The Collected Works of Sigmund Freud* as a birthday present when I was sixteen; Larry, an economics major at Yale, who sent me a book on gold and the dollar crisis during my first year in college; Phil, who introduced me to the writings of Wilhelm Reich; and on and on. I tried each interest on for size. The sad part is that I was such a willing disciple; the good part is that I learned a lot. It wasn't until years later that my friendships with women yielded such treasures. Throughout the formative years of my life, great ideas, like great literature, were the prerogative of men, and my access to them was always mediated by my relationships with men and boys.

This is not to say that I wasn't somewhat ambivalent about my Eliza Doolittle status. Receiving a copy of the collected works of Freud for my sixteenth birthday from the Brooklyn College man I was dating made me feel flattered. It confirmed my superiority to the empty-headed girls in my class, who were receiving gold hearts on chains or suitably inscribed ankle bracelets. On the other hand, you couldn't wear Freud around your neck or affirm your femininity or desirability by flaunting a Modern Library edition around the school. I pretended that I didn't want the charms and ID bracelets, but in my heart I longed for them as well. When a boy I was dating during my senior year gave me a pale blue angora sweater for my birthday, he won my heart. As a result, the relationship lasted for several months longer than it should have.

Looking back, I'm amazed at how vague, almost nonexistent, my friendships with girls my age seem to have been. Our lives revolved around boys—getting them, keeping them, getting rid of them, and then starting the cycle all over again. This made us long-term competitors and short-term allies. We started going steady early—by ninth or tenth grade—and wore our boyfriends' school rings around our necks on chains or on our fingers, wadded with white adhesive tape to make them fit. Many of the girls I knew would diet for weeks and then binge on Sara Lee chocolate cake. We spent afternoons hanging out of Nancy Solomon's bedroom window and using sun reflectors to heighten our year-round tans. Even girls who were very smart submerged themselves in eye shadow and depilatory as soon as the school day ended. While it was assumed that all of us would go to college, and most of the girls did, they went there to find husbands and having done so, usually dropped out before graduating. In those days, a popular joke claimed that boys went to college to get their B.A. and girls went to college to get their MRS.—but it was nothing to laugh at.

Although I was never particularly athletic in any other respect, basketball was a passion of mine in high school; by my senior year, I was co-captain of the team. I loved the intensity of competition, the sheer physicality of the experience, the sweat pouring over me, out of breath, gasping, every muscle aching, the feeling of pushing my body beyond pain and possibility. And, of course, the comraderie of team sports. There's never been anything like it since. But our high school didn't have a gym (no gym? no science lab? no art room?— what kind of school was this?), and so each afternoon we took the bus across town to practice at the Ninety-second Street Y. On the way home, usually flush with defeat, we stopped at one of the tiny shops that were springing up all over the city and selling pizza for fifteen cents a slice. It definitely wasn't kosher.

During tenth grade, I read William Faulkner for the first time when my English class was assigned "A Rose for Emily." After that, I read whatever works by Faulkner I could find. His writing spoke directly to me, and I felt a passionate connection to him. During a particularly terrible period of adolescent loneliness, I wrote to Faulkner telling him how much his writing meant to me and asking permission to show him some of the poetry I was writing. That he wrote back to me was a significant turning point in my life. I marveled that I could sit at a desk in my room in New York City and write words on a piece of paper that would prompt William Faulkner to sit at his desk in Oxford, Mississippi, and write back. It held out the fragile but inescapable possibility of communication between human beings, something of which I did not always feel confident, and allowed me to believe in my future as a writer. Faulkner had declined to look at my poems, saying that his seeing them was not important, that the only thing that was important was to keep on writing them and, in this way, to keep on trying to make sense out of the human dilemma. For a teenager with an enormous superego, which served as a continual brutal self-critic, and a mother who did the same, this advice was liberating.

Throughout this time, my mother remained an enigma to me. The most powerful figure in my world, dwarfing my father by virtue of both her knowledge and her taste, she had studied music at Julliard and taken college courses at Columbia. President of the PTA, able to speak French and Italian, comfortable in a world of fine damask and crystal, my private tour guide at both the Metropolitan Museum and the Metropolitan Opera, when I was little, she taught me to whittle elephants and giraffes from bars of Ivory soap and knew how to make the best cream-cheese-cookie dough in the world. She could knit sweaters and crochet afghans and create needlepoint using patterns she drew herself. She played Chopin and Schubert on the piano, whistled symphonies as she walked around the house, listened to radio broadcasts of the Metropolitan Opera each Saturday afternoon, and knew most of the arias by heart. How could such a person be so bitterly unhappy and so lacking in self-esteem? Why didn't she discover that she had the possibility to act and change her life until it was too late? I put on a black turtleneck and black tights and vowed that I would never be like her.

On days when I couldn't stand the confinement of my life any longer, I would look for ways to leave school or get out of the house and lose myself in other parts of the city. Cutting classes was never very difficult. I usually fabricated some project that required a trip to the Greek or French Consulate and easily procured a pass from the assistant principal. On Wednesdays at noon, I headed straight for Broadway and the chance to see a matinee. On other days, I might go to a museum or walk around Greenwich Village. Getting out of the house at night was more of a problem, but whenever I could, I met my friend Jane at the Seventy-second Street IND station and headed straight for the Village and the Gaslight Café. Welcome to the wonderful world of bearded beatnik poets and the first sexual stirring of an adolescent girl.

We sat for hours listening to the angry yet maudlin verse of unwashed college dropouts and overweight soon-to-be-middle-aged has-beens—all men—but in those days we didn't notice. Their every scowl and grunt sent shivers up my spine. Too young and unattractive to be of any interest to them, I both raged at and enjoyed my own invisibility. Like the proverbial moth in a cocoon, I knew that better times were coming.

For much of my childhood and most of my adolescence, I was torn between wanting to be a doctor and an actress. (In those days, women were still "actresses"; it would take another thirty years or so for them to become actors.) The high point in my acting career came in the tenth grade, when I was cast as a lead in a school production of *East Lynn*. But my excitement on winning the part was short-lived. Mr. Evans, the high-school English teacher responsible for directing the play, seemed to spend every rehearsal looking for excuses to touch my chest. One of the scenes called for me to clutch my young son to my bosom, and Mr. Evans enacted the part of the son over and over again. I coped by trying to convince myself that teachers were like doctors, and it didn't matter. But I couldn't wait for the play to end.

Unable to continue my theatrical career by appearing in school productions, I decided to branch out. I got a subscription to *Show-business* and began to look for my first break. When I learned that a movie based on Anne Frank's *Diary of a Young Girl* was going to be made and a national search for an unknown to play Anne would be undertaken, I decided to answer the casting call. Months later, I was crushed to learn that Millie Perkins, a pert young model with an up-turned nose, had been chosen to play Anne. I wondered whether I had lost out to her because I looked too Jewish.

After a while, I discovered the Living Theater, a revolutionary theater company presided over by Julian Beck and Judith Malina. During the 1950s and 1960s the Living Theater was on the cutting edge of avant-garde culture, committed to breaking down the barriers between art and politics and to using art to create revolutionary consciousness. A classmate of mine spent a few days each week doing odd jobs at the theater on Fourteenth Street, and when she offered me the chance to come along, I agreed without hesitation. Before long, I was sweeping the floor and selling refreshments, books, and pamphlets from a small kiosk in the lobby. I wasn't paid for my work, nor, I suspect, was Jessica, but it didn't matter. Judith and Julian were mesmerizing personalities, and the world they created was unlike any I had ever encountered before. The company was surely the most racially and ethnically diverse group of people I had ever known, and the way the community lived and worked together amazed and charmed me. I marveled at their easy physical intimacy and began to understand that being born into a family was not the only way to become part of one.

I watched *Many Loves* by William Carlos Williams again and again and hung around while the cast rehearsed Jack Gelber's *The Connection*, a play about drug pushers and addicts so realistic that it shocked traditional audiences when it was presented in 1959. On Julian's birthday that year, there was a kind of party in the rooms over the theater, and I watched in awe as several members of the company took turns churning the crank to make homemade mango ice cream. More than anything, I wanted to be part of that world, even though each night I went home to a freezer that boasted an automatic ice machine. I was crushed when school let out and my visits to the Living Theater were ended by my family's annual departure for our country home.

Every June, for as long as I could remember, as soon as school was out, moth balls were scattered on the carpets and sprinkled liberally between the cushions of the couches and the chairs, everything was covered with sheets, and we set out for "the country." At first, my parents rented summer houses in Belle Harbor, Long Island, and later in Connecticut. By the time I turned twelve, we had bought a house in Westport, where we spent fall and spring weekends as well as summer vacation.

The house was sold to us by two bachelors, as they were called, who had lived there together for many years. When we moved in, I inherited a gabled room with a window in the shape of a porthole that looked out on Long Island Sound. The walls were papered with deep blue-and-purple violet chains suspended against a yellow background; the furniture was country Victorian and painted a pale blue. It seemed a very improbable room for me to inhabit, and I loved it. My room in the city had been decorated by Mr. Ludwig, the interior decorator my mother used to help her furnish and refurbish our apartment. His taste and mine rarely coincided. In Westport, I nestled into the peculiarly old-fashioned room created by our two bachelor predecessors and felt at home.

But apart from the room, Westport wasn't my home at all, and I quickly came to dread going there. No kids my age lived nearby; besides, we were summer people and that meant we could never really belong. I was a city girl in my bones, living in a make-believe room in the country. I stayed up late, alternating between Jack Parr on *The Tonight Show* and the CBS late movie, eating Kraft's pimento and olive spread on Ritz crackers, cutting out photographs of James Dean, and reading novels and writing poetry.

My mother loved the house in Westport and the more casual lifestyle it seemed to allow. The furniture, which had been purchased in a single trip to a local store, was early American, and the pine wood and simple country prints were in sharp contrast to the mahogany and brocade of our New York apartment. We were the only Jewish family on the block, but my mother soon made friends with our next-door neighbors, a Leave-It-to-Beaver, Protestant family with three young children. Having friends and neighbors who weren't Jewish seemed to please my mother because it reinforced her vision of herself as a maverick and pathbreaker. She saw Westport as a place where our relative anonymity would allow us to depart from some of the more confining rules of our New York life. But to me, our stays in Westport always felt like a period of incarceration, and, in fact, they were.

My mother did not know how to drive a car and refused to learn. When I asked her why, she complained that she had responsibility for most things in the family and maintained that if she learned to drive she would simply have more to do. Using reasoning that closely resembled that of conservative women who failed to support the ERA years later, she believed that her decision struck a blow for women's rights. In reality, all it meant was that we were trapped in our house for five days a week while my father worked in the city. On the weekends, we were dependent on his good humor to take us around. Fortunately, it was never in short supply.

Mother ordered meat from a kosher butcher in Bridgeport who delivered on Tuesdays and Fridays, and she phoned in grocery orders to a local market that did the same. Except for an occasional trip to Main Street by cab, we stayed home. Years later, I thought back to my mother and our self-imposed confinement when a neighbor of mine became widowed. This sixty-four-year-old woman had never learned to drive either, a fact she shared with pride, explaining that her husband loved her so much that he insisted on taking her everywhere, even back and forth each day to her job at a local hospital. What she experienced as privileged treatment, explained by her husband as an extension of his role as her protector, ended up making her a virtual prisoner in her suburban home. One day, her husband left in the morning and never returned. He had died of a heart attack at work, and she was left stranded. Like my mother, she traded empowerment for dependency rationalized by gender stereotypes and later found that what she took to be privilege was merely powerlessness in fancy wrapping. In my late twenties, when I read Evan McCall's wonderful book *Mrs. Bridge,* about a woman who makes a similar, and fatal, mistake, I recognized the character immediately.

On Thursday nights during the summer, we went out to eat, just as we did in New York. But in Connecticut, we went to restaurants rather than hotel dining rooms. In the city, Thursday, which was known as "maid's night out," meant that we would be eating at the Savoy Plaza, where the maître d', dressed in a tux, would greet us with much seeming pleasure and where Mario, our own special waiter, also dressed in a tux, would inquire with great seriousness as to our choices for dinner. This was really not necessary, since we ordered the same thing every Thursday night. My father and brother ate grilled Dover sole, and my mother and I, being more adventurous, had a dish called *filet de sole bonne femme,* which involved cooking the fish with mushrooms in a white wine and cream sauce. Dinner was preceded by Shirley Temples for the children and Manhattans for the grown-ups and accompanied by a green salad of endive, watercress, and Bibb lettuce—greens we never ate at home. Dessert offered some latitude. My father usually ordered vanilla ice cream, but I alternated among a strawberry tart, a napoleon, or *coupe de marrons,* the last being an irresistible combination of vanilla ice cream and candied chestnuts in a thick, sugary syrup. The entire dining room staff was male, but in the powder room an old woman proffered towels and cologne in exchange for a few coins. It goes without saying that everyone was white.

Eating out represented a serious compromise on the part of my father, who took the laws of kashruth seriously but who wanted to please my mother as well. Given the choice, he preferred Ratner's, a dairy restaurant on the Lower East Side, or Isaac Gellis and, later, Fine and Shapiro, two kosher delis on the Upper West Side. Because my mother was used to Delmonico and the Savoy Plaza, he agreed to eat broiled fish out, but never went further than that. In the early days of their marriage, my mother confined herself to eating fish as well. As their relationship deteriorated, my mother began to order steaks and, in the later years, even seafood. She justified it on medical grounds, claiming that she needed the protein or iron. I followed my mother's lead, but, aside from an occasional lapse into beef, my brother stuck with his dad.

While for years Thursday night dinner meant the Savoy Plaza, there were occasional forays to the Oak Room at the Plaza Hotel across Fifth Avenue or the restaurant at the Pierre, and periodic visits to the 21 Club because my father knew its owners, the Kriendler brothers, from Mu Sigma, his high-school fraternity. I remember eating wafer-thin sandwiches made of crustless, pale pumpernickel bread that alternated with layers of incredibly creamy sweet butter, offered to me as a special treat at a birthday lunch. On several occasions, my father might attend evening meetings of the fraternity at 21, where the members discussed how to raise money for the fledgling Brandeis University. At such times, he might return home with a cardboard box of napoleons as a treat for my mother, who had a special fondness for them. This provided my parents with a once- or twice-a-year departure from their usual late-night snack, which otherwise consisted of reheated coffee and Social Teas or perhaps Uneeda Biscuits with cream cheese and jelly. They shared this small and comforting repast virtually every night of my childhood, eating off a tray table (when they were new and very popular) placed carefully between the twin beds that my father's Orthodox Judaism required. It was one of those rare occasions during which they seemed to find pleasure in each other's company.

But in Westport, we ate at the Clam Box. The Clam Box was a large and popular fish restaurant that served french fries, onion rings, cole-slaw, pickles, and every kind of fish and seafood you could imagine. It featured Formica tables, paper napkins, snappy waiters *and waitresses,* and a decidedly eclectic crowd. In the city, we would never have entered such an establishment, but in the country the rules changed. There was nobody there who might see us and set tongues wagging at our infraction, and so my father was willing to give in to my mother's wishes for a less narrow and stultifying life. After a while, my father even began driving the car on Saturday, something expressly prohibited by his religion but required by a suburban lifestyle, which included Little League games and trips to swim at the beach or the club. On some Thursday nights, dinner was followed by a family excursion to the local supermarket. Back in the city, my mother ordered her groceries by telephone, just as she did in Connecticut, so visits to the supermarket seemed like a real adventure to me and my brother. We went up and down the aisles like normal people, filling our cart with breakfast cereals, canned goods, and snacks.

There were other differences in Westport as well. Instead of having both a maid and a laundress, in Westport, one woman performed both jobs. She was always Black and always came from Bridgeport, which then, as now, was a depressed urban area with a high poverty rate and a large nonwhite population. A stone's throw from more affluent towns like Greenwich, Stamford, and Westport, it supplied a steady stream of maids, cooks, and cleaning women to white suburban families. Once or twice a week, the woman would wash our clothes in a washing machine my mother had installed in the kitchen and then hang them out to dry—in the sun if the weather was good and in the basement if it was raining. I might smile at her as I raced through the kitchen and out the back door, but we rarely spoke.

Each summer, the woman's name and appearance changed, but the pattern of her work life remained the same. Some man or men would drop her off in the morning and pick her up at night, arriving in a large, battered, and noisy car. Like virtually every other suburban area in the country, there was no public transportation to speak of and cars were essential if you wanted to work. Then, as now, it was easier for Black women to find work than it was for Black men. Ownership of cars, though, was still a male prerogative, so the men drove her to our house and drove her home and filled the time in between with odd jobs, if they were fortunate, or on the street corners, if they were not. The children, if there were any, stayed with one or another grandmother or great-grandmother, aunt, or neighborhood woman.

At one point, the same woman returned for several years in a row, and, like the more permanent help we had in New York, she became "one of the family," receiving bundles of clothes for her children and carrying home opened packages of staples and the contents of the refrigerator when we cleaned out the house for the winter. I remember her as a kind and affable woman, but it never occurred to me to ask how she survived the long winters waiting for us to return.

Now my friends who marched and chanted in the 1960s and 1970s send home bundles of used clothes to the children of the women who clean *their* houses. No longer "maids," "cleaning ladies," or "girls," but "women who clean," these women speak in the lilting cadence of the French-speaking Caribbean islands or the halting Spanglish of South and Central America or Mexico. Perhaps they speak Portuguese. And my friends, who once knew better, make no apologies for hiring these multihued women to make their beds and empty their trash. They regularly in fact, ask for my sympathy, complaining that tomorrow "Inés" or "Providencia" or "Mrs. Goméz" is coming, and that means they must clean up for her even though they're much too tired. Besides, they insist, they pay her quite well, really more than she deserves, considering how often she breaks things and how frequently she fails to clean under the couch.

At the office, my colleagues and I smile warmly as we ask Black women in imitation professional attire to type our papers or do our photocopying. We are pleased to see that they dress smartly and try to forget that they are supporting large families on a bare subsistence wage. We don't let ourselves think about the fact that they must work a second job to afford the Kmart clothes that their work requires. We'd rather not know that they depend on their less fortunate sisters and cousins who still clean houses for the used clothing they bring home and then share with them for their children. And we prefer not to think of their other relatives "back home," who sew these same garments in Third World sweatshops owned by U.S. corporations determined not to pay a union wage.

During our summers in Connecticut, in addition to a maid to clean and wash, a gardener came by once or twice a week to cut the grass and take care of the flower beds. Although our house was fairly modest by most standards and the property hardly imposing, it would no more have occurred to my mother to do without a gardener than it would have occurred to her to go out without stockings. Although she loved gardening herself, her inability to drive a car and her conviction that every house needed a gardener left her dependent on him to select and furnish the flowers that brought her so much pleasure. Occasionally on the weekend, my father would take us to a garden center, where she might choose a plant or two to fill in any empty spaces that the gardener left.

And, of course, we joined a country club. In those days, it goes without saying, such clubs were segregated. Naturally they were all white, and Jews could join only their own clubs. My family started at a private club, down by the water at Compo Beach, which catered to summer people, but later joined a more exclusive club located in a high-priced area that had a golf course and pool, but no shoreline. In spite of the absence of beach and surf, the club's higher social status meant that you needed several sponsors and an interview with the club's board before you could join. Once admitted, you were permitted to pay the hefty entrance fee that ensured your membership and granted you the privilege of paying an equally hefty membership fee each year. One of my mother's best friends was a member of the first club, and for a while, before we bought our house, we rented a three-bedroom "chalet" on the grounds, which meant we could walk to the beach every day—even when my father was at work. I was twelve or thirteen and spent the summer taking tennis lessons, drinking ice cream floats, reading books, and alternating between swimming in the ocean and floating in the pool. My mother and her friend Dora talked, played cards, or argued, and enjoyed their children together. It was a happy time. At lunch, if we were feeling decadent, my mother and I would go to the cafeteria and order half a cantaloupe with a scoop of coffee ice cream, which we ate outside under the shade of an umbrella. We rented our own cabana down by the pool that, in addition to a tiny changing room, provided us with a small porch and our own fenced-off plot of sand. Up and down the row of cabanas, each family was a mirror image of the one next door. During the week, the women luxuriated in the easy intimacy of a world without men. On the weekends, when the dads were home, the place felt totally different.

As my father's earnings increased and we were able to buy a house and became eligible to join the more exclusive club, things changed for the worse. Without a car, we could go to the club only on weekends when my father was home. My mother and I spent all our weekdays sunbathing alone, or together, on the flagstone patio at our house while my brother played nearby. On weekends, my father drove the family to the club.

During the three or four years we belonged to the club, I doubt that anyone my age ever said more than two consecutive sentences to me or ever reciprocated my awkward attempts at friendship. I would have given anything for my tanned and well-turned-out peers to pay me some notice, but they rarely did. First, we were summer people, and, second, my father did not make as much money as theirs. The girls had more expensive clothes and more of them; they dated boys who wore Brooks Brother button-downs with their jeans and drove sleek white convertibles; they had no reason to befriend me.

My mother had learned to play golf as a teenager and toyed with the thought of starting to play again, even taking a few lessons from the club pro, but she never actually played. My father, a serious and energetic tennis player since his early twenties, spent his free time on one of the two tennis courts that occupied a spare corner of the club's Gatsbyesque grounds. At Oakwood, unlike the previous club we had attended, your status was calculated based on your par, and there were no points awarded for your backhand or your serve. After a summer or two, I traded in the country club pool for a class in Latin at the local high school.

My private school did not offer classes in Latin, and I had wanted to study it for a long time. Learning Latin seemed to me like getting a piece of the rock, having a claim on the best of the past, becoming part of the tradition of educated men (*sic*). But taking a remedial Latin class at Staples High School, the only one offered during the summer, was hardly the way to go about it. The class consisted entirely of kids who had failed Latin during the regular year. Most of them were boys, and the kind of boys we referred to in those days as "hoods." Required to take Latin as part of their high-school curriculum, they wanted to spend the summer in school about as much as the country club set wanted me at their parties. The teacher was a middle-aged man who long ago had lost whatever enthusiasm he had for teaching. I began the class hoping to read Ovid and Virgil but it was not meant to be. I learned to conjugate *Agricolae est agri* and made friends with Susy Grabowski.

Susy was a reject from Sacred Heart. Actually, she attended Sacred Heart during the year and was trying to get a passing grade in Latin so that she could return. In the absence of any viable alternatives, the two of us became friends. Susy was a genuinely sweet and kind person with little interest in Latin and considerable interest in her complexion. Although no more pimply than most, Susy was preoccupied with the condition of her skin, which she feared might stand between her and the marriage that would change her life. Unlike me, who rarely thought about getting married, Susy, like my mother, believed that marriage to the right man held the key to happiness. I was never sure where Susy got the idea. Her natural father had been a drunkard and a batterer who had terrorized her childhood. Now Susy and her brother lived with their mother and her second husband in a small house in a marginal neighborhood on the fringes of Westport.

Her stepfather was a kind of handyman who did odd jobs, and Susy's mother cleaned houses. Because her mother had been divorced and remarried, Susy was thought to be in moral jeopardy by the nuns at her school. She had to work twice as hard to win their approval, which was rarely forthcoming. Because of this, Susy went through considerable pain and confusion trying to reconcile her love for her mother with the sisters' obvious disdain, and we spent a lot of time that summer trying to figure out why God and the Catholic Church thought it was sinful for Susy's mother to have divorced a man who regularly beat her bloody and why the nuns took this as proof that Susy would come to no good.

After I had known Susy for a while, she decided to show me her hope chest. I had never before known anyone who had such a thing. Girls of my class simply looked forward to inheriting the key to their mothers' safe-deposit boxes or registering at Tiffany's. Susy's hope chest really was just that, a repository of all her hopes for a better life. For as long as she could remember, she had been filling it with treasures. There were nightgowns and underwear that she and her mother had sewn, some glassware, embroidered tablecloths and napkins and other bits and pieces of a future, and a few pieces of a silver pattern that she had begun to collect. The silverware had been acquired by redeeming coupons from a food company that offered silver-plated knives, forks, and spoons in exchange for box tops and dollars. Even this means of acquiring the tableware was very expensive for her, and she worried constantly about being able to collect an entire set in time. Susy longed to be, in her words, a "lady," something her mother's marital and economic status precluded, and longed to have what she thought of as "beautiful things." But unlike many of the girls I went to school with, she was not greedy. The things she collected filled her with pleasure and held out the possibility of attaining middle-class respectability. In spite of her preoccupation with stockpiling material goods, she really wanted very little. Like my mother, she had great hopes for a better life but no sense of how she might go about shaping one. She took it for granted that she would be a wife and mother and pinned all her hopes on marrying the right man. In her case, it was clear that he didn't have to be rich, just a solid provider, clean cut and kind, someone who would love her. Until he came along, she would attend classes at Sacred Heart, try not to anger the sisters, help out around the house, and save coupons and box tops to fill her chest.

Susy had a brother who was hoping to join the navy, and Susy had a large crush on an older boy who already had. She kept a picture of him in his navy whites among her special things and showed it to me proudly, taking for granted that I, too, would be impressed by his uniform—a symbol for her of elevated status. I was careful not to disabuse her of this notion, although in my world nobody ever joined the armed services and I had little interest in the working-class boys who did. As far as I was concerned, uniforms, any uniforms, even those worn by the rabbi and cantor at our synagogue, were signs of lower-class standing. Uniforms were worn by maids, kitchen workers, parcel-post delivery men, and the guy who drove the Good Humor truck. In

Susy's world, her Sacred Heart school uniform was the subject of end-less complaints but also a real source of pride. Like a sailor or soldier's uniform, it was the ticket of admission to a better life. By association, it instantly provided a working-class person with a claim on member-ship in an institution with more power and prestige than the individ-ual herself could claim. I understood what uniforms meant to Susy, but never dreamed of sharing my own feelings about them. In the end, there were too many differences between us, and exploring them with Susy would have been cruel. Ours was a friendship of conveniences, and like so many summer infatuations, it gradually faded away.

When my mother was Susy's age, she lived in an apartment at 90 Riverside Drive and was cared for by a governess. Mademoiselle, as she called her, had been governess to the royal family of Spain until the Civil War. After that, she took care of Count Roger de Montebello, whose son Philippe went on to become director of the Metropolitan Museum of Art. Later she found her way to my grandparents' home, where she cared for my mother throughout most of her childhood and adolescence. By all accounts a kind and accomplished woman, Made-moiselle gave my mother the love and attention that, on occasion, her own mother was unable or unwilling to provide. My mother learned to speak French, to play the piano and sing, and to crochet and sew. She longed to ride a horse but was given a hoop to roll in the park in-stead. Sometimes Mademoiselle tied a series of knots in a fine gold chain and left my mother the tedious chore of untying them one by one. Con-trary to appearances, this was not a punishment but simply, at that time, an acceptable way of teaching young ladies of her class the virtue of patience. I have another of her lessons tucked away in my attic, a wisp of pale, chiffonlike cloth, once blue but now a characterless gray, on which she embroidered in fine gold thread a tiny spider caught in its web. Raised to marry a prince or at least a count, my mother married a shirt manufacturer instead. This left her understandably bitter.

Saturday afternoons during my teens often meant going to the movies with my mother at the Translux Eighty-fifth Street or the Plaza Theater. When I was eleven and twelve, I went to neighborhood mov-ies with classmates, walking with them to the Beacon at Seventy-fifth

Street and Broadway or the Loews Eighty-third a few blocks farther uptown. We watched Debra Paget and Robert Taylor or Tony Curtis and Janet Leigh in one period drama after another, and in this way acquired a very peculiar sense of history. But later, I spent Saturdays at the movies with my mother.

She always chose the films without consulting me and saw to it that I had a steady diet of romance/escape as the stuff on which to build my dreams. We saw *Wuthering Heights* and *The African Queen*, *Little Women* and *Jane Eyre*, *Seven Brides for Seven Brothers* and, of course, Garbo in *Camille*. In her heart, my mother honestly believed that she would find happiness if my father simply disappeared and she could go to Italy like Katharine Hepburn in *Summertime* and meet Rossano Brazzi. Faced with the choice of learning to drive herself or marrying a man who could afford to provide her with a chauffeur, she was raised to choose the latter without hesitation.

Sometimes we went to Saturday matinees. We saw *South Pacific, The King and I, Kismet,* and *Peter Pan.* During *Kismet,* I remember being transfixed by the beauty of Doretta Morrow's voice, only to have my rapture shattered when my mother leaned over to comment on the size of Morrow's derriere. I wondered how I would ever be able to please this woman who could find fault with the star of a Broadway show singing lyrics written to Aleksandr Borodin's exquisite melodies in a voice that could pierce your heart. If Doretta Morrow could not escape my mother's brutal judgment, what hope was there for me?

During those years, I was my mother's best and only friend. She rarely went to the movies with my father because he always fell asleep; she never went to concerts with him because he had no interest in classical music; and they went to plays together only when the synagogue or some charity held a benefit. He usually fell asleep then, too, but felt compelled to attend in order to affirm his standing in the Jewish community. Although she had a few longtime women friends, she didn't go out with them either because they had little in common. Their friendships were largely confined to the telephone, and their face-to-face meetings tended to occur on the occasional Saturday nights when two or three couples would get together to play cards.

After sundown, when the Sabbath had ended, the couples would get together to drink rye and ginger while playing canasta or bridge. At our house, these nights always ended with a late supper of Nova Scotia salmon and sturgeon from Barney Greengrass or a platter of delicatessen from Fine and Shapiro. Grossinger's bakery, around the corner on Columbus Avenue between Seventy-fifth and Seventy-sixth Streets, provided a dairy coffee cake or a pareve fruit pie, depending on the evening's menu.

My mother and father were twenty-four and forty-one, respectively, when they met, and they shared very few interests. Coming from different worlds, or at least vastly different parts of the same world, they knew very little about each other before they married and knew nothing about working at a relationship. Some years later, my mother told me that during their courtship, she believed that the long walks she took with my father on Saturday afternoons were a sign of his romantic nature. It was not until their honeymoon that she realized they were simply the way he complied with Orthodox Jewish prohibitions against violating the Sabbath. That she could have suffered under this misunderstanding for so long suggests both her naïveté and the utter lack of communication between them. This absence formed the context for their marriage and their life together.

My father believed that it was a man's duty to support his wife and children and that if he could do that well, he was a success; my mother believed the same thing, but her standards of success were higher. Rocky when my father was earning a good living, their marriage deteriorated rapidly as his earnings declined. Indeed, they both had every reason to curse their fate. They played by the rules they had been taught, but were utterly unable to accommodate themselves to the changes in the rules that came about during their lifetime. No one had prepared them for this possibility. Certainly no one had raised them to be happy.

In spite of the ample financial resources enjoyed by my family throughout most of my childhood, I was brought up to feel guilty about spending money on anything that gave me pleasure. For that reason, I always found it easy to buy dresses that were the wrong color and didn't fit, but almost impossible to bring home something I wanted unless my mother was there to buy it for me. The one exception was books. For some reason, I suppose because my mother valued them so highly herself, I was allowed to buy books whenever I wanted them and never felt guilty about doing so.

At the start of each summer, my parents took me to a bookstore on Main Street in Westport and allowed me to buy stacks of books to see me through the months until school began again. No matter how many I chose, I was never asked to put any back. And to this day, books are the one thing I can buy without any feelings of being extravagant. Most of the books we bought in those days came in hardbound editions, which probably contributed to my belief, and the belief of others of my generation, that great literature had a universal and enduring quality. Children raised on mass-market paperbacks, their bindings glued rather than sewn, or on TV and the Internet, are hardly likely to develop a similar world view. My own early interest in writing was surely motivated as much by my belief that it would ensure me a sliver of immortality as by my love of language and the pleasure that fashioning it gave to me.

Like many adolescents who feel misunderstood and alone, I depended on my books to keep me company and to take me places. Unlike that of my friends and family, the companionship they provided was always dependable and generous. This sampling of what life was like, real or imagined, at different times and in different places helped me formulate possibilities for a future beyond the confines circumscribed by the particularities of my life. I made the acquaintance of women like Emma Bovary, Anna Karenina, Elizabeth Bennet, and Isabel Archer and resolved to learn from their mistakes even as I was captivated by their beauty, resilience, and audacity. As a result, I spent most weekends locked in my room reading. This drove my father crazy. He found reading an unnatural occupation and was always after me to "do something." Reading, he told me, was all right for a rainy day, but he could never understand why any one would waste time reading when there were other alternatives. This well-intentioned comment was a constant reminder that he had no idea who I was.

In addition to the standard editions of books and the numerous cheaper volumes from Random House's Modern Library series that were popular in those days, my own library continues to house a number of special volumes that belonged to my mother and even a few that belonged to my grandmother. I am especially fond of a small, red, once leather-bound volume entitled *Friendship,* which offers its reader two essays: the first by Cicero and the other by Emerson. Its inner cover bears an inscription written in the kind of elegant hand that we now associate with women's writing, but that used to be equally the mark of a well-bred and well-educated man. It reads, "Presented to my dear friend Anna for her earnest considerations and thought by one who deeply appreciates and values sincere friendship," and is dated December 5, 1908. As precious as the book itself is the testimony it gives to a world in which young people of a certain class exchanged such volumes as proof of their deep affection and respect. Since very few of my grandmother's books were preserved, I often wonder what this volume and the person who gave it actually meant to her. Did her heart beat faster as she turned its pages, or did she accept the book reluctantly, offering perfunctory thanks? Does its persistence attest to some special meaning or to the utter and profound lack of any significance it held? What did she make of the prefatory poem by Emerson that begins

> A ruddy drop of manly blood
> The surging sea outweighs
> The world uncertain comes and goes,
> The lover rooted stays.

Did it speak to her?

I feel connected to my grandmother and her world in many ways, including the fact that I too have received a volume now and then, carefully inscribed to catch and hold some fragile moment in a past or future relationship. Perhaps someday my children will stumble on them and be charmed or perplexed by their hidden meanings too.

Over the years, I have offered copies of some of the books I have loved to my own children, giving myself the special pleasure that comes with passing on a tangible and cherished piece of the past. They try gamely to engage with them, but often do not succeed. It is clear that the books of my childhood do not speak to them. They live in a different world. My daughter, Andrea, is unmoved by Anne Frank's *The Diary of a Young Girl,* a book that broke my heart. Like her brother, she finds it almost tedious to read. A year after I offered the *Diary* to her, she comes home with a new book, *Upon the Head of the Goat,* which tells the story of a young girl and her family in Beregszasz, Hungary, during the same period. She and her classmates spend whole class periods discussing the book with a passionate intensity. In contrast to the rape and torture it recounts, Anne's story must have seemed very tame to them.

The simple truth is that every generation needs a literature that engages it on its own terms. How could it be otherwise? Will children of this world ever again read Cicero and Emerson on friendship? Does it matter? What stakes do some have in insisting that they should? Should I rejoice or weep that my daughter abandons *Little Women* after several serious attempts?

Another book I love from my mother's library is one not nearly so old but old enough to have a timeless quality about it, an edition of *The Oxford Book of English Verse,* printed on the thinnest paper imaginable, sheer as hummingbird wings, and bound in soft brown leather with a gilt embossed cover. It is a book I love to caress. There is a also a copy of *Jocelyn* by Lamartine, also bound in leather but nestled into a carefully stitched cover of red velvet and gilt threads, a gift to my mother from her governess. On the inside cover, Mademoiselle has carefully copied out a passage from Alfred de Musset which reads:

> Sans doute, tout meurent, ce monde est un grand rêve
> et le peu de bonheur que nous vient en chemin,
> nous n'avons pas plutôt ce roseau dans la main
> que le vent nous l'enleve.*

---

*To be sure, everything dies, this world is a great dream
And as for the little happiness that comes our way,
We no sooner have the reed in hand
Than the wind blows it away from us.

Hardly an encouraging piece of poetry for a young woman about to begin her adult life. But as I have already said, my mother was not raised to be happy.

This book sits on the shelf next to a copy of *Mémoires d'une jeune fille rangée* by Simone de Beauvoir, which, coincidently, also bears a quote from Musset on its inside cover page and the signature of my French tutor, who made a present of it to me when I graduated from high school. *La plus ca change . . .*

Having had a French governess, like my mother, although for only a short while, I too early acquired a good ear for French and a love of the language and rapidly outgrew the French classes provided by my private high school. Although the Spanish teacher, known, of course, as Señora, had been at the school for years, the French teachers seemed to come and go with startling rapidity. Señora was a strict teacher who kept her classes under control because the students knew that the possibility of accompanying her on her annual summer trip to Taxco, Mexico, a privilege available to her students if their parents agreed and could pay the price, was contingent on earning a good grade and behaving reasonably well. I considered studying Spanish, but for only an instant. Unlike that in French, I knew that there was no great literature or culture associated with the Spanish language. For me, Spanish meant one great book, *Don Quixote,* and Puerto Ricans—neither of which recommended the language to me. But few of my classmates shared my enthusiasm for studying French, even when their parents decided that they should do so, and without the prospect of a summer trip to keep them in line, behavior in French classes was always outrageous. This, along with the abysmally low rate of pay offered by the school, meant that no French teacher stayed very long. The good ones, all women, left in disgust to teach at more elite schools, and the bad ones, mostly men, left, according to their own reports, to pursue more lucrative careers. My favorite French teacher was a strange little man named Jacques de Buffet, who wore a mink-lined overcoat and let us spend class taking turns dancing the tango with him while he played old 78s on a portable record player. When he left after a few weeks, we were never sure whether he had been dismissed because the principal found out about our dance lessons or had simply gone off in pursuit of fresh partners. In any case, I rapidly outgrew the French instruction offered by my school and, during my senior year, ended up studying the language with a private tutor. In truth, this was less a reflection on my proficiency than on the inadequacy of the standard instruction that was offered, but it provided me with a kind of oasis in what otherwise felt like a parched existence.

One afternoon each week, I journeyed to Madame's West End Avenue apartment and studied French surrounded by her beautiful things. Although they were not of the same quality as the antiques and fabrics in my own home, they had clearly been lovingly acquired by her in the course of a lifetime, not selected somewhat arbitrarily by an interior decorator. Their charm came from their uniqueness and the easy way they came together. I felt charmed and protected. At some point during the lesson, Madame would bring out a pot of tea or perhaps a grenadine-flavored drink and some biscuits on a small tray, and we would nibble on them as we conversed. It was an afternoon to which I always looked forward.

When the year came to an end, Madame presented me with a graduation gift, a copy of *Mémoires d'une jeune fille rangée* by Beauvoir. In it, she had inscribed the following lines from de Musset:

> France, Ô mon beau pays! J'ai de plus d'un outrage
> Offensé ton céleste, harmonieux language,
> Idiome de l'amour si doux Qu'à le parler
> Tes femmes sur la levre en gardent un sourire
> Le miel la plus doré qui sui la triste lyre
> De la bouche et du coeur ait jamais pu couler!*

---

*France, Oh my beautiful country!
I have committed more than one outrage
Against your heavenly, harmonious language,
Idiom of love so sweet
That women speak it with a smile on their lips;
Honey most golden
Upon the sad lyre of mouth and heart
May never flow again.

They certainly suggested a more appealing future to me than the lines with which my mother had been similarly gifted.

Although the French, science, and math teaching at my school left a lot to be desired because the low pay and inadequate facilities were unlikely to attract particularly competent teachers, by the time I reached my junior year the English instruction was excellent. This was probably because there was an overabundance of graduates from the better women's colleges who had majored in English hoping to become writers or at least work in publishing but who ended up teaching English for a year or two at a New York private school before reconciling themselves to the inevitable marriage. Jobs in publishing were few and hard to come by and, at least in the case of women, required good secretarial skills, something that many of these Seven Sister college graduates lacked. Teaching at a small private school that allowed them perfect freedom to choose their texts and provided small classes of bright white students was a good fallback. Although salaries at such schools were abysmally low, this was not an impediment because these women had not been raised to measure their value in salary dollars or to think very much about pay equity issues. Besides, the salary at such schools probably compared favorably to those they would have received as editorial assistants in the only other jobs to which they aspired.

During the course of high-school English, we not only read *Beowulf* and Chaucer, but we often were encouraged to imitate their style in writing assignments that had us creating our own versions of lengthy prose poems in Old and Middle English. In this way, we came to feel a personal affinity for the literary traditions we were taught to value. And, of course, each book report had to conform to a formula that asked us to discuss character development, plot, and writing style and that ended with a mandatory discussion of the universal themes in the work. In this way, we came to understand that novels and short stories about the trials and tribulations of well-to-do, white men were universal and timeless. In this way, we came to own Ernest Hemingway, Herman Melville, Samuel Butler, William Shakespeare, and a host of other similarly situated writers and adopt their Eurocentric and privileged male view of life and the world as though it were coextensive with reality. And we learned to see ourselves through their eyes or become invisible if that was what was required. We did not read Richard Wright or Zora Neale Hurston but quickly came to understand the limited nature of the talent of Emily Dickinson, whom we did read, when compared with the sweeping visions and eternal values of John Milton, Gerard Manley Hopkins, and T. S. Eliot. Eliot was a particularly impressive figure throughout high school and college because of the clever way he made it impossible for anyone who was not educated exactly as he had been to read his verse. As a graduate student, I remember being particularly pleased when I began to study classical Greek and realized that by adding a knowledge of it to my facility with French and rudimentary knowledge of Latin, I would soon fulfill another of Eliot's prerequisites for those aspiring to read certain of his poems.

Whenever I got a good report card, my father rewarded me with a $20 bill. A generous man, he had no idea of how to express his praise other than with cold cash. When I announced while in my late twenties that I had decided to stop smoking, my father offered me $300 if I succeeded. Having grown up in a world where money was everything and where he had very little as a child, he was never able to develop any other frame of reference.

When it came time for college, my father wondered out loud about spending money to educate a female who would surely end up married. My mother, on the other hand, by now the victim of a bitterly unhappy marriage who had watched both her own parents and her husband lose large sums of money in the business world, was committed to financial independence for her daughter. Although she went to her death believing that the answer to her unhappiness lay in her failure to marry a man rich, charming, or worldly enough, she understood at some level that economic independence for women was a prerequisite not only for personal security but perhaps for a happy long-term relationship as well and encouraged me to get a degree and pursue a career.

In fact, like most children in my graduating class of twenty-four, I had been encouraged to look toward college throughout my high-school years and to acquire grades and honors that would ensure my admission. I was the sort of girl who was raised to be yearbook editor, student government officer, captain of the basketball team, news editor of the school paper, editor of the French magazine, and the like, and so, of course, I was all those things and more. But good grades and accolades notwithstanding, I knew that where college admissions were concerned, my family lived in the wrong part of the country and practiced the wrong religion. The rigid quotas placed on New York City Jews made it very unlikely that I would ever go to one of the Seven Sister colleges regardless of how well I did. I alternated between frustration over the clear injustice of it and feeling that somehow it was my fault. I just didn't measure up.

My interview at Wellesley was painful. I wanted to get in so badly that I could hardly keep myself together. That's how overwhelmed I was with the possibility of going there and the fear that I wouldn't be accepted. Interviews at Radcliffe, Mount Holyoke, and Barnard went a little better because I didn't want to go to any of them quite as much. Besides, by then I was probably numb.

My interview with the admissions officer from Oberlin deserves a paragraph of its own. He conducted interviews at a hotel in midtown, probably the New Yorker or the Biltmore. I was nervous as I dressed to meet him and spent a long time worrying about what to wear. Back then, I believed that each college had its own distinctive look and thought that it was essential to turn up at the interview looking like one of its own undergraduates. Having little basis on which to develop my imitation of an Oberlin freshman, I settled for the usual skirt and blouse and crossed my fingers. Halfway through the interview, the man, noting that I was Jewish, looked up from his notes and asked, "How Jewish are you?" To my shame, I was so surprised and disoriented by his question that I actually tried to answer it.

High-school graduation was held on the stage of Town Hall on West Forty-third Street, and the senior prom took place at the Starlight Roof of the Waldorf. The Junior-Senior luncheon that year was held at the Sherry Netherlands, and I was on the committee that made the rounds of a select group of hotels in order to examine the facilities, discuss the menu, and negotiate the cost. Dressed in our Saks Fifth Avenue clothes, we carried our sixteen- and seventeen-year-old selves straight to the banquet manager's office and began to hone the skills that we were expected to use throughout our lives to orchestrate social and charitable events for our husbands, families, and communities. The managers and staff at these hotels were properly deferential. They understood that whatever status their age, experience, gender, and race afforded them—since they were, of course, all men and all white—was more than offset, in this context, by our class position.

We graduated at Town Hall and danced at the Waldorf because New York was our town. We never doubted it for a second. We grew up in a world that was covered in the *New York Times*. Our parents' class privilege guaranteed us a future. In my case, I believed that it could even compensate for being Jewish and being female, although I suspected that it could not obliterate their consequences entirely. Certainly, it could not keep me safe. But it could give me the illusion of power and prerogative and the reality of privilege, and it could make them all seem like my due. Not privilege at all, just the way things were, the way they were supposed to be.

3

Becoming Educated

❖　❖　❖　❖　❖　❖　❖　❖　❖　❖　❖　❖　❖　❖

September 1960, born and raised by my mother to go to Wellesley or Mount Holyoke, I find myself, through blunder and design, about to enroll as a seventeen-year-old freshman at the University of Chicago. The beginning is inauspicious. My mother and brother accompany me from New York to Chicago, but we make the trip by train because my mother is afraid to fly.

My trunk, which was shipped ahead, still has not arrived, and I borrow sheets and towels from Marcia, who has the room across the hall. My roommate is not there when I arrive, but she has already unpacked and left her mark: an iridescent crucifix. It is mounted on the shelf above her bed directly in my line of vision but safely out of her own. I will go to sleep and wake up each day with a neon Jesus. As it turns out, the two of us are perfectly matched. She grew up in a small, midwestern town and has never seen a Jew before. She spends our first days together trying to determine whether I have horns. This rooming arrangement lasts for less than a semester, and we are both relieved.

I am at Chicago because after having been rejected by every school I applied to, in a panic, I remember Peter Barlow, a senior boy I had a crush on when I was thirteen. Knowing nothing about Chicago, not having seen Peter in four years, and never having talked to him in the first place, I decide to apply to the University of Chicago because I have a vague memory that that's where he went. This approach to decision making is perfectly consistent with the way I had made choices during most of my life. A veritable Eliza Doolittle, I continue to read books, adopt interests, and make excursions based on the tastes and predilections of boys and men I know. Is there really any better way to choose a college?

During a hastily arranged interview in the middle of May, I explain my dismal board scores in math by pointing out that Albert Einstein failed math. My father uses a business contact, the merchandise manager at Spiegel's, a large mail-order-catalog company based in Chicago, to find a professor at the university who will intercede with the admissions committee on my behalf. A week later, I receive a letter welcoming me to the class of 1964. In spite of being relieved and happy to have a college to go to, I was mortified that it was necessary to depend on my father—who had never even attended college—to get me into one. How ironic. In spite of all my hard work, it is ultimately my father's old-boy network that seals my future. And this is a man I regard as a failure because he never reads and does not value ideas.

Four months later, at eight o'clock in the morning, I am sitting in another cavernous lecture hall, once again surrounded by white male students, and I am waiting for the professor to appear. The class is Chemistry 101, and many of the other students are, like me, pre-med. The professor, a Nobel Prize winner in chemistry, enters the room. In an exercise carried out at countless other elite institutions, one that will be featured many years later on *The Paper Chase,* a television series about Harvard Law School that was popular in the 1970s, the instructor tells us to look to the left and look to the right and announces that at the start of next year, at least one of us will be gone. Did I know then that he was talking about me?

Consumed with a passion for medicine, I find any pretext I can to wander the halls of nearby Billings Hospital and breathe in the delicious hospital smells. These meanderings transport me back to the summer during high school when my pediatrician arranged for me to work in a medical research lab at St. Luke's Hospital in New York City. I spent one glorious summer catheterizing rats to collect data on enzymes and never realized that all the scientists were men and even the rats were white. Now I wander the halls at Billings and know that this is where I belong. I am thrilled to be a pre-med student actually on my way to becoming a doctor. I feel confident in spite of my professor's sober warning.

My dorm at Chicago, which had been designed by Eero Saarinen, one of the best-known architects of the mid-twentieth century, was new and strikingly modern, in contrast to the older and more dignified classroom buildings and lecture halls. While the rooms in which we slept and lived were the cinder-block rectangles of the period, the lobby of the main building, the one that housed the dining room and then opened onto a courtyard leading to the dorm buildings themselves, was spacious and airy. The furniture, in definitive primary colors, was as striking as the large windows and comfortable seating areas that formed the lobby. Living in spaces so markedly different from any I had ever occupied before seemed like an appropriate new beginning for the college experience that I hoped would establish my independence.

The formal orientation that brought each first-year class to the campus early was preceded by several informal, although no less institutionalized, rituals. Even before we had finished unpacking our trunks, the stairs outside the dorm were lined with male undergraduates fingering copies of the new student directory and jockeying for the best place from which to inspect the new arrivals. Several times a day, we ran this gauntlet of upperclassmen who shouted out their evaluations and tried to match names and photos with faces and chest measurements. It was difficult to know whether to feel flattered or offended.

One night, my friends and I go to a mixer at ZBT, one of the Jewish fraternities. I am utterly unprepared for the experience. The basement room is packed with people, and everyone is guzzling beer. I meet the senior who will pin me in the winter and buy me an engagement ring in the spring, and I meet his best friend, who will take me to his room and tell me that what I need is a good lay. This is a line that young women hear over and over again during their college years—and before and after, too. Boys offer it up as an invitation and as a judgment, as a kind of universal cure: you needed one if you were tense and cranky; you needed one if you had a cold; you needed one if you were having trouble sleeping; you needed one if your grades were poor; but, most of all, you needed one if you failed to welcome their advances. And, in that case, it was no longer merely an invitation but a threat.

Every Thursday afternoon, the entire first-year class, roughly six hundred of us, enrolled in Humanities 101-2-3, gathered in Mandel Hall to hear a lecture on music, art, or literature. Like everyone else, I complained about these mass lectures, but since we were told that they were the price we had to pay for the much touted small group discussion sessions, we learned to tolerate, if not enjoy, them. I strain hard to hear what I am expected to in the phrases from Copland's *Appalachian Spring* and Mozart's symphonies; I watch the endless slides of Picasso that take us from his cubist period to his blue period to his mistresses' periods; and I try to follow the rigid interpretations of T. S. Eliot and e. e. cummings to which we are expected to acquiesce. At the end of the year, I will come close to flunking my comprehensive exam because of my inability or refusal to reduce all the meanings in Eliot's "Prufrock Revisited" to a single letter on a multiple-choice grid. The only thing that will save me is my grade on the essay part of the exam, but essays here count very little in contrast to the hard knowledge that is tested on the more manly objective sections of the test.

In Humanities 101-2-3, I discovered Jane Austen and rediscovered Henry James. Our discussion sessions met several times a week and were held around large round wooden tables that, we were led to understand, were used to situate students and faculty on the same plane. Although the symbolism and the goal, replacing hierarchy with collegiality, was appealing, I wasn't sure that the round tables had anything to do with me.

In theory, the system was designed to ensure perfect freedom to comment and disagree. Grading was to be impersonal and remote and based entirely on comprehensive examinations at the end of each year. The round tables were designed to undercut the authority that might accrue to a professor based on his position at the front of the traditional classroom. But in spite of these efforts to stimulate intellectual exchanges and undercut authority, the patriarchal relations that characterized the university and formed its character made it clear whose voice had a right to be heard. The male students brought a sense of entitlement with them into the classroom, and women like myself understood that they were lucky to be there at all. While it was true that anyone could offer up any comment they chose, there was a particular style and form which guaranteed that your comments received a respectful hearing and that form and style was gender based. Attending class at the University of Chicago was like entering an all-male club on visiting day—you were always waiting for the bell to ring, signaling that the visit was at an end.

Within a few days of arriving at the university, I learned that it was inappropriate to use the title "Dr." when addressing a professor who had earned a doctorate. Chicago practiced a kind of reverse snobbery that I confess, appealed to my own sense of elitism, and I quickly learned to refer to my professors as "Mr.," the preferred form of address. This was a practice I had to learn to discontinue when I later enrolled at New York University. I never learned what to call female professors because I never had one.

Chicago turned out to be a mixed blessing. I loved the huge Gothic buildings and the odor of entitlement that wafted through them. I loved being able to look out the window of my dorm room and see Frank Lloyd Wright's Robie House just across the street. I loved drinking boilermakers several times a week at Jimmy's on Woodlawn and acquiring a taste for "the beer that made Milwaukee famous," while eating hamburgers that were clearly *traif.* I even loved listening to the bells from Rockefeller Chapel that woke me too early every Sunday morning. But even I could not help noticing that many of the professors treated female students with a kind of supercilious and condescending contempt. This was less true of the older faculty and more often the case with the brash young men who ran discussion sections and taught freshman comp. In their classrooms, even the most serious questions asked by female students often disintegrated into muddled rambling. The slightly deprecating smirk they adopted, listening with their arms crossed and pressed against their chests, made you feel that whatever you said was simply wasting valuable class time. I remember being particularly humiliated by the comments of an English comp. professor who likened my, by then, eighteen year old's prose to "a used car dealer's jargon." In my attic, I still have a box that contains a sampling of papers from that first-year writing course. This particular man's comments were easily identifiable. Unlike the other instructors who wrote in blue or black ink, he used a red ballpoint pen to leave his mark. His comments on one of the last papers I did for him were at least partly responsible for my decision to drop out of college at the end of my fourth quarter at UC. I reproduce them here:

> It is baffling to deal with a paper like this because you have put so much into it, and it's so bad. When I compare it to a movie magazine or to the *Cosmopolitan* I'm not attempting to be idly insulting. You have, in point of fact, duplicated their impossible style, their coy euphemisms, their cute vagueness, their bubbling triteness. Until you can see that an expression like "to the interest of practically everyone" is pointless and trite and appalling, there's nothing I can do for you. D–

Could he really have believed that these comments would help me to be a better writer? Would a female professor have been so unapologetically arrogant?

The assignment for that particular paper had been to write a description of an enjoyable experience. The paper I turned in described an afternoon, several years earlier, when a fifteen-year-old friend and I had gone out to lunch, pretending to be young married women one of whom was having an affair with the other one's husband. Aspiring actresses, we would improvise this scene in the midst of a crowded New York City restaurant and see how believable we could make it. As I explained in the paper, we modeled our characters on Eloise in Salinger's short story "Uncle Wiggly in Connecticut." The description is hilarious. Its comic quality is enhanced by the slightly ironic, slightly amused, slightly condescending attitude my eighteen-year-old self adopted as I reflected on this teenage adventure. The style is, of course, meant as a parody. One can hardly imagine what it was like for a young, white, male English instructor at the University of Chicago in the spring of 1961 to be asked to comment on such a paper.

The previous quarter, and with a different instructor, I had written my way through the standard variety of composition class assignments. When it was time to write an argument, I decided, as an exercise, to try to defend the appalling business practices of John D. Rockefeller, a man whose career had captured my interests in high-school social studies. My paper, "John D. Rockefeller: Tyrant or Tycoon," argued against the claim that Rockefeller had been an unprincipled man who had used deceptive practices to amass his fortune. Adopting a viewpoint that was not my own, I maintained that there was nothing particularly callous or unethical about the way Rockefeller had conducted his business and built his empire. I used a modified "might makes right" argument to justify his practices and went on to attack my heroine, Ida Tarbell, suggesting that her criticisms of Rockefeller had been largely lacking in substance and had succeeded primarily by appealing to the emotions of her readers. This paper received favorable comments and earned me a B plus. However, there was still room for improvement. Commenting on my opening line—"History has a way of classifying people . . . "—the instructor circled the word "history" and substituted "men." Who can say he was wrong?

At the University of Chicago and throughout my undergraduate and graduate training, I learned that success was contingent on being one of the boys, and I did my best to become one. I adopted the pitbull approach to classroom discussions, attack first and think about it after hours. I learned to lower my voice several decibels and worked hard at giving it a round and full quality so that my comments would get a hearing, in contrast to the soft and flimsy voices of my female peers, whose fragile timbre floated directly to the ceiling and filled me with embarrassment.

From an early age, I understood that the world was divided according to gender and understood clearly who got what spoils. From the time I learned to read by reading books with Allen Waller, the high-school friend who introduced me to great literature, I understood that girls were silly and frivolous and that boys owned the past, the present, and the future. It was clear to me that my only hope of bypassing the law of primogeniture was identifying with the male point of view. I did so with a vengeance.

In the fifth grade, when our class of twenty-five divided into two clubs based on sex, I happily became the only girl in the boys' club. Since the primary activity of the boys' club was looking up the skirts of girls in the class, I spent most of my time back at the clubhouse, actually behind the piano in the corner, where I prepared endless bowls of strawberry Jello and chocolate pudding by mixing the content of the packets I pilfered from home with hot water from the bathroom tap. Although assigned to my role as cook, housekeeper, and nurturer for the boys by fairly crude, sex-role stereotyping, I quickly learned to internalize those stereotypes and, along with them, contempt for things female. I decided that girls were empty-headed and not to be taken seriously and that the things that interested them were inherently lacking in value. The problem with adopting this mode of survival was that, in spite of myself, I was a girl and there was little I could do to change that. But girls had very limited choices in those days: either you were attractive, sexual, and stupid, or you were ugly, smart, and thought like a boy. I decided to be smart.

One of my best classes at UC was the year-long required course in the social sciences that provided an introduction to government and economics. We used a text called *The People Shall Judge,* which had been compiled by the social science faculty and contained a variety of primary-source readings on the birth and evolution of the Republic. Its title page quoted the following dramatic lines from Locke's *Second Treatise:* "Who shall be judge whether the prince or legislative act contrary to their trust? . . . The People shall be judge; for who shall be judge whether the trustee or deputy acts well and according to the trust reposed in him, but he who deputes him." Locke's writing seemed very radical and visionary to me, and I took away from both the book and the course a deeply felt commitment to the rhetoric and the ideals of the American experiment as well as a profound disappointment with the way those ideals had been woven into the fabric of the nation. My professor for the course was Maynard C. Krueger, who had served as Norman Thomas's vice-presidential running mate on the Socialist ticket in 1937. A wonderful and gifted teacher, Krueger often delivered his sharply critical examination of the material we studied with a gentle sense of irony that appealed to my own sensibilities.

As it turned out, Krueger was an excellent and worthy successor to one of my best high-school teachers, John Clem. When I think of Mr. Clem, I see him sitting hunched over in his chair, not behind a desk, but part of the classroom landscape, wearing his usual rumpled gray suit or green corduroy jacket, a Chesterfield dangling from his mouth. A habitual smoker, even during those rare times when he was not actually smoking, Mr. Clem had a tiny shred of white cigarette paper permanently attached to his lower lip. Never a particularly animated or lively teacher, he held our rapt attention by the force of his steady and dependable intelligence. Like Krueger, he refused to take things at their face value and used gentle irony to encourage us to question what we might otherwise have taken for granted. None of us could ever figure out how he had ended up teaching at this third-rate private school or why he stayed.

At the heart of his low-keyed teaching style was his habit of asking interesting but unexpected questions and then actually waiting for us to respond to them. The fact that they were real questions, not merely rhetorical, meant that you had to think about them to fill up the silence. If none of us offered a response, he usually moved on without offering any answer himself; thus the question remained suspended, at least in my mind, initiating a chain of questioning that would continue long after the class ended.

Over the years in Mr. Clem's classes, I learned to recite and apply the eight rules of critical thinking, wrote research papers on the Truman Doctrine and the Marshall Plan, and did an independent study of the Cuban revolution even as it was occurring. I wrote a paper on the *Dred*

Scott decision and stumbled into reading Mathew Josephson's brilliant indictment of early capitalism, *The Robber Barons*—and was never the same. It was also in Mr. Clem's class that, for the first time, I discovered a woman in history who had had a role in changing it: Ida Tarbell. From my studies and my reading, I developed a strong sense of respect for the ideal of democracy and a deep sense of anger over the race and class injustice that it was clear to me was part of our nation's history.

By the time I entered the University of Chicago, my politics were very confused. Raised by parents who identified with the liberal wing of the Republican Party (Jacob Javits and Nelson Rockefeller), who were vehemently pro-business and anti-union, and who managed to combine their laissez-faire Jewish liberalism with a fairly conservative and rigid worldview grounded in Orthodox Judaism, I had a difficult time reconciling the various contradictory strains of their weltanschauung with the one I was trying to shape for myself.

In part, my politics were shaped by the boys I knew. I had dated boys from Brooklyn College who were liberal and boys from Bard who were alternative and boys from Yale who were conservative, and had learned something from each of them. I read the *New York Times* and the *Journal American* at home and the *Herald Tribune* at my great-grandfather's house. My high-school report on conditions in Batista's Cuba convinced me that Fidel Castro was a real revolutionary hero. In 1957, when he visited New York and stayed *uptown* at the Theresa Hotel—not in midtown at the Waldorf, to my amazement and delight—I went alone to join the cheering crowds that lined the streets to welcome him to the city. In fact, I shimmied up a lamppost in Central Park all the better to see him.

To my eternal shame, I campaigned and voted for Dwight Eisenhower, my parents' candidate, instead of Adlai Stevenson, during the mock election held in my fifth-grade class. By high school, my readings of Dred Scott and the Josephson book made me passionately committed to fighting racism and class privilege. While I was in Maynard Krueger's class learning to read *The Federalist* and the Constitution with a critical eye, I was also a member of the campus Young Republican Club and one of its most enthusiastic and vocal recruits. In three short years, I had gone from cheering Castro's victory to demonstrating against him in Chicago's Loop, chanting "Cuba, Sí; Castro, No." But in this respect, I was not unlike thousands of other Americans who followed our government's lead.

My presence at the national Young Republican Convention held at Loyola University, which featured an address by Barry Goldwater, is harder to explain, as was my close association with the extreme right wing of the Republican Party in the form of the Minute Men. Basically naive about politics but committed to fighting injustice and championing democracy, I found myself in Chicago during the zenith of Mayor Richard Daley's autocratic rule and was persuaded to fight corruption by working to defeat him. In my mind, Daley's career and continuing candidacy embodied all the evils I wanted to address, and, as the daughter of self-proclaimed Republicans, I was happy to join the campus chapter of the Young Republicans and get to work. I spent long days canvassing the South Side of the city, going door to door to challenge the inflated voter registration rolls typical of Chicago politics in those days. My enthusiasm for this activity and my effectiveness at ferreting out voters who listed cemeteries, garbage dumps, and vacant lots as their home addresses even made me the target of a law suit when I incorrectly challenged the status of a longtime Daley supporter who lived, as it turned out, in a building that was not immediately visible from the street. Only the fact that, at seventeen, I was underage saved me from a protracted legal encounter.

I watched the 1960 presidential debates between Kennedy and Nixon with other students on a large television at UC's Reynold's Club, but I was one of the very few in the room rooting for Tricky Dick. I campaigned hard and enthusiastically for Richard Nixon, and a newspaper clipping from this time includes a photo of me at a rally holding up a large sign on which I had written "U of C Bookworms Like Dick, Other Worms Like Jack." Fortunately, I was too young to vote.

When I needed some quiet time, I walked the few short blocks from my dorm to the Oriental Institute. My affinity for museums developed early, the result of frequent trips to the American Museum of Natural

History, which was just a stone's throw from our apartment house in New York City. Although I never found the statue of Teddy Roosevelt outside the front entrance or the dark halls filled with stuffed animal carcasses particularly welcoming, regular visits with both my family and my elementary-school classes made the museum feel like an extension of my personal space. I knew it so well.

On those Saturdays when my mother and I did not go to the movies or attend a theater matinee, we often prowled the galleries of the Metropolitan Museum of Art. To this day, going to the Met feels like going home, and I am often surprised to find so many other people there when I visit. As a teenager, I developed the habit of hiding out in the museum to regain my equilibrium whenever my life seemed out of joint and found that it always helped to be in the company of old friends. When our family's reversal of fortune required my mother to take on her first paying job at the age of fifty-eight, she went to work in the museum gift shop, and when a good friend decided to help me celebrate my fiftieth birthday by returning to some of my favorite lifetime haunts, it was only natural that our day should begin there. Throughout my life, I have taken pleasure and comfort in visits to art museums, where the beauty and persistence of the treasures they house has made me feel safe. The Oriental Institute performed that function for me while I was at Chicago. It was a great place in which to get lost or lose yourself because it was always empty and it was a lot closer than the Art Institute—an El-ride away, downtown.

Both the dorm and my classes are integrated at Chicago, and for the second time in my life I find myself in a world where at least a few of my peers are Black or Asian—very few. It was 1960, and I don't remember much, if any, racial tension on the campus—either because there wasn't any or because I was removed from it. All the campus graffiti and chalk marks in the surrounding neighborhood were about drugs and peace. My memory is that the number of kids who weren't white was very small, and I had the impression that many of the Black students did some kind of work on campus to help pay their tuition and room and board. But like most schools, Chicago was divided into various groups with little interaction among them. While it was rela-

tively easy for an individual to move into or out of the groups themselves, each group was a self-contained world and showed little interest in the others. The Black girls in my dorm who were cute and
perky, and those who dressed and acted white, seemed to have little
difficulty being accepted, at least superficially, in the white world
(whether this was a happy or an unhappy circumstance is for them to
say). The others remained on the margins, largely invisible. At Chicago, gender, not race or class, continued to be the dominant discourse
in my own life because there was little to contextualize my whiteness
or my class position and everything to make me focus on my sex.

Initially excited at having entered the world of higher education,
I grew increasingly disillusioned with what the University of Chicago
had to offer. Nothing I did could make me feel at home there. Used to
being patted and praised by my teachers, my failure to excel left me
feeling confused. By the spring quarter, I had stopped going to many
of my classes. I had taken refuge in the novel I had begun writing,
and I was auditing a course in Serbo-Croation—a sure sign of my
desperation. My best friend, Marcia, and I spent hours critiquing the
androcentric nature of the institution, but did so without benefit
of that word, which would not become popular for another decade
or two.

Weekly phone calls home made it clear that all was not well with
my parents. Each time we said goodbye, I felt like I was abandoning
my mother all over again. Letters written to me by my eleven-year-
old brother were filled with unhappiness over the deteriorating condition of my parents' marriage, something he did not understand but
could not escape. When I returned home briefly that May to attend
my grandmother's funeral, my mother's loneliness was palpable.

I stayed on at the university for the summer but moved out of
the dorm. Although nominally sharing an apartment with two other
women students, I spent most nights a few blocks away in the apartment of my fiancé, which he rented with two other men. Paul and I
had been dating since that ZBT party early in the fall, and we had
become engaged in March. He had just graduated from the university with a degree in history and would begin working toward a

master's at the Business School on a fellowship in the fall. Feeling like a misfit at the university, I thought a lot about quitting school and getting married. My short-term plan was to work at a local bookstore and earn money by writing for pulp magazines. But in spite of my English instructor's assurance that I had mastered their impossible style, all the true-confessions articles I submitted came back with rejection slips. My long-term plans were nonexistent.

My parents liked Paul but did not think he was a good marriage prospect. He and his younger brother, who also attended UC, had grown up in Margate, New Jersey, near Atlantic City, and their father sold insurance—but not very successfully. In my mother's eyes, it was not a good match. And, of course, she was not anxious to see me marry so young. Paul, who was a really nice person, sensed my mother's reservations and was worried about his ability to support me in style. Over my protests, he had decided to get an MBA rather than do graduate work in history because he was concerned about his ability to earn a good living. During July and August, our relationship and my life at the university began to unravel. There were just too many pressures. By the time the summer quarter ended, I was on academic probation, a hair's breadth away from being asked to leave, and Paul and I had broken up. I packed my bags, withdrew from the University of Chicago, and went home.

Not used to failure, I returned to New York seriously depressed. Having spent most of my high-school years thinking about college and the chance for a serious education, I didn't know what to make of my experience at Chicago and my failure to do well there. I found myself living at home again, trapped in a life I couldn't control. My parents' relationship, problematic in the best of times, was deteriorating under the financial pressures caused by my father's declining earnings. My closest friend, Marcia, was in Chicago, although she too had dropped out of the university and was living at home and attending Roosevelt University in the Loop. I started reading the want ads and thought about killing myself.

Being unskilled and unqualified for any interesting job at a time when the want ads were still segregated by sex and men got to be administrative assistants while women got to be typists, clerks, and secretaries, I settled for a job as a receptionist working the switchboard at Chester Gore & Co., a small advertising agency on Fifty-fourth Street, just off Madison Avenue. As it turned out, I had stumbled by chance on an office that could have been the setting for a weekly TV sitcom. Mary Tyler Moore would have loved working there. Getting dressed up and taking the E train to Fifty-third and Madison each morning made me feel at least twenty and was a world away from 8:00 A.M. lectures in Cobb Hall. In a matter of days, I went from being an eighteen-year-old college dropout to being a poised receptionist with teased hair, sitting in a well-appointed waiting room, wearing stockings and heels, and earning a salary. Sitting at the reception desk surrounded by pastel walls and sleek furniture, and readying my smile each time the elevator doors opened, only the daily letters to and from Marcia reminded me that things had ever been different. When I thought back to my year at the University of Chicago, I realized clearly that I hadn't belonged there. Raised to attend Wellesley or Radcliffe, how could I have known that Chicago would be all wrong?

Although my job was undemanding, the people were pleasant, and when I showed an interest in writing copy, they were willing to help me learn more. I continued to have responsibility for the switchboard and reception area, but I began to work on other projects when the board was slow. My first real foray into advertising found me working on a direct-mail advertising campaign designed to persuade potential owners of the Silver Cloud Rolls Royce that there was nothing ostentatious about such a purchase. Research had shown that many potential buyers were reluctant to own a Rolls because they thought of it as a status-flaunting car. My job was to persuade financially solvent business executives that buying a Rolls Royce was really a sensible, practical investment. This involved convincing them that in the long run, a Rolls Royce was a more economical and dependable choice than other less expensive cars. Some of my time was spent writing copy, and some of it was spent placing calls to men who were listed in a directory of millionaires and trying to persuade them that by purchasing a Rolls they could enjoy both the fruits of their wealth and a sense of their own frugality.

Before long, as a reward, I was offered a promotion. I would leave the switchboard and go to work as assistant to the president. While in many respects the job amounted to being no more than a glorified secretary, it served as the primary route for advancement available to women at the agency. I was told that working in that position would familiarize me with every aspect of the business in addition to introducing me to all the clients. After a couple of years of apprenticeship, I could expect to become an account executive.

The prospect of a raise and my own office, even if it was little more than an anteroom next to the president's, was very tempting. I was still eighteen and very anxious to affirm my hold on adulthood. The promotion held out the possibility of a seriously adult career and life. I began to fantasize about having my own apartment and earning a good living. But did I really want to spend my life selling Rolls Royces and persuading people to drink Grand Marnier, another of our clients? Michael's Pub was nice, but did I really want to take up residence there? In fact, I felt almost as out of place on Madison Avenue as I had at the University of Chicago. It was clear that I needed to spend more time composing a life.

In the end, the offer of the promotion scared me back to school. I was afraid that once I could afford an apartment of my own, I'd never be willing to give up my financial independence no matter how unrewarding the work. I didn't take the job for the same reason some people are afraid to try drugs—the fear that I might like it, or at least like my new lifestyle so much that I'd be hooked and be willing to do anything to keep it. In my heart, I was still a pre-med student, and I decided to go back to school.

Having decided to return to school, I filled out an application for New York University and waited for the spring semester to begin. It never occurred to me to consider looking for a school that might suit me better, and I never considered returning to Chicago. Where school was concerned, I felt like a terrible failure and assumed that going to NYU was a kind of penance that was necessary to perform.

It was all I deserved. As it turned out, after reviewing my transcript, the members of the admissions committee at NYU were not at all sure that they wanted me even if I was willing to do penance, and it took some persuading, this time on my part, not my parents, to get me admitted.

I had grown up referring to New York University, derisively, as NYJew. I thought of it as a place where not very smart Jewish kids went because their parents could pay the tuition, and I was more than slightly embarrassed to be going there myself. In many ways, it reminded me of the private school I had attended—a place to bide time. Unlike Chicago, it did not have a reputation for being a place where undergraduates routinely got excited about ideas. In addition, because it was a large commuter school, there was no sense of community. I hung out at a coffee shop down the block from the main building, but that was a poor substitute for either a dorm room or a commons. On the other hand, Washington Square Park was right outside the front door. Before and after class, I could prowl the streets of the Village, no longer as the high-school interloper of my younger days but as someone who belonged. Most important, unlike Chicago, where it was harder to both fit in and stand out, I understood the rules of a place like NYU and knew how to do well there. In the end, I was admitted and received an excellent, if not an indulgent, education.

It was at NYU that I finally took my first college class taught by a woman, and I was not pleased. My experience in elementary and high school had made it clear that women were suited to teaching the early grades as well as "soft" subjects like English, but that men did the real teaching. My year at Chicago had confirmed this early impression by failing to include any contact with female faculty members. As it turned out, Vilma Cavallero, my political science teacher, was no more than an adjunct. While some men without doctorates were full-time instructors, the women, when there were any, were usually adjuncts. Although I could not have articulated my dissatisfaction at the time, one of the reasons I resented having her teach the class was that I understood on some level that my own status was contingent on that of my instructor and, in the scheme of things, there was nothing lower than a female adjunct. My reaction to Cavallero was interesting not only because of what I felt about her but, equally important, because of the implications it held for my feelings about myself. But that never occurred to me. I had so completely internalized a male perspective that I didn't realize that in dismissing her, I was devaluing myself. In fact, she turned out to be a very good teacher.

New Year's Eve 1962. I am in a third-floor apartment somewhere in Chinatown, the only white woman at a holiday party. For some reason, my friend Charlotte Li, another student at NYU, has decided to bring me along, and for the first time in my life I am in a room where no one else is white. The realization dawns on me gradually but isn't a cause for alarm. White people carry their privilege wherever they go; I knew my minority status was only temporary.

We ended up sitting on the floor, drinking beer, and talking. After a while, when the others forgot that I was there or stopped caring, they began a round of mocking impersonations of a popular media ad for China or Japan Airlines, one that offered the weary (male) business traveler the services and attention of a demure, exotic, patient, charming, and docile stewardess who, it promised, would cater to his every whim. The implications were both clear and insulting. I laughed along with the others but felt acutely uncomfortable. Even though I had been repelled by the ad long before the party, I felt somehow personally tarnished by it and even personally responsible, as though my whiteness made me guilty of unintentional complicity. On some level, I understood that, my good intentions notwithstanding, the Chinese students at the party were "us" and I was one of "them," a beneficiary of the racism in the ad even if I had not initiated it. Had it been ten years later, in the flush of the women's movement, I might have been able to take refuge in my gender, but at that time I had not yet begun to think deeply about sexism, and, besides, the gender issues were inextricably bound up with the racist stereotype. I was left holding the bag of my race. The fact that I do not remember which airline used the ad is interesting too. Can it be that I do not remember because my ignorance of ethnic and national differences among Asian peoples was so great that I didn't know enough to distinguish between

China and Japan or think it important that I be able to do so? Would most other white Americans care?

At NYU, I had once again declared myself a pre-med student and a biology major, but by the end of my second semester reluctantly decided to abandon the sciences. At both NYU and Chicago, surviving in the pre-med program felt like trying to swim upstream against the current. It was just too difficult. Some women, of course, persisted, but most did so in spite of the program and climate, not because of it. I sometimes think that the right adviser could have made the difference, but I never had one. My biology professor was an excellent teacher but a cold and distant man who did not encourage personal conversations or disclosures. Discussing my plans and hopes for a future in medicine and soliciting his advice never crossed my mind. I would have felt ridiculous. I wanted to be a doctor but couldn't find a way to see myself as a scientist. I continued to feel poorly prepared in the sciences and entirely unprepared in math. The chilly climate for women that pervaded both areas did nothing to help me overcome my fears, and I blamed myself entirely for what I saw as my inevitable failure. Years later, reading the work of Sue Rosser, Bonnie Spanier, Evelyn Fox Keller, Evelyn Hammonds, and others, I found out that what I took for personal failure was at least partially grounded in an institutionalized sexism in the sciences that was as yet barely identifiable by me.

Faced with the need to declare a new major, I didn't even consider English in spite of the fact that I loved literature and spent much of my time reading novels and literary criticism. I ruled out English without a thought because in those days being female and saying you were an English major was equivalent to saying you were a space cadet. Every one knew that if you were a girl and couldn't figure out what to major in, you majored in English or elementary ed., and I refused to become one of the girls. It was a case of cutting off my nose to spite my face.

Reluctant to stigmatize myself by taking too many English courses, I managed to study literature by taking the equivalent of a minor in classics as well as a year-long advanced French lit course that began in the Middle Ages with the *Chanson de Roland* and *Tristan et Iseult* and ended in the twentieth century with Sartre's "Le Mur." Like *The People Shall Judge*, my French text is still on my bookshelf. Some years ago, when my daughter brought home a seventh-grade English assignment that required identifying The *Song of Roland* and telling a little about it, I dug out volume one of the French texts. But when she sought my advice about which language to study, I guided her firmly toward Spanish.

In addition to literature, I was fascinated by the history and culture of ancient Greece, which my studies taught me was the cradle of civilization. I studied the tragedies and comedies of Greece and Rome with Lionel Casson and read as many historical novels as I could to supplement the history, religion, economics, and geography I was learning in my other classes. On Saturdays and Sundays, I took to wandering through the galleries at the Met that housed the statues and artifacts of the ancient world; by my last year in college, you could have picked any object among them at random, and I could have given you a fairly accurate account of what life was like in the polis or the region and could have described the part played in it by the object in question. I longed to travel to Greece but lacked both the money and the proper traveling companion.

In the course of my studies, and without any evil intent on the part of my professors, I learned to see the world through the eyes of the ancient Greeks, easily adopting a Eurocentric worldview according to which everyone else was a barbarian. For me and my classmates, the globe was shrouded in darkness, with the exception of the Greek city-states, which emitted a hundred points of light. The status of women in ancient Athens was murky at best, although we did learn that some woman on the island of Lesbos had written poetry. Class issues were glossed over and prettied up, as, of course, was slavery, and sex between men was presented as an inevitable outgrowth and defining characteristic of superior social position and education. Apparently, it was always carried out in a context of intellectual camaraderie or tutelage and was clearly acceptable, since the alternative to sex with men was sex with women. A kind of unacknowledged misogyny provided the context for our study, and, like any eager student, I managed to make it my own without question. Perhaps most interesting of all, although there was sex between men in the ancient world, there was clearly no homosexuality and certainly there were no homos in the curriculum I studied.

When I read Nietzsche a short while later, I began to understand why it was possible for upper-class Greek men to engage in sex with other men and yet still not be "homosexuals." Nietzsche pointed out that first came the men (*sic*) and then came the determination of what was right and wrong based on their conduct. He criticized Christianity for replacing values that originally celebrated the deeds and behavior of strong and powerful individuals with values based on the needs of the weak, to which the mighty are then expected to subordinate themselves. Extrapolating from this philosophy and applying it to contemporary society, I began to understand that in some real sense, right and wrong are defined by the behavior of those with social and economic clout, the right gender, the right color skin. When those people do things ,they *become* right or are judged differently than when identical acts are committed by people with a lower socioeconomic status. Women who have babies outside of marriage are unwed mothers if they are the wrong color or class or both, while white women of means, especially if they are celebrities, become "single parents" whose lifestyle is often romanticized and admired. When people who are neither middle class nor white live together without benefit of marriage, they "live in sin," while those of us who are white and middle class "cohabit" or form "nontraditional families." When upper-class Greek men engaged in sex with others of their kind, it was an expression of the purest kind of love.

The point holds from the ridiculous to the sublime—working-class African-American women who cornrow their hair have occasionally been fired from their jobs for failing to groom themselves appropriately, but white upper-class women and celebrities who adopt that hair style become the subject of a photo-essay in a fashion magazine. Wealthy white suburban teens who on occasion "borrow" a car and go for a joy ride are understood to be carrying out a prank or transgression of youth that is likely to earn them a mild reprimand, while urban teenagers who are the wrong color, class, or both will end up in a juvenile detention home, or dead, for doing the same thing. Some years ago, I was surprised by the conclusions contained in a study that compared the behavior of two groups of adolescent boys. One group consisted of high-school students in a wealthy white suburban school district, and the other consisted of boys in a juvenile detention home who, for the most part, were poor and/or nonwhite. As it turned out, members of these two groups had committed essentially the same kinds of acts of law-breaking with the same frequency during their teens. Whether they found themselves completing high school at seventeen or doing time seemed to be entirely a matter of their race and/or class.

It took me a long time to come to this and other similar realizations because so much of what we are taught makes race, class, and gender privilege invisible or actively teaches students not to use these forms of oppression as categories for analyzing experience. By treating hierarchy as natural, and race, class, and gender privilege as the inevitable outcomes of innate superiority, our curriculum rationalizes unequal treatment by making it appear to be, alternatively, just, necessary, or inevitable. The "right" men can take other men as lovers without being homosexuals, the right women can have babies without being married and still not be unwed mothers, and the right people can have more than they need or can possibly use, without being greedy, irresponsible, or wasteful.

But I attended NYU as an undergraduate between 1961 and 1964 and was a long way from being able to articulate the perspective from which I was being taught. While I possessed a developing awareness of class, gender, and race issues, I did not yet understand the role they played in constructing what counted as knowledge and the force they exerted on the way in which both research and scholarship were defined and carried out. I certainly had no understanding of the Eurocentric nature of the curriculum. Although a number of Black scholars had already begun to identify and decry that perspective, I would not become aware of it until the publication of Martin Bernal's *Black Athena* in 1987. Bernal, of course, was a white man.

After dropping out of the pre-med program, I changed my major to government with a pre-law specialization. My classes in government stand out in my mind because of how unremittingly boring the professors were and because of the simplistic anti-Communist perspective that defined the department—a fact that was obvious even to me. The treatment of Marx was worst in the courses on Soviet history and government taught by the department's expert in that area, a man so thorough and industrious that he had even married a Russian woman and brought her home with him. This man managed to cover all of modern Soviet history without ever taking either Marx or Lenin seriously, although, of course, we heard a great deal about Stalin. During one of the few class meetings when the previous night's reading might have led us to expect a serious discussion of Marxism, he simply announced that there were five reasons why Marx was wrong and proceeded to write them on the board. Having done so, he dismissed Marxism with a sweep of the eraser and went on to the next topic. For my part, I found the readings from Marx and Engels fascinating, and the professor's cavalier attitude toward them only served to increase my interest.

The most interesting single class I ever attended in the government department was one on international relations that met in the midst of the Cuban missile crisis in the autumn of 1962—while the world waited to see who would blink. The day after the Soviet Union had deployed its missiles, we were seated as usual in a classroom in the main building waiting for the professor to arrive. Like many of my peers, I believed that we were precariously perched on the verge of World War III, and only the nature of this particular course explained why I was willing to make the subway trip downtown to attend class on a day when the end of the world seemed so near. What attracted me was the feeling of self-importance that came from discussing breaking events in a professional context. Attending that class was, for the moment, as close to world power as I could imagine getting and certainly brought me closer to the action than my mother, who was consigned to sitting at home in front of the television.

The other reason I remember that particular course is because it was taught by a professor who managed to unnerve his female students by staring deep into our eyes whenever he spoke to us. In this way, he gave the impression that he was quietly but methodically removing every stitch of clothing from your body even as you sat engaged in a seemingly civilized conversation about the ramifications of some piece of foreign policy or the suitability of some proposed topic for a term paper. Like the other women in the course, I avoided going to his office unless it was absolutely necessary and, when it was, always persuaded a friend to come along and stand outside in the hall.

In spite of my interest in classics and the number of courses I had completed in that area, I felt completely unprepared to take the required introductory philosophy course and postponed taking it as long as I could. While novels and even the *Chanson de Roland* might be accessible to girls, philosophy, in my mind, was clearly off limits. I considered it a male domain and felt inadequate when confronted with the prospect of studying the great writings of Plato and Aristotle in the same way that my eighth-grade self had been intimated by the thick history text used by tenth-grade students at my high school. I wondered how I would ever be able to succeed in the course. Once I enrolled in "Introduction to Philosophy" during my junior year, my fears were confirmed.

On the very first day, the professor, Milton Munitz, entered the classroom and proceeded to define our topic by writing *philo* and *sophia* on the board in ancient Greek and asking who among us knew what the words meant. This opening exercise was hardly designed to elicit information from us, since we were, for the most part, a motley collection of untutored freshmen and sophomores unlikely to be schooled in the language. What it did for me, and probably for the other students as well, was confirm whatever feelings of inadequacy I brought with me into the class. After a suitable silence, Munitz translated their meaning, writing "love of wisdom" on the board. As I copied the words dutifully into my notebook, I learned the subtext of the lesson, which was about who had knowledge and the attendant power and who did not. I did not, you will note, learn very much about the business of philosophy because other than being suitable for inclusion as a multiple-choice or fill-in exam question, the phrase "love of wisdom" has very little value. It told us absolutely nothing about what philosophers actually did, nor did it provide any idea of what we would be doing for the next semester. Like so much that continues to pass for education today, it was designed less to empower than to subdue. But at that time, I was impressed, copied the phrase in my notebook, and went home with what I surely believed to be a treasure.

As it turned out, learning about the business of philosophy followed pretty quickly because, apart from his unfortunate beginning, Munitz was a fine teacher. I sat in the first row of his class, a technique I adopted early in my career at NYU, understanding that only this proximity to the instructor would assure me of getting called on and being noticed, and I listened hard. Some years later, I was interested to find that studies confirmed my intuition that while male students are called on regardless of where they sit in a classroom, females do best when they make the seat selection I had instinctively chosen.

The class began by reading Plato's *Republic*, and, to my surprise, I found it enthralling. In part, this was probably because we used a highly readable translation by F. M. Cornforth, and in part it was because of the variety of techniques Plato used to make his ideas accessible to readers with different interests and learning styles. He did so by offering multiple accounts of his most important ideas, directing one account to those who do best with quantitative reasoning, one to those who respond to analogy and symbolism, and one to those who prefer straightforward narrative. Although I wouldn't have used the phrase at that time, *The Republic* was the first text to make me think about the issue of cognitive diversity and to offer a model for addressing it.

My second model in this respect was a person, not a text. A few years later, I went to hear H. Rap Brown address a rally at the Fillmore East and ended up getting a lesson from a master teacher. Like another brilliant orator, Malcolm X, he moved back and forth between sophisticated, almost academic, language and street talk. In the course of making a point, he moved effortlessly between flawless English and the kind of basic street language and idiom that was accessible to people without very much formal education. What impressed me most on hearing Brown was how little was lost in the reformulation and how much remedial education was carried out in the course of a seemingly polemical address.

What impressed me when I read *The Republic* for the first time was that Plato seemed genuinely concerned with finding ways to communicate his ideas. This was in sharp contrast to many other scholarly texts, which were written more to impress and subdue than to engage or empower the reader. In contrast to my expectations, philosophy seemed to offer exactly what I had hoped college would provide—an opportunity to wrestle with ideas. This was in such happy contrast to so many of my other classroom experiences that I quickly signed up for another course.

The course I selected seemed an obvious choice for me. It was entitled "The Philosophy of Democracy" and was taught by the chair of the department, Sidney Hook, who was also one of the stars on the NYU faculty. One of more than a hundred students who came to listen to Hook twice each week, I was fascinated by the man and the topic and never said a word. It was not the size of the class that intimidated me—other classes at NYU were equally large—but the man himself. I knew that if I spoke, I would stumble over my words and, worse yet, reveal my utter stupidity. He would know at once that I did not belong in his class and would respond to my question or comment in a way that held me up to ridicule. Fresh from Plato's dialogues, I knew he was either Socrates incarnate or the ultimate Sophist, and, in either case, I would be no match for him. This feeling of inadequacy was further strengthened when Hook invited Ernst Van Der Haag to fill in for him during one of his absences. Where did men like these get their verbal facility and intellectual breadth? What did it feel like to know so much and have such confidence in your own thinking and speaking skills? I knew a few male students who at least could mimic the style of these men, but I looked at myself and could find no possible connection to them and their ability and power.

A few days after the course ended, I received a postcard from Hook, written in his own hand, that said: "An excellent examination paper in 'Philosophy of Democracy'! I was utterly floored. In recent years, I have often wondered what exactly I wrote in that paper to make the great man take notice, but when I searched through a box of papers and letters from that time, I discovered that I had saved the postcard but not the paper.

Ambivalent about what to do after graduation, during my senior year I applied to several law schools as well as to a few doctoral programs in political science. I was graduating with a pre-law specialization and found the classes I took in English constitutional history and U.S. constitutional law particularly satisfying. I was attracted to the rigor of thought that the law seemed to demand, and I was interested in the underlying philosophical or theoretical issues raised by the court cases I had studied. On the other hand, I wasn't convinced that going to law school made sense for me. By all accounts, going to law school was like entering a convent or, more correctly, in those days, a monastery. The only law students I had ever known were men who seemed to spend all their time memorizing cases and precedents. They seemed to have little time to think broadly and less time for their personal relationships. What attracted me to law, as to medicine, was its potential to make an impact on people's lives, but the three-year credentialing period loomed before me as interminable.

Doing graduate work in political science seemed the obvious thing to do, but the prospect of teaching government for the rest of my life was unappealing. Apart from the one or two courses I had taken in political theory, my experience at NYU made me think that teaching government was like being a plumber. By that I mean that as modeled by the department, the discipline seemed less concerned with exploring broad theoretical issues than with tinkering with the pipes. I wasn't convinced that I would be able to teach courses in government for thirty or forty years without becoming bored. On the other hand, teaching college seemed like one of the few viable futures I could contemplate. When Sidney Hook called me into his office and offered me an assistantship in philosophy, it seemed to solve all my problems.

Teaching philosophy appeared to open up possibilities rather than close them. Doing graduate work in the field seemed to allow me to envision a future of thinking about everything rather than something. And so a day after talking to Hook, I applied to the graduate program in philosophy at NYU. It was a good thing, too. None of the other schools accepted me.

For the most part, being a graduate student at NYU was not very different from being an undergraduate, except that the classes were smaller and more intense and there were no women at all on the philosophy faculty and hardly any women students in the department. The last suited me fine. The few women who managed to stay in the program were tough. We had to be. We had learned to shout out our comments and interrupt our classmates—only girls waited to be called on. We struggled with whatever inclination we might have had to offer constructive or supportive criticism in the course of class discussions and instead drilled ourselves to go for the jugular every time. As it turned out, I was still weak in one area; like most women, I was still more likely to ask a question than to make a statement. Fortunately in philosophy, this gender-based tendency isn't as significant a drawback as it might be in other arenas—for example, the corporate world.

The main reason I was attracted to philosophy was that it held out the possibility of continuing to study and think about a broad range of issues and fields instead of having to specialize. I could continue to pursue my interest in science by working in the philosophy of science; I could continue to read novels and work in the philosophy of literature; I could do epistemology and metaphysics and aesthetics and philosophy of history; and, of course, I could study political philosophy and classical civilization. Throughout my education, I had been looking for connections and finding discrete disciplines; philosophy seemed to be a subject where I could think about big questions instead of little ones and where I might pursue the connections between ideas and areas of thought instead of having to stop at the artificial boundaries imposed by academic departments. In this respect, my year at Chicago had not been lost on me. I knew that knowledge couldn't be reduced to the shoebox categories of a traditional college catalog, and

I saw training in philosophy as a way to find an academic home that would not be limiting. Several years later, this would be a bone of contention between me and Sidney Hook when he insisted that I begin to specialize if I hoped to get anywhere in the field.

One reason I enjoyed my initial graduate studies in philosophy was because I had taken so few courses in the discipline as an undergraduate and liked the challenge of new material. I studied analytic philosophy with Paul Edwards, epistemology and metaphysics with Milton Munitz, Aristotle with Harmon Chapman, and existentialism and phenomenology with William Barrett. Edwards was perversely brilliant and fascinating, although I disagreed with him most of the time. He was a slight, odd-looking man with a sharp and impatient intellect that was hard as ice, razor sharp, and often brittle. On the other hand, he was an unusually kind and sympathetic person who treated his students as individuals and who was capable of sympathizing and empathizing with problems in their lives. He was also fair and just. I did some work for him when he was editing an introductory textbook and later when he edited the *Encyclopedia of Philosophy*. He gave me credit in both books and paid me for my work—not something that every full professor would have done.

Harmon Chapman had all the intellectual tenderness that Edwards lacked and taught both Husserl and Aristotle with extraordinary grace and a quiet devotion. He was moving toward the end of his teaching career by the time I studied with him, but he approached each text, even those he had taught for many years, as though he were encountering it for the first time. Passages in some of Aristotle's treatises that would fail to excite even the most motivated student continued to fill him with reverence and delight, even after what must have been innumerable readings. He lacked the drama and certainly the caustic wit and innate pessimism that Edwards carried with him, but Chapman inspired us with the simple and unconditional love he felt for the philosophy he taught.

I was sitting in Chapman's class in the late afternoon, on November 9, 1965—the night that much of the East Coast experienced a massive blackout. Even after the lights had been out for several minutes and the room was growing dark, Chapman continued to lecture. No one spoke for some time, but when it became impossible to take notes any longer, a student pointed out our plight and the class came to an end. But nothing less than a power failure affecting six or seven states on the East Coast could have persuaded Chapman to set aside Aristotle's *Metaphysics*.

Having an opportunity to study with William Barrett was like a gift. Reading Heidegger, Husserl, and Sartre with him was a treat; studying Hegel's *Phenomenology* with him was unforgettable. The pages that I labored over at home came alive in his classroom. Lines of text that seemed ponderous and unwieldy burst into color in the course of his lectures when he mined their hidden gems. Where the rest of us might see only words, he found references to history and culture in every line. The breadth of his interests and knowledge made him a fascinating lecturer, all the more so because of the lack of self-importance with which he shared his enormous knowledge and talents.

On the other hand, Barrett could be very erratic. A brilliant class might be followed by one equally brilliant or succeeded by a mumbled, jumbled, chaotic lecture lacking both focus and content. At such times, it was clear that his mind was simply elsewhere, and we waited for it to return. I picture him now, wandering into class wearing his winter overcoat and gray and red muffler, carrying his large briefcase, his uncut graying hair looking windblown and disheveled, blinking at us as though he, too, was amazed that he had ended up in this very place and this very time. A man of many talents and interests, he once gave me a recipe for wine-soaked baked peach halves stuffed with amaratti biscuit crumbs that made my mouth water.

Although I held an assistantship in the department from the very first, it paid very little and so it was necessary for me to piece together part-time jobs to help pay for my tuition and expenses. By the time I entered graduate school in September 1964, my father was sixty-five years old, had been fired from his job, and was suffering from Parkinson's disease. My parents continued to send me money each month, but the dramatic reduction in their income and the fact that my brother was still attending an expensive private school meant that their resources were severely stretched.

After graduating from high school, my father went to work as a salesman for the shirt manufacturing company where his older brother Philip was employed. Later, when my uncle bought the business, my father became vice president of the firm. When Uncle Phil died suddenly in the mid-1960s, the business reverted to his son Harvey, my father's nephew. In spite of the familial relationship, my father was really never more than an employee of the firm, and once his nephew took charge and the two began to disagree on policy, his position began to decline until he was forced out of the business entirely.

My mother was bitter over my uncle's failure to provide a secure future for my father and even more bitter over my father's failure to insist on such a provision. My father was crushed by the treatment he received from his nephew as well as by my mother's reaction to it and, finally, by his diminished ability to provide for his family. Having grown up poor and with little opportunity to develop a wide range of interests and talents, he measured his success entirely on the basis of his success as a provider. When he made good money, he felt good; when he made less, he felt like a failure. Being forced out of the business broke him. By the time he fell ill, my father hadn't played tennis in years. His only other interest or outlet was his religion, but once he was dealt the double whammy of losing his job and his health, his faith was sorely tested. I don't think that he ever really wavered in his belief, but I know that he was at a loss to understand why God would have done this to him. He continued to daven each day, but the comfort he had always found in prayer was considerably diminished. In the end, the resulting financial and emotional strain, combined with the onset of Parkinson's disease, precipitated a decline from which my father never recovered.

Even as things became more difficult, my parents still paid my tuition and my mother managed to find $100 in the budget each month to help me out. It was enough to cover the $95 rent on my minuscule Sullivan Street apartment but not enough to cover expenses. After I earned my master's degree, I was able to support myself with adjunct teaching. But during my first two years of graduate school, I worked at a series of temporary jobs obtained by registering with several of the office temp companies that operated in the city. Sometimes the temporary agencies sent you to a law firm or doctor's office to fill in for a sick or vacationing employee, which usually meant answering the phone or serving as the receptionist in a reasonably comfortable office, but on other days you could end up doing the most menial and repetitive clerical work—isolated in a factory or warehouse anteroom. The worst job I ever had consigned me to a week of filing invoices at a lamp factory. This was literally back-breaking labor—impossible to imagine unless you've done it. Almost thirty years later, I can still remember the ache in my arms, neck, and back and the dizziness in my head and stomach, the nausea that resulted from hours of leafing through faded invoices and filing them in the appropriate order, the hundreds of tiny paper cuts that stung my hands. When the pain got too bad, I would stop and run my hands under cold water, but it never helped for more than a few moments. I have often thought of that experience when people argue that certain traditionally male jobs deserve higher pay than women's office work because of the physical demands they make. Because we have learned to see the world through men's eyes and our standards continue to reflect their experience and interests, we tend to define demanding physical labor in terms of the number of pounds carried. In this way, the physical burden and cost of so much of the menial labor performed by women continue to be rendered invisible.

Shortly after completing my stint at the lamp factory, I went to register at yet another employment agency, looking for a permanent part-time job, and was offered a job at the agency itself. I took it without hesitation.

The agency was small, with a Madison Avenue address. It consisted entirely of two people, Byron Jacobs and Bernard Stein, whose first names combined produced the company's name: the Byron Bernard Agency. As the only "girl" in a "one-girl" office, I served as the receptionist, answered the phone, did the typing, and performed whatever other clerical tasks were needed. The men were pleasant, the job was undemanding, the hours were convenient, and the filing was minimal. On some quiet afternoons, I even managed to read some philosophy before leaving for one of my early-evening classes. I considered myself fortunate and hoped that the job would last until I finished my studies. Unfortunately, it didn't last long.

Both the partners were well-dressed men in their early thirties who occupied identical, well-appointed, side-by-side offices. Stein seemed to be the brains of the operation, while Jacobs had the good looks. Stein had a picture of his wife and two young children sitting on his large desk. Jacobs was single and, based on phone conversations I overheard, had a very active social life. My first weeks at Byron Bernard were fairly uneventful, and so I was completely unprepared for what happened one morning when Stein asked me to bring a file into his office. Since he was on the phone, I placed the material on his desk and started to leave the room. He signaled to me to wait, put the receiver down on his desk, walked across the office, put his arms around me, kissed me passionately on the lips, walked back to his desk, and resumed his conversation without missing a beat.

I was astonished and had no idea how to respond. Although it sounds melodramatic to say so, for an instant I honestly felt as though I were losing my mind. I knew what had happened and yet couldn't believe that it had. I felt that I must be mistaken and yet knew that I wasn't. My first thought was not to make a scene. I wanted to avoid calling attention to myself. Besides, since this was just the kind of thing that Rock Hudson was always doing to Doris Day in the movies, I remember thinking that only a bad sport would make a big deal out of it. I was torn between embarrassment and guilt. I wondered what I had done to provoke his behavior. I couldn't imagine how I would ever face him again. As it turned out, this wasn't a problem. When he left the office for lunch a short time later, he acted as though nothing had happened. In fact, he acted as though I wasn't even there. I think I was as humiliated by this treatment as by the kiss itself. Shortly thereafter, and without ever confronting him, I quit and went back to the temp jobs I thought I had escaped.

During the spring semester of my second year in the program, I made an appointment with Milton Munitz in the hope of obtaining a graduate fellowship for the following year. In Hook's absence, Munitz was serving as chair of the department. At the time, I was William Barrett's graduate assistant, but the previous year, I had worked for Munitz and so we knew each other very well. Because of my assistantships, the high regard my professors expressed for my work, and my standing as Hook's protégé, I was optimistic about receiving one. But after listening to my request, Munitz explained patiently that the department had to reserve fellowships for male students who might have families to support.

In the end, I was given a fellowship—or at least a piece of one. I don't remember exactly how it happened, but it is likely that Hook interceded for me on his return. I was allowed to share the A. Ogden Butler Fellowship in Philosophy with another (male) student. Getting even a part of a fellowship made me feel adequately validated, but in the end, it didn't help my financial situation very much; the stipend it carried amounted to no more money than the $600 I had been receiving as a graduate assistant. This meant I still needed to work to pay my expenses.

I received my master's in June 1966 and was fortunate to get a full-time instructorship at what was then Hunter College in the Bronx beginning in the fall. This was rare for graduate students in philosophy in the metropolitan area. Even with the large number of colleges and universities in the area, the small size of undergraduate philosophy departments and the relatively high concentration of graduate students meant that most people had to piece together a living by adjuncting at three or four schools before and often even after earning their doctorates. I was recommended for the job by Sidney Hook and interviewed and hired by Peter Caws, who was then chair of Hunter's department. It was probably my good fortune to have sought my first full-time job from a man whose wife was a serious scholar in her own right. Getting the instructorship meant that I no longer had to do office work to support myself, but it also meant that I would have to teach a full load while preparing for my comprehensives and writing my dissertation. I felt seriously underprepared to tackle any of the above, but tremendously excited to have the job and be getting on with my life. I resolved above all else not to be a boring teacher and to remember my friend Jane's warning that even the worst instructors have one or two faithful students who allow them to deceive themselves about their ability and the regard in which they are held. Jane knew because her own father was a professor who, in spite of being unrelentingly boring, had a small following of his own. I promised myself I would try hard not to be boring.

4

Getting It Right

❖ ❖ ❖ ❖ ❖ ❖ ❖ ❖ ❖ ❖ ❖ ❖ ❖ ❖

The summer before my job at Hunter began, I was initiated into college teaching by adjuncting at the University Heights College of New York University. Hired to teach two courses in the history of philosophy, I spent literally every minute that I wasn't teaching preparing for them. As it was, I barely managed to stay a chapter ahead of the class. I took endless notes on yellow legal pads and then used those notes to lecture each day. I read every secondary source I could on Hobbes, Locke, Berkeley, Hume, Descartes, Leibniz, and Spinoza and hoped that no one would ask me a question that I could not answer. No one had ever talked to me, not even for five minutes, about the art of teaching, and there was never a senior faculty member around to ask how I was doing or offer advice. I was so nervous that summer that I lived on Kaopectate.

When my mother learned that I would be teaching in the Bronx, she immediately offered to buy me a car. This kind and generous offer was prompted by her belief, which I suppose I shared, that it would be impossible, or, rather, wholly undesirable, to travel from my apartment in the Village all the way to the Bronx on public transportation. In fact, it is entirely possible that my mother literally did not know that one could travel from Greenwich Village to the Bronx by subway.

In my family, traveling to another borough was equivalent to crossing the state line; it required a car.

By this time in my mother's life, she had probably taken the crosstown bus on a handful of occasions but certainly had never ventured into the subway, and she would die at the age of sixty-seven, a lifelong New Yorker, without ever, to my knowledge, having done so. In our world, you traveled by taxi or by car, preferably one driven by someone else. I ended up with a bright red 1966 Plymouth Valiant that I promptly nicknamed Charlie after the man who had been my biology professor at NYU three years earlier.

At Hunter, I was assigned to teach four sections of "Introduction to Philosophy," an undemanding but boring schedule. The text I used was one of the then standard philosophy anthologies designed for the introductory course. Entitled *Philosophical Problems* and edited by Maurice Mandlebaum, Francis Gramlich, and Alan Ross Anderson, of the eighty-three readings included only one was by a woman, Ruth Benedict, and *she* wasn't even a philosopher. All the rest were written by men, and virtually all the men were white. Since I had not been taught to think that race, class, gender, and sexuality mattered as categories of experience, I did not notice. Thoroughly schooled in a tradition that defined the white, European, male, privileged voice as universal, I never considered the exclusion of women and people of color from the text as an issue. I was in the business of seeking truth, and I knew that truth had no gender and no race. I understood my role in the classroom to be that of shepherding students through an encounter with the great ideas of civilization. I would expose them to ideas and arguments that would challenge some of their most deeply held beliefs, and throughout this journey I would remain neutral and objective.

I was so good at doing what I had been taught that at the end of my first semester, a group of students in my introductory philosophy course came to me and said, with awe and appreciation, "We've been in your class all semester, and we still don't know what you think about anything." This, mind you, in a course in which we discussed such questions as "Does God exist?" "Is there life after death?" and,

"Is there such a thing as free will?" I was flattered and pleased. Like my professors before me, I was simply "presenting both sides" and allowing my students to think for themselves.

When I look back on that course and others that followed, I am amazed at the worldview I was teaching under the guise of neutrality and universality. Implicit in my syllabus was the notion that wisdom was the special attribute of one race, one sex, and one class, and thus one particular way of thinking about the world and framing questions was the only model for intelligence and rationality. That this way of defining knowledge and framing arguments made the experience and wisdom of most of the world's people either invisible or irrelevant never occurred to me. Nor did I understand that I was presenting a Eurocentric worldview. Since it had never occurred to me that it was possible to place any other experience, history, or culture at the center of my focus, I could not identify the perspective from which I taught. For me it was not a perspective, it was "reality."

As one of a minority within the profession, I felt privileged to be allowed to teach and write philosophy at all; lurking somewhere in the back, and occasionally at the front, of my mind was the belief that I was somehow a fake and the fear that I would one day be found out. Over the years, I have discovered that many women in academia live with this same fear. We wait patiently for the ultimate compliment from our professors and our peers, the one that assures us that we are so good we think like a man, but the flip side of this expression of approval is, of course, the dismissal we constantly fear and sometimes receive as well.

At Hunter, I shared an office with the other junior members of the department, who were, of course, all men. We shared a large room in the basement of the building, and each of us had a desk in it. The classics scholar with gold-rimmed glasses and a neatly manicured beard who had graduated from Princeton, a protégé of Gregory Vlastos, sat near the door; next to him was the nice Jewish boy ethicist who epitomized Phil Ochs's definition of liberals—two degrees to the left of center in good times and ten degrees to the right when it affects them personally. At the other end of the room sat a streetwise linguistic analyst with working-class roots and style, who had been raised in a lower-middle-class Jewish home in Brooklyn. I forget exactly how many others there were, but I remember well what an eclectic and spirited bunch we were. Although all of us complained about the lack of private office space, the fact that people with markedly different intellectual predilections shared the same space meant that conversations often took place that bridged both schools and periods in philosophy and that were carried on across interests, even weltanschauungs.

In some ways, sitting in that office was a continuation of my course work at the University of Chicago, where the organization of degree requirements by area (social sciences, humanities, and so on), rather than discipline, guaranteed that we would see, or be forced to make, connections among ideas. Conversations in that basement office might begin from very narrow positions or interests, but the diversity in the room guaranteed that they would move outward instead of imploding on themselves, as academic arguments so often do. Of course, that was hardly the reason we found ourselves sharing space. Our physical situation was the result of material necessity, not intellectual design, and the senior members of the department were safely ensconced in their own private offices one floor above.

In retrospect, I think that walking into that office was very much like walking into a men's locker room or at least what I imagine it would be like to enter one. The culture of the space was so clearly defined by the men who occupied it, and I was the "other." Of course, I was "other" not only because I was female but also because I was the youngest person in the room, no more than twenty-three and still a graduate student taking courses toward my doctorate. But clearly my gender was the primary difference I brought with me. It was a difference I thoroughly enjoyed. I did not consider being the only woman in the group a problem—rather, I considered it a privilege. Once again, it distinguished me from the rest of my gender and allowed me to claim the life of the mind as my own. Or, if not exactly my own, as something to which I might lay some claim. The relationship the men assumed toward me alternated between treating me as a colleague and as a kind of mascot or kid sister. I think that is how Malcolm X described his position in the all-white middle school he attended in seventh grade. As one of the two brightest children in the class but the one who was different, he was treated as a mascot or a pet—with affection but without respect.

My colleagues were friendly and accepting and in many ways provided, at least in the beginning, what remains the most cordial and collegial atmosphere I have ever experienced during my teaching career. There was genuine camaraderie among those of us who saw ourselves as young, smart, and up and coming, and there was affection and support on the part of the older, more established men who ran the department. On the other hand, the absence of a critical mass of people of my own kind—people who were women—meant that any time my teaching style or collegial behavior departed from the male-defined norms already in place in both the profession and the department, it was called into question. Two years later, when a new and rabidly misogynist chairperson took over the department and decided to get rid of me, one charge against me was that too many students came to visit me in the office to talk about the class. The assumption was that if you were a popular teacher who had close relationships with your students, you probably weren't teaching the hard stuff. In that male-defined world, any differences in style had the potential to end up making me look as though I were unprofessional. Can it be true, as I have been told, that the chairperson actually explained his desire to remove me from the department by announcing to several of my colleagues that he considered women the niggers of the profession?

My years teaching at Hunter in the Bronx were an important transitional period in my life. They were concurrent with the early years of the Vietnam War and constituted for me a time of political and personal awakening. In the beginning, I did not have strong feelings about the war. Most of the people I knew opposed it, but I remained unconvinced. I prided myself, however, on keeping an open mind and believed very much in the importance of having an opportunity to hear both sides of the question. A turning point came for me when a liberal, antiwar colleague of mine named Lewis Schwartz became concerned about the failure of the media to present "the other side" with respect to the war. Convinced that the media were airing only prowar propaganda, Lewis began collecting money from other like-minded academics with the goal of purchasing an hour of prime-time TV and using it to present the American people with a thoughtful antiwar perspective. Two networks refused outright, privately expressing fears that if such a program were aired, they would have trouble with the FCC when their licenses came up for renewal. The third network, ABC, was willing to consider such a program only on the condition that half the air time be devoted to presenting a prowar position. This, they assured my colleague, was required by their obligation to be fair and unbiased. Since in his eyes the prowar position was already receiving more than enough air time, he was hardly willing to spend the money collected from antiwar activists to provide yet another forum for that point of view.

I was astounded by the position that the networks took. My colleague's modest proposal, purchasing a single hour of TV time to present an alternative view of the war, seemed mild indeed and in the best spirit of democracy as I had come to understand it. The suggestion that people at the highest levels of government would bring pressure to bear to keep this information off the air was extraordinary to me. I was additionally astonished when my colleague's contact at one of the networks tried to justify its reluctance to sell the air time by explaining that after an evening news report that had depicted a particularly brutal bombing raid on a Vietnamese village, the network had received a call from the White House expressing President Johnson's displeasure with the reporting. The complaint was accompanied by the suggestion that future newscasts would be carefully monitored, perhaps by the president himself.

The other lesson I learned from this abortive attempt to use the airwaves to express a position I did not yet hold was that at times the insistence on presenting "both sides" might in practice and under certain conditions undermine the possibility of opening discourse rather than encourage it. A short time later, when I began to read some of the writings of philosopher Herbert Marcuse, his discussions of repressive tolerance and one-dimensional thinking seemed to apply easily to the way in which the U.S. government and the media were attempting to limit both thought and access to information.

My disillusionment with the liberal paradigm was further reinforced by the furor that erupted when Angela Davis, a member of the Communist Party USA, was scheduled to appear as the guest on a late-night TV talk show shortly thereafter. In response to protests, it was agreed that Davis would be permitted to appear only on condition that she be followed immediately by someone presenting the opposing point of view. The implication was clear. This rebuttal would serve as a kind of instantaneous antidote to the poisonous doctrine that Davis could be expected to spread. Davis, a former student of Herbert Marcuse, quite rightly refused to agree to these terms. I learned another lesson about free speech and who enjoyed it, and I began to understand something more about the way in which discourse can be limited in the name of being fair, neutral, and objective and under the pretense of simply "presenting both sides."

After my first or second semester at Hunter, I began to teach an occasional elective. Given the opportunity to teach political philosophy, which was my specialty, I organized the course around questions of rights and responsibilities within the modern nation-state. The course began with traditional readings from Hobbes, Locke, and Rousseau, examining the basis of political authority and asking under what conditions government relinquishes its claim to legitimacy. These were, of course, the pressing issues of the day. The course then explored the liberal freedoms by reading John Stuart Mill, who was later joined on the syllabus by both Herbert Marcuse and Robert Paul Wolff. This was followed by a section on resistance and revolution, which began by discussing civil disobedience using readings from Plato, Thoreau, King, and Gandhi, and ended up with readings from Marx, Engels, and Lenin. Over the next six years, I taught that course many times, and, depending on the semester and the political issues of the day, it might include writings on anarchy, a reading of Frantz Fanon's *Wretched of the Earth* and Shulamith Firestone's *Dialectic of Sex*, and, in its final permutation, works by André Gorz, Paul Sweezy, Paul Baran, and others offering an analysis of power and powerlessness in the advanced capitalist state.

If I had to identify three thinkers who had shaped my understanding of personal responsibility and moral agency, they would surely be Plato, Thoreau, and Sartre. Teaching Plato and Thoreau in the context of the turmoil of the late 1960s and then the early 1970s was for me a truly revolutionizing experience. Like many of my students, and a few of my colleagues, I listened to the news on WBAI–Pacifica, listener-sponsored radio, each evening and watched my country become more and more deeply involved in a war that I came to understand as antidemocratic in the most profound sense of that term. As I contemplated the economic, social, and political policies of the day, domestic and foreign, being carried out by my government and the havoc they were wreaking on people's lives, I began to find Thoreau's words compelling.

It is very difficult to capture and convey the climate that existed at U.S. colleges and universities during that period because it was so different from campus life in the later years of the twentieth century. Students who spent the morning discussing theories of the state in their class might well be engaging in civil disobedience on the campus a few hours later. Rather than undermining the enterprise of education, this situation actually enhanced it. The classrooms were alive with energy, and many of the students, certainly those who were politically active, took serious responsibility for their own education, which is no longer always the case. Traditional barriers between teacher and student were replaced by feelings of comradeship that grew out of respect and mutual accountability. In sharp contrast to the apathy that replaced it, the consensus of the time was that it was both possible and necessary to work toward a better society and that all of us shared the responsibility for doing so.

Among the early targets for student protests were the army recruiters who were allowed to come on campus to recruit soldiers for the war. In the beginning, when a recruiter was scheduled to be on campus, antiwar students simply penciled themselves in for all the appointments in the day; when that no longer was effective, they staged sit-ins, blocking the halls and stairways that provided access to the office where the recruiters were located and daring the college to take action against them. By the end, feelings ran so high at Hunter that one day students surrounded a car carrying two recruiters onto the campus and held them hostage for hours until they agreed to leave. This last tactic was finally successful in discouraging their visits.

In addition to mobilizing to keep recruiters off campus, many of us were engaged in some form of draft counseling. It was impossible for me to read Thoreau and not take this obligation seriously. For so many of us during this period, there was no distinction between intellectual and political work, nor was there a serious question, David Hume notwithstanding, about how to bridge the gap between the "is" and the "ought," between thought and action.

After a while, Congress passed a law making draft counseling a crime. Antiwar activists responded by organizing a mass meeting at Town Hall presided over by Benjamin Spock, David Delinger, and others. Standing on the very stage from which I had graduated at the start of the decade, they challenged the law by breaking it openly and invited us to join them. Hundreds of people in the hall, myself included, rose to their feet to join in this public act of civil disobedience. Later we signed the draft notice of one of the young men present, sharing publicly the responsibility for counseling him to avoid the draft. Although the government portrayed us as radicals intent on destroying the fabric of America, this simple, nonviolent, public act of law-breaking seemed to me to be in the best tradition of Thoreau's writings on civil disobedience. It reflected my best understanding of how a responsible citizen in a democracy was required to act. It was the appropriate way to respond to Thoreau's challenge to us to be "men first, and subjects afterward."

Although Thoreau's famous essay on civil disobedience relied exclusively on the male pronouns, I was hardly a feminist then and did not take offense. It never occurred to me that he might have expressed himself differently. Certainly the injunction to be "women first, and subjects afterward" would not have had the same ring as his original formulation. Still the fact that I was not a man and could not be one and that, since women were not subject to the draft, I had no draft card to return or destroy seemed to compromise my status as a moral agent. In a world where heroism is defined by putting "women and children first," it was not entirely clear to me how I could be either a hero or a patriot.

When the women's movement first began to focus our attention on language challenging the exclusive use of the male pronoun and words like "mankind" and "humanity," a common retort was that of course these words included women too. But a close reading of most historical texts fails to support this contention. When Thoreau wrote, "Let every man make known what kind of government would command his respect, and that will be one step toward obtaining it," it is difficult to believe that he was picturing women as citizens. When Hobbes, in *Leviathan*, wrote on "the Natural condition of mankind as concerning their felicity, and misery," it is impossible to believe that he meant to include women even once when he used the word "men." And so it goes. I have always been delighted with the ultimate feminist rejoinder to the claim that this attention to language is "trivial," the suggestion that if the use of the pronoun is so inconsequential, we might as well use "she" and "her" instead of "he" and "him" for the next several hundred years. I have rarely met a man who shrugged his shoulders at this modest proposal and said "why not!"

As opposition to the war in Vietnam mounted, the protests on college campuses began to escalate and students sought ever more dramatic ways to permeate the conscience of the average citizen. At one point, the students at Hunter announced that they would napalm a dog. This dramatic announcement was designed to focus attention on the destruction of Vietnam and the suffering of its people, but the students had no napalm and never intended to harm an animal. The response to the announcement was incredible. Animal rights' activists and humanists from every corner of the city and beyond registered their outraged protest, and the students were denounced in the press and on the airwaves in every term imaginable. But no one seemed to be able to transfer their horror over the proposed mutilation of a single dog to opposition to dropping napalm indiscriminately on hundreds of thousands of human beings. When asked to choose between a poodle and a gook, as the Vietnamese were often disparagingly called, they chose the poodle every time. The same thing happened repeatedly over the next several years each time a group of demonstrators threatened or actually carried out the desecration of the American flag. People who were not affected by the sight of ravaged hamlets, burned-out fields, and mutilated Vietnamese children were reduced to a frenzy at the prospect of witnessing the destruction of a piece of cloth.

The earliest mass demonstration against the war held in Washington took place at the Pentagon in October 1967 and has been recorded for posterity by Norman Mailer in his book *Armies of the Night*. Hardly a hardcore antiwar activist, I went on the demonstration partly out of curiosity and partly to accompany my husband, who was already strongly opposed to the war. I returned from Washington a committed antiwar activist.

My change of heart and mind was the result of three things that happened during the course of that weekend. The first was the government's decision to greet the demonstrators by massing hundreds of National Guard troops around the Pentagon dressed in full military regalia. I will never forget my sense of disbelief on encountering the troops, their gas masks in place, bayonets in hand. I could not believe that the government would bring forth such a show of force in response to a peaceful protest by citizens of conscience. By doing so, I understood that it had ceased to be *my* government—not because of any decision on my part to withdraw my allegiance, but because its refusal to distinguish between civil disobedience and self-interested criminal conduct did not leave me room to exercise my conscience and still claim a fundamental loyalty. It was the presence of the troops in full battle gear, not any action on the part of the demonstrators, that instantly transformed us from citizens into outlaws.

The second pivotal event of the weekend was the government's decision to use tear gas against the demonstrators. As I ran from the fumes, I understood that the government had chosen to cross a line that changed the premises of citizenship irrevocably and that in some profoundly important sense, by doing so it chose not to be my government. Getting teargassed during a peaceful protest was something that in my mind happened in other countries. It could not be happening here.

The third thing that happened that weekend was the failure of the nation's press to accurately report the events of that Saturday afternoon and Sunday morning. Although I did not spend the night with those who were supporting the nonviolent, civil disobedience occurring on the steps in front of the Pentagon, I returned early the next morning to stand witness. As we passed around copies of the early edition of the *New York Times*, we were incredulous at the difference between the report in the paper and the event in which we had participated the previous day. Many of the demonstrators, myself included, turned to the reporters and photographers who ringed the demonstration and chanted "Shame." Several years later, I would not be surprised when I learned that the *New York Times*'s description of police activity during the efforts to end the student siege at Columbia University had been written and filed before the police ever set foot on campus. It has been suggested that the resulting coverage was a more accurate reflection of the overlap between membership on the board of trustees at Columbia and membership on the editorial board of the *Times* than of what actually took place there.

Back at Hunter, I was continuing to learn other lessons as well. Unlike the students I had taught at NYU uptown, who were almost entirely white, my students at Hunter always included a small number of Blacks and Hispanics. City University had adopted a policy of open admissions, and its highly successful SEEK program provided poor white and "minority" students who entered the university under its auspices with an array of support services that resulted in an impressively high retention and graduation rate among those who participated.

The "minority" students in my introductory philosophy classes usually sat together at the back of the room and didn't say very much. As a young and inexperienced teacher, I had little sense of how to involve them more directly in the class; as a young, white middle-class woman, I felt a real chasm between us that I was at a loss to bridge. The class was studying Descartes's *Meditations,* in which the philosopher sets off in search of something that is absolutely true. To this end, he invokes a universal doubt and ends up questioning the existence of everything in the world, including himself. By discarding anything of which he is not absolutely certain, Descartes finally arrives at his famous Cogito, "I think therefore I am," which then serves as the bedrock of his philosophy—a self-validating truth that is beyond question. At the end of a class on the *Cogito,* a group of my Black and Hispanic students waited to talk to me. Their message was that I was okay but that they really couldn't make much sense out of Descartes. After talking to them for a while, it became clear that actually they understood Descartes very well—they simply couldn't believe that he was saying what they thought he was. Over the years, I have come to understand that very often when students in a philosophy class say they don't understand, what they mean is they can't believe that anyone would make that claim or they can't imagine entertaining it seriously. Part of the job of teaching working-class students is finding ways to empower them enough so that they have the confidence required to be able to say, "I understand, but I disagree."

My students' discomfort with Descartes proved to be another turning point in my intellectual life. Their response to his writing made me begin to wonder how differences in class, race, and gender might affect students' reading of Descartes's *Meditations* and other classic texts. While my more privileged students at University Heights College of NYU seemed able to treat ideas as puzzles or games to be engaged with for the sheer pleasure of the exercise, many of my students at Hunter lacked this ability, which I had been taught to equate with high intelligence. They seemed to take ideas with deadly seriousness. While the students at NYU could enjoy engaging in the Cartesian doubt, asking themselves whether there was any reason to think that the earth, the sun, the moon, the clouds, or the sky, even their own bodies, existed, my students at Hunter found Descartes's project uninviting, even absurd. How could these students, for whom material life was such a brutally clear reality, take seriously the ramblings of a man sitting by the fire in his cap and nightshirt who seems to question whether he exists at all? Why should they?

Like crossword puzzles and double crostics, entertaining epistemological idealism is an interesting way to pass the time, but it hardly seems appropriate to make the ability to think such thoughts a basis for determining intelligence or a prerequisite for graduating from college. The fact that I enjoy the epistemological puzzles raised by both empiricism and idealism is quite beside the point. The issue is whose "reality" is validated by making Descartes the father of modern philosophy and allowing his questions and, worse yet, his attempts at answers frame the issues for the modern period. By constructing a curriculum—worse yet, a culture—around such an idiosyncratic worldview and then calling it knowledge, we have privileged the distorted perspective of an infinitesimal fraction of the world's population. It makes about as much sense as reducing "art" during certain periods to the portraits of members of wealthy families and consigning everything else to the dustbins of history.

As I began to understand the difficulty that some of my students were having with Descartes, I began to think in new ways about the classical writings that I was teaching. Instead of beginning with the assumption that some of my colleagues adopted, that my students' difficulties were a sign of their inadequacy, I decided to operate from the premise that their discomfort was a sign of Descartes's inadequacy. I decided to ask the students to make allowances for his limitations, and, in order to do so, I spent more time discussing the context out of which Descartes's writings and worldview emerged. Where previously I had simply presented an *intellectual* context and history for his writing, treating ideas as though they existed in relation to one another but in no particular relation to material conditions, my teaching now began to reflect more of a materialist worldview. Along with my students, I asked why someone might end up posing the kinds of questions that Descartes did. I told them about his experiences at La Fleche, the Jesuit school he attended from the age of ten, where, because he was the son of a well-to-do family in the area and a precocious student, he was allowed the privilege of staying in bed to "meditate" while others were up and about doing chores. While it was unlikely that those who had to clean the floor or work in the garden or, perhaps, make Descartes's bed would spend time wondering whether they had arms and legs, just as it was unlikely that most women whose lives were so firmly grounded in their biology as well as in their social role might ask such questions, it made perfect sense that someone in Descartes's situation might engage in this kind of alienated speculation.

I shared with my students the suggestion offered by some commentators that Descartes's philosophy may have reflected in part the fact that he had very poor eyesight and that his sense of the world and his relation to it had been acquired while looking at everything through a pair of poorly ground lenses. I did this not to dismiss Descartes but to help my students understand that ideas are the products of material reality as well as intellectual engagement.

In addition, in order to elicit their interest and their sympathy, I went out of my way to talk about the radical nature of Descartes's intellectual and personal mission in relation to the Catholic Church. I described the "negotiations" that led from the original publication of Descartes's *Discourse on Method* in French, a language accessible to a fair number of people, to its final version as *Meditations on First Philosophy* written in Latin in order to significantly limit its audience. This was a condition that the Church required in order to give its imprimatur to the text, since publishing the work in Latin would safely limit its readership to those who were less likely to be misled by Descartes's hypothetical doubt of God's existence. As I began to understand that ideas had a political significance as well as an intellectual history, I was able to make more sense out of what I was teaching and to present formerly inaccessible ideas to my students in ways that empowered them.

This did not mean that I taught Descartes as a capitalist running dog. It simply meant that in addition to sharing my own delight with the intellectual puzzles that emerged from Descartes's writing, and examining the progression from Augustine to Aquinas to Descartes that reflects the evolution of "modern" philosophical thinking, I was able to talk about Descartes as a thinker with a particular race and class and gender and to speculate on how those variables shaped his thought. If Descartes could be understood as limited by his own race, class, and gender, then my students could engage with him as an equal, a product of his own personal and historical moment, as were they. I could encourage my students to see ideas as weapons in a political struggle as well as puzzles in an intellectual tradition. When Descartes was presented in this way, many more students were prepared to follow him through his universal doubt and to entertain a philosophical position they might otherwise have dismissed as ridiculous. I could assure them that their puzzlement was not a result of a lack of intelligence on their part but an understandable reaction to the intellectual enterprise they were being asked to entertain, and then I could give them a hundred reasons, intellectual and political, why it was important to read and grapple with Descartes and his worldview.

When I think back over my teaching career, I am embarrassed by how many of my colleagues have felt contempt for working-class students of all colors, mocking them for their inability to engage with highly abstract, often desiccated and elite thought presented to them as though pearls were being thrown to swine. I think back to some particularly unpleasant colleagues who seemed to delight in announcing that each year the students got worse, who never failed to ask me, almost gleefully, at the start of each school year whether I, too, wasn't appalled at how unintelligent and lazy the latest group of students appeared to be, as though the standing of these men somehow rose or fell in inverse proportion to that of their students. I am still at a loss to understand why a teacher would take a class's poor performance or lack of interest as a sign of the students' inadequacy rather than a sign of his or her own failure as a teacher. I think back to the dean at then Paterson State College in New Jersey who patiently explained to me in the early 1970s that we taught philosophy to our Black and white working-class students in order to civilize them. When I hear his voice, I hear the voice of those who oppose a multicultural curriculum today and maintain that a curriculum that includes the diverse perspectives, knowledge, and culture of women and men from all classes and all racial and ethnic groups from around the world will impoverish rather than enrich our education. What they take to be the mark of their own superiority is really a measure of their own ignorance.

My own mother had a passion for caviar, and my brother and I were raised to enjoy it as well. In fact, during one period of my brother's life, when he was a particularly picky eater, his daily and improbable after-school snack was a beluga caviar sandwich on Wonder bread. While I still consider caviar a wonderful delicacy, I know that those who laugh at paying enormous sums of money for a tiny heap of fish eggs are right. In some ways, teaching philosophy is like making a meal of those fish eggs and dismissing those who do not share our taste. In the great march of history, they are the ones who will have the last laugh. This has not stopped me from eating caviar on occasion, but it certainly has stopped me from thinking of myself as superior because I do.

In those days, of course, I was less sure. I often felt like an interloper in a field of brilliant minds, all of whom were men. I could read Kant's *Critique of Pure Reason* and Hegel's *Phenomenology*, but I couldn't conceive of a woman writing those books and I understood that the measure of real intelligence was the ability to do so. It would be several more years before feminist academics would begin to create a field called "women's studies" and before books like Kate Millet's *Sexual Politics*, Toni Cade's *Black Woman*, Shelia Rowbotham's *Woman's Consciousness, Man's World*, Juliet Mitchell's *Women's Estate*, and Rayne Reiter's *Towards an Anthropology of Women* would appear. I had not yet begun to understand the ways in which the scholarship produced by disciplines as traditionally defined reflected a narrowly male and privileged point of view that was then treated as universal. That there were no women on either the graduate or the undergraduate philosophy faculty at NYU, that, to my knowledge, no one ever required us to read a book written by a woman during my entire tenure there, that virtually every student was white and most were men—all struck me as a reflection of a natural hierarchy of intelligence and ability. The fact that some few of us were allowed to occupy the margins of the circle of the initiate was both a testimony to the fluidity of the system and an indication of our own personal limitations.

Although most days I spent my mornings and early afternoons teaching, by four or five o'clock in the afternoon, I was back to being a graduate student and was concerned with preparing for my qualifying exams and finalizing a topic for my dissertation. After hearing that I had attended the antiwar demonstration at the Pentagon, Sidney Hook, who was my adviser, indicated that he was not pleased. He asked if it was I who had written those dirty words on the walls, referring to the widely televised "Fuck the War" slogans that had been painted with spray cans by some of the more enthusiastic demonstrators. I wasn't sure whether his question was a real question, one that he expected me to answer, or simply a peculiar way of expressing his disapproval. I wondered whether my reign as the department's golden girl was coming to an end.

My relationship with Hook was always problematic. On the one hand, he was clearly committed to women's equality and prided himself on giving the few female students in the department the same opportunities as the men and even went out of the way to mentor us. On the other hand, Hook was enormously paternalistic toward me and toward other women—a cross between a doting grandfather, a shy suitor, and a playful colleague. One day he asked me to come to his apartment, instead of his office, for a conference about my dissertation. I don't remember why. Perhaps he had been ill. At his suggestion, we took a walk together, and I remember being amazed when he tucked his arm through mine. The fact that he would never have done such a thing with a male student doesn't even need to be said. This intimate gesture, innocent though it was, was hardly appropriate, but it was typical of the kind of relationship we had. I knew that Hook had real affection for me, but I could never trust its basis. Was I his mascot or his student? His granddaughter or his fantasy? Whenever I said something he thought clever or insightful, he made me feel more like Hedda Gabler than Annie Oakley. Did he take me seriously? As our disagreements over the war broadened, I suspected that he rationalized our differences by telling himself that I was under my husband's influence. In this way, he would have been able to tolerate the disagreement without holding me responsible for it. This was made easier by the fact that I was married to another philosophy graduate student whom Hook did not think very much of.

Our widening disagreement over the war became a cause of increasing concern as I got closer to selecting a topic for my doctoral dissertation. Although I would have preferred to do a dissertation in political philosophy, I decided that doing so might lead to direct conflict with Hook and other members of the department. Instead, I decided to write about Charles Sanders Peirce's theory of truth, a topic wholly removed from the politics of the day, or so it seemed. Peirce, a brilliant and original thinker, was an American philosopher who, along with William James and John Dewey, formulated American pragmatism. I was fascinated by Peirce's work because it was both wide-ranging and unwieldy. Peirce had never written a single complete account of his philosophy. Instead, the body of his work is contained in eight volumes of collected papers. I was fascinated by the prospect of extracting a coherent account of a portion of his work by integrating and reconciling his writings on widely divergent topics. In addition, I was attracted to Peirce the human being, a man who was something of a misfit in the glittering world of Boston intellectuals who were gathered at Harvard during the late nineteenth and early twentieth century. When I told Hook that I wanted to do a dissertation on Peirce's epistemology, he immediately volunteered to be my adviser, assuring me that no one in the department knew as much about Peirce as he did.

The part of Peirce's theory that I found most interesting was his claim that ultimately logic rests on ethics, which rests on aesthetics. This peculiar and provocative, almost poetic, claim is hardly the basis for Peirce's considerable reputation, and it was hardly an aspect of his thought that attracted the sympathy of Hook or the other members of my committee. To make matters worse, the more I wrote and thought about Peirce's unusual attempt to ground what we ought to think on how we ought to act and, in the end, on what we ought to admire, the more I noticed similarities between his way of thinking about the relationship between thought and action and the way in which Herbert Marcuse was seeking to ground revolutionary change and vision in art and culture. I had set out to do a dissertation that would avoid politics but, unsurprisingly, found that everything either was political or had political implications and consequences. Only an idiot could have thought otherwise during this period. To my credit or my shame, I resolutely put these interests out of my mind, refusing to allow them to spill over into my dissertation, and tried to keep to the straight-and-narrow path. As every graduate student knows, the point of writing a dissertation is to earn a degree, not necessarily to say anything that is personally meaningful.

As my involvement in the antiwar movement increased, Hook and I spent more time bantering about our opposing views than we did discussing my dissertation, and somehow no matter how much rewriting I grudgingly did, my committee seemed to find ever more reasons to withhold its approval for my defense. Hook finally confided that the problem was another member of my committee, who was put off by my political activism. According to him, the logician Richard Martin had learned that I had contracted to co-author a book on Marcuse's thought and considered this proof that I was unworthy to write about Peirce. When I confronted Martin, it was clear that my interest in Marcuse had in fact offended his sensibilities, and he told me that I would have to spend at least an additional year grappling exclusively with Peirce's writings if there was any hope for my degree. Shortly thereafter, I was sexually assaulted by another member of my committee, who then told me that I would have to spend the next two years working very closely with him if I had any hope of getting to my defense. I did what any sensible woman would have done in those pre–Anita Hill days; I abandoned my dissertation and gave up all hope of getting my degree.

Because I had taken a job at a state college in New Jersey two years earlier and had already been promised tenure the following year, it was possible for me to abandon my dissertation without having to give up my teaching career. After leaving Hunter in the Bronx, by then known as Lehman College, I had secured a position as an assistant professor at then Paterson State College in Wayne, New Jersey. At that time, the state of New Jersey still had in place a law that granted tenure after a three-year probationary period. This meant that candidates for tenure presented themselves for evaluation in the fall of the second year. Tenure was voted at one of the board of trustees' fall meetings and took effect at the start of the following academic year. At the time I came up for tenure, I had passed all my qualifying exams and had completed a draft of my dissertation. As was customary in such situations, Hook wrote a letter on my behalf, saying that he expected me to go to my defense shortly and be awarded the degree. He spoke of my abilities as a teacher and a scholar in glowing terms, and on the strength of his recommendation, my publications, teaching evaluations, and other professional activities, I received tenure easily. Even without a doctorate, I seemed assured of lifetime tenure as an assistant professor.

Although I never did receive my terminal degree, some years later, with the help of a suit filed with the Equal Employment Opportunities Commission (EEOC), I was able to obtain a promotion to the senior ranks. My suit claimed "equivalency," citing the selection from my dissertation that had been published as an article in the *Journal of the History of Philosophy* in the fall of 1975 as evidence that, although undefended, the dissertation was a publishable work.* It also pointed to the body of professional work that I had produced over the years, claiming that it was more than equivalent to the record of a "similarly situated male" psychology professor who had been recommended for promotion based on equivalency that same year. In my case, although the college's Promotion Committee had recommended both equivalency and promotion, the college president had overruled the decision. Among other things, when the president's representative met with the Promotion Committee to explain why he was rejecting its recommendation, he made it clear that he did not consider my work in women's studies relevant. To respond to this position, and in order

---

*"Charles Sanders Peirce's Defense of the Scientific Method," *Journal of the History of Philosophy* 13, no. 4(1975): 481–490.

to create a promotion file that closely paralleled that of my male colleague who had sought external validation for his scholarly contribu-
tions to his field, I sought and received letters about the value of my
work from colleagues all over the country. Even before my case at the
EEOC received a formal hearing, it is my understanding that the college received counsel that it would lose. To my surprise, at the regularly scheduled board of trustees meeting both the "similarly situated
male" and I received our promotions.

Originally located in the city of Paterson, as Paterson's nonwhite
population had increased over the years, the college moved to its
present location on two hundred or so acres in lily-white Wayne.
Having begun as Paterson Normal School, it had then become Paterson State Teachers College and, only recently, Paterson State College.
A few years after I arrived, it would change its name once again, although not without student protest, to the William Paterson College
of New Jersey. In 1997, the college became William Paterson University. By taking the name of one of the early governors of the state, the
college attempted to sever or at least blur its last remaining link with
the city of Paterson. This, it was assumed, would aid the college in
attracting white middle-class suburban students who would feel comfortable in Wayne, but who would have no interest in attending school
in Paterson.

When I first began teaching at the college, there was not as yet a
philosophy department; however, all students were required to take
a course in the philosophy of religion. The course was offered under
the auspices of the Department of Professional Education, which became my temporary academic home. During my first semester, my
entire teaching load consisted of four sections of this course. To my
mind, this was even worse than being consigned to teaching four sections of "Introduction to Philosophy." As an atheist, I could think of
no more unfortunate fate and began to think that perhaps there was a
God after all.

The course I taught began with a consideration of the traditional
proofs of God's existence, including those by Anselm, Augustine, and
Aquinas. Since a section of the introductory course was often devoted

to these proofs, I had already taught them many times. I was less interested in discussing whether they proved God's existence, since I assumed that everyone could see that they did not, than I was in exploring the worldview they implied and the paradigm of thought and argument they offered. It turned out that the interests of my students were somewhat different.

My usual approach to teaching the proofs was to give the strongest and most persuasive presentation of each one that I could and then invite my students to dismantle it. After spending some time explaining Aquinas's "Five Ways," I turned to a young woman in the first row and asked what was wrong with Aquinas's argument. She gasped, turned pale, and responded in disbelief, "You want *me* to criticize Aquinas?" It was then I learned that for the most part, students at Paterson State came from traditional and fairly conservative Christian backgrounds, many of them from Italian, Irish, or Polish Catholic families, and that many had attended parochial school throughout their childhood. These were the girls who had grown up being told that it was unladylike to wear patent-leather shoes because they allowed boys to see under their skirts. As it turned out, Paterson State was a good choice for them; throughout most of the 1960s and until a year or two before I arrived, women students and faculty at the college had been bound by a strict, gender-based, dress code that prohibited them from wearing slacks or trousers (forget about jeans), even during the worst northern New Jersey snowstorms.

Although the college was located no more than half an hour from the George Washington Bridge, my students were markedly different from those I had taught in the city. There was just a sprinkling of African-American and Latino/a students at the college, hardly any Jewish students, and very few Muslims either. Most of the students had never visited New York or even spent the night away from home, and most were among the first in their family ever to go on to higher education. While some of the women, who were overwhelmingly white, might have entertained the fleeting hope of attending colleges away from home in neighboring Pennsylvania, most came from families with limited resources, and their parents used whatever money they had been able to set aside for education to send their sons away. The female students were lucky to be in college at all, and many were there over their fathers' strong reservations against sending their daughters to college in the first place.

As I got to know the young women in my classes, I discovered that almost without exception they were majoring in early childhood education or speech pathology. When I tried to encourage several of them to think about going on in philosophy or another liberal arts discipline, I discovered that the price many had to pay to come to college in the first place was the promise that they would major in one of these two fields because these were the only areas that their parents thought appropriate for women. Even parents who believed that their daughters should become wives and mothers could see the virtue of having a career in elementary- or secondary-school teaching to fall back on if the family went through hard times, or to pursue in the few years before the children started coming, in order to save money for a down payment on a house.

When I arrived in 1969, no more than 4 or 5 percent of the college's students were African-American, and even this poor representation was a recent improvement, the result of a building takeover the previous spring. At that time, twenty or thirty members of the Black Student Union had taken over one of the main campus buildings and resolved to remain there until the college agreed to increase its "minority" enrollment and to open the curriculum to Black studies. One of the beneficiaries of that demonstration and the subsequent change in recruitment policy was a young woman named Caroline, who was one of the very few Black students, perhaps the only one, in my introductory sections. Caroline had attended high school in Paterson and, like most or all of the other Black students I met, had been tracked through the commercial course rather than the college preparatory program. At the age of twenty-six, hearing Caroline's story was a revelation to me, one that in retrospect makes me cringe at my own naïveté. Coming from a small private school in New York where it was assumed that everyone would go to college, I never really believed that schools tracked their students toward different futures based on their race, gender, or their class, even though my own experience at a segregated private school made it very clear that this was the case. Although I realized that my own educational opportunities had been limited somewhat by gender, I continued to hold fast to the American ideal of school as the great equalizer that provided unlimited possibilities for upward mobility to *anyone* who worked hard and had the right stuff. In this respect, I was not unlike many others, then and now, who cannot think critically about such issues, even in the face of countervailing evidence, because of the overwhelming power and attraction of the rhetoric of American democracy. The ideal of equal treatment and justice for all is so compelling that reality often pales in relation to it, and we fail to "see" anything that might force us to loosen our hold on this cherished piece of American lore.

Although she was an articulate, motivated, and intelligent young woman, Caroline had been encouraged by her guidance counselor to think about a career as a seamstress. The story she told me closely resembled Malcolm X's experience in junior high, which he wrote about in his autobiography. When Malcolm expressed an interest in becoming a lawyer, his teacher urged him to think about a future as a carpenter, since he was good with his hands and would always get work because white people liked him. Somehow, Caroline had managed to gain admission to Paterson State, but her lack of preparation left her at a clear disadvantage in relation to students who had come through the college preparatory program. Like many others, Caroline had to work close to a full-time job in order to pay for her tuition, books, and other expenses. Because getting to the college was almost impossible using public transportation and the dormitory space was very limited, like most students she was dependent on a car for transportation. Once at the college as one of a very few Black students in any course she took, often the only one, she was left largely to herself. Of course, most of the students and faculty would have told you that they had no objection to her attending the college and were perfectly willing to befriend her as long as she proved herself. When I think back, I am humbled by the courage and determination of the hundreds of Black students, like Caroline, who endured daily isolation as they pursued their education at white schools. And I am saddened and embarrassed that so many of us who could have done more thought that we were doing enough simply by not opposing their presence.

As I got to know her, I began to wonder what the curriculum we were teaching had to offer students like Caroline. And I found myself thinking again about the "minority" students I had taught at Hunter in the Bronx and their reaction to Descartes. I began to wonder whether the classroom process and culture functioned to empower some students and to disempower or silence others, and I began to ask how I could modify my teaching style and content in order to reach all, instead of some, of my students. As I got to know Caroline better, I began to think a lot about at what personal cost she came to the college. Who were her friends? Where would she find them? Who would smile at her in the hall? And I saw that many of my white students were very much as I had been in high school. They did not mean her any harm, but it would never occur to them to offer her their friendship. A few years later, I began to notice that the few faculty of color at the college made a habit of greeting warmly any other person of color—student, colleague, or maintenance worker—whom they passed whether they knew them or not. I thought back to Caroline and understood.

Like many of my peers, in the late 1960s and early 1970s, I was beginning to think about the politics of education. Much of the discussion during the period focused on the ways in which both the form and the content of education reproduced hierarchy in general and class divisions in particular. Issues of gender and race were discussed as well, but most often they took a back seat to class. Similarly, although some traditional scholarship and research came under indictment for being political, more attention was paid to pedagogy and institutional structures than to the curriculum or the canon. In the early 1970s, Edgar Friedenberg wrote books and essays in which he argued that the real lessons our students learned in school were not in the curriculum but in the school culture—the kinds of treatment they received, and thus came to expect, from those in authority. And, of course, Paulo

Friere's *Pedagogy of the Oppressed*, which appeared in 1970, prompted many of those who were just beginning their teaching careers to experiment with new teaching techniques and new and more collaborative ways of structuring the learning experience.

A few years later, in April 1973, I would participate in a conference that signified the start of attempts to make the philosophy curriculum more genuinely inclusive and relevant. A paper I had written using Plato's "Allegory of the Metals" to examine the ideology of racism in contemporary U.S. society was selected for presentation at a conference on "Philosophy and the Black Experience," which was funded by the National Endowment for the Humanities and held at Tuskegee Institute in Alabama. In addition to providing me with an opportunity to meet and talk with some of the leading intellectuals and activists in the Black movement, including Harold Cruise,whose book on the Black bourgeoisie had just appeared, and the almost legendary C. L. R. James, whose kindness to me I will never forget, participating in the conference provided me with my first trip to the Deep South.

Unbeknownst to me, several of those of us who were invited speakers had flown into the Birmingham airport on the same plane from Kennedy, and a car was sent from Tuskegee Institute to transport us to the campus. In addition to me, the group consisted of two Black men, one of whom was a clergyman. Along the way, we stopped for a bite to eat at a large cafeteria in a shopping mall where I was painfully aware of the highly defined absence of any other Black people in the dining room. In the parking lot on the way back to the car, we passed an older white woman who was struggling to carry two large grocery bags. One of the Black men in our group offered his assistance. After he had placed them on the back seat of her car, she called him back and I watched in amazement as she handed him a quarter. He was wearing his clerical collar at the time.

In the course of that encounter, I came to understand that relationships between Blacks and whites occur within a context of white racism that has been established quite apart from the intentions or desires of the participants. My profound embarrassment and discomfort as we sat in the car making small talk and trying to ignore the humiliating encounter did not absolve me entirely of responsibility for it. I was acutely aware that the color of my skin and the history of privilege it bought me circumscribed whatever relationship might develop between the man and me. In future years, on numerous occasions, I would be painfully aware of the ways in which historically structured differences in privilege repeatedly limited and qualified my friendships with other women and men, particularly those who were not white. One of the least recognized costs of racism is the loss of so many unrealized friendships.

The Tuskegee conference occurred at the time when academics and activists were in the midst of the volatile debate over how to respond to the racist pseudoscience about race and IQ that was being promulgated by William Shockley and Arthur Jensen. One session of the program was given over to a refutation of their research by a Black biologist from Howard University. She covered every inch of the board with data that exposed their shoddy research methodology and with arguments that refuted their conclusions. The audience, which, as in all sessions, was predominantly Black, was split almost in half between those who were impatient with the time and energy she was devoting to what was clearly not science, but racism, and those who felt that such a careful refutation of that work was a valuable and necessary contribution to the debate. I found myself agreeing with the more radical point of view of the first, and younger, group and wondered what valuable work of her own this talented woman might have produced in the time she had spent painstakingly refuting theirs.

As the opposition to the war in Vietnam continued to grow around the country, even fairly conservative and insular student bodies like that at Paterson State began to hold teach-ins, candlelight vigils, and marches. By this time, some of the students at the college were veterans who had come to school after serving in Vietnam and who were attending the college under the GI Bill. Members of the newly formed Vietnam Veterans Against the War, these young men provided some of the most impassioned and courageous leadership in the antiwar movement.

Shortly after the United States had invaded Cambodia in April 1970 and after students protesting that incursion had been fired on and killed by National Guard troops at Jackson State and Kent State, students and faculty at schools all over the country began staging marches and sit-ins to demonstrate their outrage. We held a candlelight vigil at Paterson State, and, to the amazement of other faculty, several of the women faculty involved, including myself, wore jeans to campus—a college first. Jane Fonda, Tom Hayden, and Holly Near came to speak at the college, and we began organizing opposition to the war in earnest.

Two years later, in the spring of 1972, the ongoing protests over national and international events came to a head on campus over the firing of a young woman from the History Department who many felt was being let go because of her politics. When a group of student and faculty protestors, who had marched to the college's administration building seeking to make their grievances known, were informed that the college president was off campus and unavailable to meet with them, they staged a sit-in in his office. Other students and faculty filled the lobby of the building in support of the demonstrators, and Ralph Schoenman, a controversial public figure at the time who was serving as Bertrand Russell's secretary and principle administrator of the War Crimes Tribunal, joined the demonstration. Schoenman had been on campus to give a lecture. When he discovered that the majority of his prospective audience was otherwise occupied, he decided to join the audience instead of waiting for the audience to join him.

James Karge Olson, the college president, returned to campus and met with those of us who were occupying his office. But when hours of discussion and negotiation failed to result in a promise to reconsider the faculty member who was being fired, protestors were given an ultimatum: leave the building by a specific time or face serious disciplinary action. After the deadline had passed something like forty students and seven faculty members, including myself, remained. All the students faced some kind of disciplinary action that resulted in brief suspensions. The fate of the faculty was less clear. The college administration decided not to attempt to break the tenure of the five permanent members of the college faculty who had remained in the building, but was less sure about how to proceed in my case. Although I had been voted tenure four months earlier, the state's tenure statute required that an individual serve the first day of his or her tenure year in order for tenure to take effect; it was not entirely clear in which category I fell and how it was in the college's interests to treat me.

The state's attorney general was called in for an opinion, and the president and board of trustees met to decide my fate. Fortunately for me, the president was a civil libertarian with a longtime involvement in the American Civil Liberties Union, and the chair of the board of trustees was a progressive rabbi who had participated in many civil rights marches. After deliberating for some time, they decided not to risk establishing a dangerous precedent by trying to break my tenure.

Coincidentally, it turned out that the board chair was an NYU graduate who enjoyed a close relationship with Sidney Hook. I learned later, from the rabbi himself, that when Hook heard about my involvement in the sit-in, he offered to destroy his original letter in support of my tenure and to provide a new version, backdated, that would make it easier for the college to terminate me if it so chose. I heard the story several years after the fact and thought briefly about contacting Hook to ask whether it was true. Unfortunately, I knew it was without ever asking.

Looking back, it's difficult to make sense out of that demonstration. What did I think I was accomplishing by sitting in the president's office? Why was I willing to risk my job and my future by being part of it? What did sitting in a college building in Wayne, New Jersey, really have to do with the Vietnam War? The answer is, everything and nothing. Nothing in a simple straightforward telling of the events of that day will make clear why I felt I had to stay. To understand, you would have had to experience the rage and the despair that alternately buffeted those of us who were constantly looking for ways to publicly differentiate ourselves from those who were guilty of complicity or silence. Civilians were being tortured and killed in Southeast Asia. Young Americans were being sent to kill and die or were being forced to abandon their country, their families, their friends, their past lives, and flee to Canada. Students who looked just like us or just like our students were being shot and killed as they tried to bear witness in peaceful protest. People everywhere were trying to find ways to testify to their opposition to U.S. policy. On May 3, 1971, more than twelve thousand antiwar protestors would be arrested by police and military units in Washington, D.C., as they tried to bring the government to a standstill. A slogan of the times cried out: "Stop the Madness, Stop the War." In order to a stop the war, sometimes it felt as though you had to be part of the madness.

As the war continued, many of those active in the antiwar movement began to adopt a more comprehensive critique of U.S. society that included attention to issues of race and class, even gender. The disproportionate number of African-American and Hispanic men who had fought and died in the war in place of their more privileged white brothers, the poverty documented a decade earlier by Michael Harrington in *The Other America* and exacerbated by a domestic economy that had chosen guns over butter, the Stonewall rebellion, and the cumulative experiences of women in the civil rights and antiwar movements all began to shape a new and more inclusive political agenda for the nation.

One August in the early 1970s, I served as a coordinator of the Hiroshima-Nagasaki days of remembrance and protest, which were held each year on the anniversary of the bombing of those Japanese cities. That year's New York City demonstration was notable because it was one of the first major demonstrations to posit a relationship between expenditures on the war in Vietnam and issues of quality of life at home. Increasingly large segments of the antiwar movement would replace a narrow focus on ending the war with the demand to "bring the men *and* the *money* home." In this way, we would connect the lack of adequate funding for education, health care, and housing in the United States with the money being spent on the war effort. Sponsored by the Vietnam Peace Parade Committee, the August demonstration brought together an unprecedented coalition of diverse community groups united around this new and more inclusive theme. The major event of the week was a mass march to City Hall, where a few members of the City Council would accept a petition demanding that money currently used to fund the war effort be returned to New York to provide basic human services to the city's people. The actress Viveca Lindfors read the text of the proclamation for us on the steps of the building and then handed it to the council representatives.

Another of the coordinators of this demonstration was a man named Lou Salzberg, who identified himself initially as a photographer for *La Prensa*. Lou and I and my then husband, Karsten Struhl, had been given the responsibility for coordinating the protest after having volunteered to do so during an organizing meeting at the Vietnam Peace Parade headquarters. It was probably my first, certainly no more than my second or third, visit to the headquarters, and, apparently, the same was true for Lou. The fact that we three unknowns were allowed to coordinate this large demonstration simply by virtue of volunteering is testimony to the openness of the process in that organization as well as its naïveté. In my experience, and contrary to the media's stereotypical portrayal of antiwar demonstrators, the people at Fifth Avenue Peace Parade were a collection of very ordinary citizens who cared deeply about both the war and their country. Seasoned political activists might have known better and would have been less likely to make it so simple for agents and provocateurs to infiltrate the organization and hold leadership positions in it. But as it turned out, everyone there was already doing more than their share; when we three volunteered, they were glad to be able to share the burden of the work with new people who brought new energy to the group. In those days, it was the government, not the majority of people in the antiwar movement, that constantly reflected both a paranoia and a predisposition toward violence.

People in the organization, including myself, were particularly pleased about Lou's participation because he was working class, a vet, and Hispanic. This made him an ideal recruit to the antiwar movement, which was very self-conscious about its largely white and middle-class composition during the early years. When it came time to divvy up responsibilities, Lou, who was a freelance photographer, pointed out that because he had an answering service it would make sense to route all inquiries about the demonstration through his phone, and so we listed his number on every flyer that went out. Little did any of us know that several months later we would see Lou identified on the front page of our morning papers as the secret government witness who would testify against the Chicago Seven at their trial. Lou's phone number on our demonstration flyers had given the FBI direct access to all our plans and allowed it to acquire a complete list of the most active participants. After reading the story in the *New York Times*, Karsten and I went up to the Peace Parade offices, wanting to share our feelings of astonishment and betrayal with others who must be experiencing them, too. That we found no one there we knew well enough to talk to at any length indicates how peripheral our connection was to the organization. Only the sign that someone had taped to the bathroom door, renaming it "The Lou Salzberg Memorial Trophy Room," served to acknowledge the story that appeared on the front page of the *New York Times*.

Although my phone had been tapped for some time, as was the case for so many of us with even minimal participation in the antiwar movement, my involvement with Lou ensured that the FBI would keep me under close watch. I thought back to the many afternoons and evenings that Lou had spent in our Sullivan Street apartment—talking about the war, the country, our lives, his kids—and wondered what he really made of it all. Ironically, during the months we worked together planning strategy for each of the events that would form part of the Hiroshima-Nagasaki week protest, it was Lou who was always proposing strategies that had a great potential for confrontation or were likely to lead to violence. We spent a lot of time reining him in to make sure that things did not get out of hand. In our minds, we were clear that we were asking people to participate in a peaceful demonstration and seeking to build alliances among many community groups, not provoke a violent melee.

Years later, in 1989, when I obtained copies of my FBI files under the Freedom of Information Act, I wasn't surprised to find that they were fairly extensive. I was surprised, however, to read the recommendation that I be included in the ADEX, which meant that the government considered me so dangerous that I was among those scheduled to be rounded up and placed in detention immediately if the FBI thought that there was significant reason to arrest militants. Among the damaging pieces of information contained in my file was the report that I had written a letter to one of my United States senators, Harrison Williams, protesting the way several students at William Paterson College were being harassed by the FBI. As I recall, FBI agents had appeared at the students' homes (they lived with their parents) at five o'clock in the morning, dragged them out of bed, to their parents' horror, and pummeled them with questions about another student they were trying to locate. When I learned of this incident, I organized a group of faculty at the college to write a letter in protest. All of this was duly noted in my file, along with the observation that my signature appeared at the top. This same file page recommends that I be placed on the ADEX. Clearly in those days, writing a letter to a senator was the act of a dangerous citizen.

The publication of Betty Friedan's *Feminine Mystique* in 1960, followed ten years later by the publication of *Sisterhood Is Powerful*, edited by Robin Morgan, Toni Cade's *Black Woman* and *The Dialectic of Sex* by Shulamith Firestone, and then a host of other books, anthologies, and journals signaled a new beginning for the women's rights movement, which had been so visible more than a century earlier.* At first, I began integrating some of the new feminist analysis into my political philosophy syllabus, but before long I began to develop a new course: "Philosophy of Sexual Politics." I started teaching this women's studies course within the philosophy department in the early 1970s using an assortment of duplicated essays and articles, along with a few books, to piece together a syllabus. A few years later, this course served as the basis for my collaboration with Alison Jaggar on one of the first women's studies text-anthologies published in the United States, *Feminist Frameworks: Alternative Theoretical Accounts of the*

---

*Betty Friedan, *The Feminine Mystique* (New York: Dell, 1970); Robin Morgan, ed., *Sisterhood Is Powerful* (New York: Vintage Books, 1970); Toni Cade, *The Black Woman: An Anthology* (New York: Signet Books, 1970); Shulamith Firestone, *The Dialectic of Sex* (New York: Bantam Books, 1972).

Relations Between Women and Men (New York: McGraw-Hill, 1978, 1984, 1993).

Alison was teaching at the University of Cincinnati at the time, and although we had never met, we discovered through friends that we were developing and teaching similar women's studies courses under the auspices of the philosophy departments at our respective institutions. In 1974, we began a correspondence that involved exchanging copies of our course outlines and sharing relevant essays and articles as we came upon them. Since some of the most interesting work in the fledgling women's studies was being published in small journals and mimeographed newsletters, or was simply being circulated informally, all of us who were developing women's studies courses counted on informal networking for material we might not discover individually. Alison and I finally met in the summer of 1975 when I traveled to Ohio to attend the National Socialist Feminist Conference, and we used the opportunity to begin work on *Feminist Frameworks*.

Teaching women's studies courses in philosophy has always been regarded as suspect by the white male philosophers who have, for the most part, defined the discipline. Only the happy circumstance that John Stuart Mill met Harriet Taylor and was moved to write *The Subjection of Women* has given the topic some small degree of legitimacy. Interestingly enough, over the past thirty years, some of the most breathtaking theoretical work in feminist theory has been produced by thinkers trained in philosophy who have then used that training, combined with an interest in politics and sociology broadly defined, to produce some of the most thoughtful critiques of traditional epistemology, metaphysics, and ontology. For the most part, this work still has not been recognized as real philosophy or incorporated into the field. Many of the most widely used introductory texts in philosophy continue to resemble the one I used so long ago at Hunter College in the Bronx.

Unsurprisingly, many of the women who began to develop women's studies courses and to write the new feminist theory had been active in the civil rights movement or the antiwar movement or both and were part of what was called the New Left. As a result, many women struggled to find a way to incorporate a concern with women's issues into the hierarchy of issues they already embraced. Since most of the men who were politically active in these movements were quick to denounce a concern with women's issues as bourgeois or traitorous, many white women understood that it was necessary to subordinate gender to class in order to prove themselves, just as Black women were expected to place the race struggle ahead of women's equality issues in order to do the same. As a result, many white women who were active in the New Left spent a great deal of time trying to find room for sexism and women's oppression within the categories and analysis in Marx's early writings.

This led to heated debates over whether the situation of women as a group could best be understood by treating us as a caste, a class, or a sex. Some even formulated an internal colony model of women's oppression. Frances Beal, who was New York coordinator of the Black Women's Liberation Committee of the Student Nonviolent Coordinating Committee, attempted to analyze the situation of Black women and their relations to Black men within capitalism in a now classic essay: "Double Jeopardy: To Be Black and Female." I was part of a group of philosophers who banded together in an organization called M.A.P., which would later spawn the Radical Philosophy Association. We met twice a year to debate theory and practice around these issues and to find ways to make philosophy relevant and useful in the struggle for social justice. It was also common at this time for some white feminists, as in the nineteenth century, to draw parallels between the oppression of women and the oppression of Black people. As Black feminist theorists such as Deborah King have since pointed out, using this analogy told us little about those who were both women and Black and, in fact, was one more way of ensuring the invisibility of that group.

Friedrich Engels's *Origin of the Family, Private Property and the State* helped legitimate feminist attention to the family in the same way that John Stuart Mill helped women in philosophy work on women's rights theory. However, the prevailing view among men on the left was epitomized by a prominent member of the Progressive Labor Party, also a CUNY faculty member at the time, who explained to some of us one night that there was no point in helping his wife with either the housework or their children because no real gains for women were possible until after the revolution. During the time he offered his comments, his wife was busy in the kitchen preparing food for his friends and comrades who filled their small apartment and, no doubt, hoping that their two young children wouldn't be awakened by all the noise. A thoroughly apolitical person, she spent much of her married life in a state of deep depression for which doctors prescribed an elaborate combination of antidepressants and amphetamines. Her story was not uncommon.

The shift from a focus on women's equality to a focus on women's liberation among some women theorists and activists brought with it serious attention to process and form as well as content. I remember an evening session at an early Socialist Scholars Conference in New York City when Marlene Dixon was the featured speaker. Dixon taught sociology at the University of Chicago until 1968, when she was fired for her radical and feminist activities. She was an early leader of the women's movement whose articles, such as "Why Women's Liberation?" were widely read, and her session drew a crowd.* Humorless and intense, Dixon followed her talk with a question-and-answer period during which she steadfastly refused to call on any of the men in the room. After having his raised hand ignored for quite some time, one of the men erupted in anger. Why, he asked, was Dixon calling on women who had just raised their hands when his hand had been up for so long? Dixon responded that in the past, women were consistently disadvantaged when they sought to participate in public conversations, and so in order to really give women an equal opportunity to participate, it would be necessary to give them preference for a time. She would call on men only when there were no longer any women who wished to be heard. A few of the men became furious, but most took this policy in their stride. Perhaps they thought that she wasn't really serious, perhaps they found it more amusing than threatening,

---

*Marlene Dixon, "Why Women's Liberation?" *Ramparts*, 1969.

or perhaps, for a moment, they saw its fundamental fairness. For my part, I was astonished, charmed, and embarrassed. On the one hand, like many women in the room, I was both amazed and delighted at seeing a woman on the left exercise any power at all, and, on the other, I was slightly embarrassed to be the recipient of this arbitrarily bestowed, if peculiarly appropriate, privileging. In an instant, she had turned the "natural order" upside down. I had spent my life surrounded by men who never hesitated to claim their turn to speak and who were rarely intimidated from doing so even by the fact that someone else, especially a woman, was already speaking. The man I had come with was an excellent speaker who was quite used to taking and holding the floor and who assumed that it was his right to do so. How I envied his sense of prerogative. When I realized that for the remainder of the evening, if I raised my hand, I would be recognized but he would not, I was disconcerted but not dismayed. It felt so right. It felt like justice. I remember that he made some jokes about how he'd better stick close to me and behave himself, and I remember enjoying, for once, a small feeling of power, even pride.

Dixon's conduct of that meeting had an enormous impact on me. Although I did not find her personality particularly appealing, I felt empowered by what she had done. Equally important, what happened that night showed me very concretely that things could be different. For the first time, I was able to understand what a different social order might feel like. Dixon's exercise made it clear that it was possible to change the rules that governed behavior between women and men and, in so doing, alter power relations and change prerogatives. I don't think I had really understood that until that moment. Certainly, I hadn't experienced it. Another lesson that was reaffirmed for me that night was that equitable treatment and equal treatment were not always one and the same.

While I never again participated in a meeting where men were forced to keep silent until all the woman had spoken, over the years I have participated in many different meetings that relied on feminist techniques to ensure that everyone in the group had an equal opportunity to participate. These feminist practices, used in single-sex and mixed groups, have included adopting the rule that no one speak twice until everyone who wishes to has spoken once, the practice of going around the room and giving everyone an opportunity to speak without having to volunteer or to be called on, and the process of using rotating chairs or facilitators so that everyone can have an opportunity to develop leadership skills and confidence. In addition to the goal of sharing power among participants, they are designed to encourage collaborative rather than competitive group interaction. Over the years, they have formed the core of feminist pedagogy and have been adapted for classroom use by teachers of both sexes who believe that issues of power and privilege in the classroom need to be addressed in order to enhance the learning environment for all students.

Like many other women of the time, I was profoundly affected by the analysis of patriarchy that was pivotal to many of the important writings of the day. Both Marxist feminism and radical feminism seemed to demand that we examine the ways in which marriage and the family and compulsive heterosexuality perpetuated the subordination of women. In this respect, Firestone's analysis of "romantic love" along with essays by Charlotte Bunch, Ti-Grace Atkinson, and Shelia Cronin had a profound impact on many of us who were coming to understand that the personal was political. It was not long before I began to use these writings to examine my own life.

I had married without enthusiasm at the age of twenty-four, mostly to appease my parents and his, who were disturbed that we were living together, and I was increasingly uncomfortable with my married state. Even as a teenager, I had been bitterly resentful of the double standard according to which I was raised. Like many other young people of my generation, I was deeply critical of what I considered the hypocritical ways in which my parents and their friends lived their lives. The 1970s brought with them wonderful possibilities for creating new relationships and new forms of the family, and I was eager to explore them. Along with many others on the feminist left, I rejected the artificial distinction between the public and the private that relegated women's lives to a subordinate sphere; however, my own belief that the personal was political was as firmly grounded in Jean-Paul

Sartre's writings on freedom and responsibility as it was in any feminist texts.

I had been teaching Sartre for years, and selections from both Beauvoir's *The Second Sex* and Sartre's *Existentialism and Humanism* were included in the introductory philosophy text *Philosophy Now*, which I had co-edited. A popular text as soon as it appeared in 1972, *Philosophy Now* was designed to remedy the deficiencies of the kinds of books available to me when I first started teaching introduction to philosophy at Hunter College in the Bronx. Each time I taught the book, I was forced to call into question many of my own life choices. In one selection, Sartre outlines his theory of radical freedom and inescapable responsibility, according to which human beings are said to create themselves in the course of acting on their choices. The heart of his philosophy is contained in the following often quoted passage:

> When we say that man chooses himself, we do mean that every one of us must choose himself; but by that we also mean that in choosing for himself he chooses for all men. For in effect, of all the actions a man may take in order to create himself as he wills to be, there is not one which is not creative, at the same time, of an image of man such as he believes he ought to be. . . . I am thus responsible for myself and for all men, and I am creating a certain image of man as I would have him to be. In fashioning myself I fashion man.*

Because Sartre believes that human beings create both values and meanings in the course of making choices and because he believes that there are no values apart from those choices (and no God to appeal to for guidance), human beings are left with the burden of creating their own humanity.

In spite of Sartre's reliance on male nouns and pronouns in this passage, I have always taken it to heart. Like Sartre, I believe that we have an inescapable responsibility for creating morality through the

---

*Jean Paul Sartre, "Man As Self-Creator," in *Philosophy Now*, ed. Paula Rothenberg Struhl and Karsten J. Struhl (New York: Random House, 1972), p. 37.

life choices we make. I also believe that it is the source of our freedom and our dignity. But living according to such a set of beliefs is no easy task. Each time I taught Sartre, I found myself forced to confront my own hypocrisy. Of the two examples Sartre provides to illustrate his philosophy, one called me to task every time. He wrote, "If I decide to marry and to have children, even though this decision proceeds simply from my own situation, from my own passion or my desire, I am thereby committing not only myself, but humanity as a whole, to the practice of monogamy."*

The fact that I was married but did not respect the institution was a major contradiction in my life. It was not monogamy itself that troubled me but the nature of the institution, which seemed to be about possession and control. Even as a very young girl, I had a sense that, somehow, marriage was fundamentally degrading to women. While my friends were fantasizing about the long white gown they would wear one day, I found nothing appealing about the require-ment that I announce my virginity to the community at large by walking down the aisle dressed in this way. The white gown was such an obvious symbol of virginity and of society's right to control it that I felt it would be mortifying to appear in public wearing such a dress, and I wondered why other girls didn't find the prospect equally degrading.

Many years later, as I began to read radical feminist critiques that analyzed marriage as a patriarchal institution, I began to understand the source of my early intuitive discomfort. The romantic love that was born in the modern period didn't seem very far removed from the days of trading blankets and oxen for women, and I hardly thought of myself as some man's prize. Stories about villages where the entire population waited under the wedding-night chamber for the bride-groom to display the bloodied sheet from the marriage bed convinced me that I wanted no part of this institution even before I heard stories about women who were returned *to their fathers* in disgrace if the sheet failed to show any blood.

---

*Ibid.

The more I read, the worse it got. We were only a few generations removed from women who lost all their rights upon marrying. Women who could not own property, had no right to their own paycheck, could not make a legal claim to their own children. Why would I want to be part of this institution? Where other women seemed to delight in referring to their "husbands," the word stuck in my throat. I did not want to have a "husband," nor did I want to be anyone's "wife." I preferred to be a "person." Because the man I had married shared these political views and because we had married to please our families, not ourselves, in the beginning I felt no contradiction between being married and disparaging the institution. Ours didn't feel like a real marriage. In fact, being married to each other felt largely irrelevant. At least this seemed true when I was not teaching Sartre.

On the days I taught Sartre, and during the weeks leading up to and following those classes, I was acutely aware of the untenability of my position. In that class and in others, I often presented the feminist critique of marriage while wearing my own wedding band. My mother had often quoted to me the maxim, "Do as I say, not as I do," urging me to learn from the mistakes in her life, not replicate them. But if Sartre was right, it was impossible to use words to reject the reality of the values I created by the choices I made. If marriage was degrading to women, why was I married? Or as my mother might have said on another day, "Talk is cheap."

Over the years, my husband and I had outgrown each other and the life we shared. When I finally ended my marriage, which was flawed in so many ways, it was a relief. There were no children to provide for, and the property we had was easily divided. I used a then widely circulated feminist do-it-yourself divorce manual and represented myself in the uncontested divorce proceedings. I read the manual, photocopied and then filled out the forms it provided, and, when it was necessary, called on Anne Elwell, a supportive feminist attorney for advice.

On the day I was scheduled to appear, I went to court with a friend who would serve as a witness in what I took to be a thoroughly pro forma appearance. Little did I know that the judge who was sitting that day would be enraged by the prospect of a woman, and a lay person at that, coming into court to represent herself. We sparred for a while, and then he sent me out of the courtroom like a child who had misbehaved, with the stern warning that the next time I appeared before him, I had best come represented by an attorney. This thoroughly humiliating experience confirmed what I already knew, by getting married in the first place I had involved the entire society in what should have been a private relationship between me and another human being. I deeply resented having to ask the court in the person of this judge to allow me to end that relationship, and, like many other women during this period, I swore I would never make that mistake again. Unlike many of them, I kept my promise.

My decision two years later, at the age of thirty-four, to build a life with Greg Mantsios, then a colleague at William Paterson, and to have children with him without being married was as much a reflection of my privilege as of my politics. For many women, being legally married provides whatever limited protection they have in their relations with the men to whom they commit their lives and with whom they have children. As women continue to earn substantially less than men, regardless of what kinds of jobs they perform, and because so many women are dependent on their husbands' employment for whatever health coverage and pension benefits they can claim, marriage is often a necessity, not a luxury. The fact that my earnings as a college professor placed me in the top 10 percent of income in the country and that my job carried with it health and pension benefits meant that I had the financial independence and the security that is a prerequisite for autonomy. The class privilege that I carried with me from my childhood, the nice home in the suburbs, the station wagon, and the clothes and other accouterments of a middle-class life identify me as a woman with a certain position in society. I could have my children outside of marriage without becoming "an unwed mother" and without giving birth to "bastards."

People reacted in interesting ways to my first pregnancy. Several male colleagues were clearly shocked, not by my marital status, which they probably didn't know, but by the fact that a woman they knew to be an ardent feminist would choose to have children. For them, the two were incompatible. Because I did not give birth to my first child until I was thirty-five, many people had assumed that I did not intend to have children. Evidently, this conformed to their stereotype of a woman who was both a feminist and a political activist. They found my pregnancy very disconcerting. Other people were disturbed by our failure to marry. I remember a conversation with Greg's aunt on Memorial Day weekend just days before our son was born. What was the problem, she wanted to know, were we afraid of making a commitment? For me, that question got to the heart of the matter of why we were not married. From reading Sartre, I had come to believe that the most profoundly serious commitments we make are those we live each day—that they must arise from our willingness to claim and exercise moral agency and that they are diminished, not enhanced, by institutionalization. Choosing to have a child with another person seemed to me to be the most extraordinary commitment possible. I wondered about the values of a society that would fail to identify it as such, that somehow mistakenly confounded selecting china patterns and bathroom towels with moral commitment. When I talk to young women in college who are engaged to be married, I am often amazed by how little they have thought about the enormity of their decision. So often it seems that the trappings of getting married—selecting a gown, planning the reception, furnishing an apartment—are all distractions that undermine the women's ability to make conscious decisions about the kind of future they want and the kind of relationship they will build with their partners. I have always wondered why anyone would want to marry someone they had never lived with or, worse yet, been intimate with, and find it remarkable that so many parents wish this fate for their children.

Greg and I had been close friends for several years when, in the summer of 1976, we decided to travel to Mexico together. Having very limited resources, we made the trip by car, sleeping in the back seat at rest stops in the United States and heating cans of baked beans and chunky clam chowder on a Coleman stove we kept in the trunk. After six weeks of pitching our tent in cow pastures and on top of ant-

hills along the Old Panamanian Highway, we decided that living together would be easy and began doing so on our return. That fall, I
joined Greg in attending a study group that met weekly on the Lower
East Side. When our first child, Alexi, was born a year and a half later,
he attended those meetings with us, sleeping on a quilt on the floor
or in the arms of one or another of the group members. It was here
that I began to fill in some of the gaps in my education in the area
of race.

The group was fairly evenly divided between members of the Old
and the New Left. The older members, in particular, many of whom
had been active in the Communist Party until 1956, brought with them
a long-standing commitment to the fight against racism. Together we
studied Black history, and for the first time, I had an opportunity to
reflect in a serious way on the role that race oppression had played
in the evolution of social, political, and economic institutions in the
United States. Members of the study group shared their memories
of events like the trials of the Scottsboro boys and the Puerto Rican
nationalists as well as their experiences in the North integrating Woolworths and middle-class housing developments such as
Stuyvesant Town, and working in organizing drives at garment factories in the Deep South. From them, I acquired a deep sense of history and an understanding that the struggle for justice and freedom
must span many generations and will endure even in the face of inevitable major and minor setbacks. I also began to understand that
racism was a white problem and that it was necessary for white people
to assume responsibility for dealing with it. Whatever contribution I
made to the group came from my insistence on the importance of the
"woman question" and the need to integrate issues of gender along
with race and class into our understanding of history and of contemporary social problems.

During this time, many of us in women's studies were coming to
understand that it was impossible to adequately deal with issues of
gender without talking about race and class as well. From the very
start, gender had included issues of sexuality for most of us. Early
gender role socialization demanded attention to issues of family and

sexuality as well. Heterosexuality and the politics of vaginal orgasm were subjected to serious critical scrutiny, and some of the most powerful theoretical work was produced by radical feminists who argued that feminism was the theory and lesbianism was the practice. But an awareness of race and, to a lesser extent, class had been largely absent from the work of white, academic feminists. Many white women writing in the field had mistakenly begun to generalize the experience of "women" from their own limited experience without realizing that in doing so they were simply universalizing the experiences of white women of privilege.

My own work in women's studies had been grounded in some awareness of diversity issues from the start, but now I began to study and teach about issues of race not simply in order to "include" the reality of all women's lives but from my position as a white woman who had a responsibility to deal with racism in the broadest sense. Doing so raised serious questions for me about integrity and privilege.

As a woman who had serious doubts about the appropriateness of men teaching women's studies, I had to ask myself under what conditions it was appropriate for me, a white woman, to teach about race. I realized that my reasons for excluding men from teaching women's studies had to do with issues of power and empowerment. Placing male faculty in the position of authority in such classes seemed to suggest that even when studying their own experience, history, and culture, women needed to defer to men's knowledge and insight.

I was well aware that some of my male colleagues routinely used their classrooms to harangue women about their own subordination. They set themselves up as experts on the oppression of women and then proceeded to ridicule those women who had not yet developed a sophisticated understanding of their own situation. Under these conditions, women's studies hardly served to empower women. These same men often slept with their students outside class as part of the broad, extracurricular learning and consciousness-raising experience they thought it their duty to provide. Many thought that women's liberation was a synonym for sexual liberation, which they understood to mean that women should sleep with any man who showed an interest and do so without expecting commitment or, in many cases, even kindness. But clearly there were other more constructive ways in which men might teach and mentor.

After the early phase in the development of women's studies, it became clear to me that at a certain point it would be necessary to allow, even encourage, men who were feminists to teach and write in the field. Like their female colleagues, men would be credentialed by the use of a feminist perspective and a feminist pedagogy. These male faculty could effectively reach students who might be unable or unwilling to hear me or other women faculty.

In much the same way that I understood that real change would require that men own sexism and assume responsibility for dismantling it, I understood that white people had a responsibility to learn and teach Black history and work toward dismantling racism. The challenge was to do both in ways that empowered the victims of oppression and that challenged privilege, including the privilege of those who did the teaching. This, of course, has always been the challenge and the responsibility of feminist teachers in the classroom—whatever subject they teach.

Around this time, the curriculum at William Paterson College was undergoing one of the periodic revisions to which the higher education curriculum is routinely subject. At the start of the 1980s, under the direction of the Carnegie Commission and other such agencies, colleges and universities around the country were moving to reassert control over the curriculum which had become increasingly flexible and student friendly in response to the student activism of the late 1960s and 1970s. The concern expressed by these education watchdogs was that students educated within this curriculum were entering the world of work with inappropriate expectations about autonomy and job satisfaction. Corporations claimed that their profit margins were being adversely affected by workers who talked with their feet if they were unhappy with conditions in the factory or the workplace.

The new curriculum being fashioned by colleges and universities for the 1980s would produce more docile workers by dramatically increasing the number of required courses that all students had to fulfill as part of their core requirements and would dramatically decrease the opportunity to take electives. At the time this new curriculum was under consideration, both Black studies and women's studies were extremely popular programs, attracting large student enrollments. It was clear that the new curriculum would change this situation dramatically.

In the fall of 1980, faculty in women's studies and Black studies at the college joined together to approach the curriculum committee considering these changes and proposed creating a three-credit requirement in "racism and sexism." The new course would be titled "Racism and Sexism in a Changing America." I have written about the process by which the requirement was created and our early experiences teaching the course.* Here I simply want to note that the course was designed to be team-taught and that my own education has been considerably enhanced by the fact that over a period of years I have taught the course with three different African-American male colleagues, each of whom was trained in a different discipline. That team-teaching experience, along with my work in the study group, made it possible for me to begin seeing the world through the eyes of people who were "different" from me. I began to hear and then to ask the questions that my Black colleagues brought with them and began to use their perspective to specify and contextualize my own.

We learned from each other. As my African-American colleagues began to understand why I thought it was important to refer to women by that term and not some other, I began to understand that it was important to replace the word "slave" with phrases like "Africans who had been enslaved" or "Black people held in slavery." I learned to ask

---

*Paula S. Rothenberg, "Integrating the Study of Race, Gender, and Class: Some Preliminary Observations," *Feminist Teacher* 3 (1988): 37–42; "Integrating the Study of Racism and Sexism in a Changing America: A Case Study," *Journal of Thought* (December 1985): 122–36; and "Teaching Racism and Sexism in a Changing America," *Radical Teacher* (Decmeber 1984): 2–5, reprinted in *Politics of Education: Essays from "Radical Teacher,"* ed. Susan Gusher O'Malley, Robert C. Rosen, and Leonard Vogt (Albany: State University of New York Press, 1990), 33–45.

when and how Africans became enslaved rather than begin the course from a perspective that, implicitly, treated that condition as natural to them. I began to listen with a third ear and to find new or hidden meanings in essays and books that I had read many times already. I "saw" race, along with gender and class, in places where it had been invisible to me because of the narrowness of my limited experience and knowledge. For me, the goal of helping students see the world through many different people's eyes continues to be a primary and laudable aim for undergraduate education.

One of the most valuable parts of the team-taught class for our students was the opportunity it gave them to watch us interact and, in this way, model how a man and a woman, a Black person and a white person might talk, banter, argue, discuss, and disagree, with respect, even affection. Few young people today have an opportunity to watch this kind of cross-race, cross-gender interaction. Differences in race, class, and gender consign people in our society to different and separate worlds, and many find it impossible to imagine what collegiality or friendship between occupants of these worlds might look or feel like. Over the years, Leslie Agard-Jones, one of my teaching partners, and I have made joint presentations at conferences about our work. Whenever we do so, faculty audiences seem as engaged by the nature of our collaboration and interaction as by the actual content of the presentation. Witnessing this kind of friendly collaboration between a Black man and a white woman is so rare that, to this day, faculty who attended one of our presentations years ago stop me at conferences to remark on it and to share their memories.

But in spite of the obvious benefits of team-teaching, few colleges are willing to make the financial commitment that supporting it requires. As one college official told me, we don't support team-teaching because we are unwilling to pay two people to teach the same class when only one of you can talk at a time. And so after a while, I began to teach the race, class, and gender course by myself. Fortunately, I was often able to carry the voices and the perspectives of my African-American colleagues and other with me. Nonetheless, the continuing absence of a critical mass of people of color, students and faculty who trace their heritage to different parts of Latin America and to Asia as well as to Africa, means that our efforts to create a genuinely inclusive curriculum, scholarship, and pedagogy are seriously hampered.

One of the outgrowths of the required course on race, class, and gender at the college was the evolution of a group of faculty who began to meet on a regular basis, once a month, to discuss the newest scholarship in women's studies, multicultural studies, lesbian and gay studies, and other fields. While some of the participants regularly taught the required course, others had no plans to do so. They participated because of the lively intellectual and personal interactions that occurred and, in the end, began to incorporate the new materials and perspectives into whatever courses they taught.

In addition to helping encourage and facilitate a slow but persistent transformation of the broader curriculum at the college in this way, the seminar helped identify campus climate issues that needed to be addressed. As a result, on a number of occasions the group lobbied for specific programs, policies, and support services that would enhance campus life. In spite of British philosopher A. J. Ayer's logical positivist claim that there exists an unbridgeable chasm between facts and values, discussions at the seminar frequently led to a recognition of the necessity to take action. For example, a discussion of issues of heterosexism and homophobia in the classroom led to a more general concern with the situation of lesbian and gay students on campus and ultimately to a meeting with the counseling service to request that a counselor specially trained to counsel lesbian and gay students be hired. A theoretical discussion about sexual violence against women led to an intense conversation about sexual harassment on campus, with the ultimate result that members of the seminar took responsibility for writing and then lobbying for the implementation of the college's first sexual harassment policy, an activity that took several years.

As one of the first chairs of the college's sexual harassment panel, I worked with other faculty and administrators to help refine and enforce the policy once it was in place. It was a thankless and frustrating task. From the start, the committee spent the majority of its time discussing how to protect the rights and future careers of accused harassers. While it is obvious that this should be a concern of any such group or policy, it was ludicrous that several committee members seemed more concerned with this aspect of their responsibility than with protecting and empowering the women students who were routinely harassed by male faculty, which was, after all, their primary charge. I had endless arguments with one member of the committee, a woman and self-defined feminist, whose preoccupation with the First Amendment freedoms paralyzed the committee's work. As a frequent beneficiary of the protection of those freedoms, I value them highly, but I also understand that they were written by privileged white men to protect the freedoms (and privileges) of men of their class. Over the years, they have proved useful to some of the rest of us by extension or by good fortune. At issue now is whether we will interpret them in ways that continue to prioritize the interests and values of a small group of already privileged people over the emerging rights and needs of other subjects and agents.

The debate over "free speech" is a case in point. If you begin with an absolute commitment to protecting free speech, then, of course, you defend the right of people to use whatever racist, sexist, or homophobic language they like. If, however, you begin with an unwavering commitment to ending racism, sexism, and homophobia, and define the task of democracy as achieving this end, then you will deny such inflammatory hate speech the protection of the Bill of Rights and will argue that in doing so you are extending and enlarging, not diminishing, democracy. In fact, you will claim that hate speech itself undermines free speech because it silences so many. Which of these approaches to rights' theory is ultimately victorious will not be a matter of which argument is superior, since both can be framed persuasively. It will depend on the success of political struggle in the real world because, in the end, action shapes thought just as much as thought leads to action. The history of democracy over the past two centuries is a history of ever broadening the circle of those who are understood to be citizens with claims to legal standing and civil rights. At first, those who seek to expand the definition of a citizen and reinterpret the meaning of the Constitution are denounced as radicals who are seeking to destroy our way of life; later they are embraced as men (*sic*) of vision and humanity. There is little reason to think that this will not be so this time around.

How to deal with issues of sexual harassment is another case in point. The Bill of Rights was never intended to leave room for dealing with sexual harassment. Beginning with its premises and forcing sexual harassment procedures to conform to them when they are rigidly and narrowly interpreted and enforced will result in the silencing and victimization of women. A more constructive approach is to begin by recognizing the serious nature of sexual harassment complaints and the pervasiveness of the harassment of women of all ages and then asking what kinds of policies and practices will protect women and others while creating a campus and workplace climate that is respectful of and liberating for us all.

Unfortunately, on my campus and many others I have visited, the sexual harassment policies written and adopted over the past two decades have not changed things very much. Only a tiny fraction of the women harassed on campus ever bring their stories to the appropriate members of the campus community, and of those who do, most are too frightened and embarrassed to bring even informal charges against their harassers. Sadly, in my experience, in those cases where formal charges were brought, most of the harassers have gotten off very lightly, and most of the women have had to endure extraordinary emotional stress with minimal support from the highest officers of the college or university in question.

In the first full year that the sexual harassment policy was in effect at William Paterson College, three formal charges of sexual harassment were brought under it, one of which was against me. In the course of helping to facilitate a faculty-staff workshop about sexual harassment, I had used some very strong language to describe the way women are often portrayed in contemporary culture. One of the participants, the head of the college's MBA program at that time, was offended by what he called my "gutter language." Evidently unfamiliar with the distinction between "mention" and "use," he filed charges against me. In his letter, he suggested that the best way for the college to prove its commitment to a harassment-free campus was to fire me.

We had come full circle. Here was a white man attempting to use the college's fledgling sexual harassment policy to "protect" himself and other men from having to *listen* to accounts of how women are portrayed and brutalized in a sexist society, rather than having the policy serve as a mechanism for protecting women from that behavior. It would have been funny had I not known of at least three young women on the campus who were in terror and despair over indescribable harassment by male professors that they were afraid to report. The following semester, two of them dropped out of school. Yet in this man's eyes, people like me were the problem, and it was he who was the victim. Worse yet, he reported proudly that he was filing the charges as the father of four daughters and seemed to somehow believe that in attacking me, he was protecting them. He could not tolerate a world in which his daughters might have to listen to ugly descriptions of degrading treatment, but considered the words themselves and a woman who would use them as his enemy, rather than the behavior that put his own daughters in jeopardy.

In the end, the African-American woman who represented the college administration in the complaint process rejected his claim; however, in an effort to be all things to all people, she required, as part of her decision, that I apologize for having offended him. Fortunately, the college president, another white male, who had the final say, found in my favor and did not require an apology—either because he didn't think one was necessary or because he knew me well enough to know that I would never consent to make one. I have always been grateful to him for the integrity he showed in the case and have always been disappointed in her for her failure to do so—but then, she had more to lose.

5

Fifteen Minutes

❖ ❖ ❖ ❖ ❖ ❖ ❖ ❖ ❖ ❖ ❖ ❖ ❖ ❖

"Political Indoctrination Supplants Education in Nation's Universities" read the headline of the September 16, 1990, column written by
the conservative syndicated columnist George Will, and he was talking about me. In the fall of 1987, the first edition of my college text
Racism and Sexism in a Changing America had been published and,
within a short time, had sparked a national debate. The text first received national attention in the spring of 1990 when the English faculty at the University of Texas in Austin decided to use it as part of a
new approach to teaching composition to first-year students. The required English course would be renamed "Writing About Difference—
Race and Gender" and would use Supreme Court cases and other
relevant materials, from my book and other sources, to teach students
how to construct well-written, well-reasoned arguments while developing critical thinking skills. A secondary benefit of this curricular
change was that it would increase students' awareness of differences
in race, class, and gender by providing space in the curriculum to think
and talk constructively about these issues.

The decision at the University of Texas was very much in line with
curricular changes occurring at other schools around the nation.
Increasingly alarmed by the volatile nature of racial tensions on campus and by the increased visibility of sexual harassment and expres-

sions of homophobia, many colleges and universities were seeking opportunities to integrate consideration of these issues into their curriculum in order to diffuse them. But one member of the English department at Texas was disturbed by the faculty's decision. Alan Gribben, a member of the National Association of Scholars (NAS), a notorious right-wing faculty group, denounced the new course as "the most massive attempt at thought control ever attempted on campus," and then, ironically, mobilized the NAS as well as conservative journalists around the country to carry out just such a campaign against the new course and my text.* They were partially successful. As a result of an extensive campaign, which also involved letters to members of the board of trustees and alumni of the University of Texas, the book, although not the new course, was jettisoned by the department. The ripple effect of their campaign continued for many months, sparking what came to be known as the "culture wars." National and regional news magazines and newspapers, including *Newsweek* and *Time*, as well as *U.S. News & World Report, New York,* the *Village Voice,* the *Wall Street Journal,* the *New York Times,* and the *Washington Post,* ran cover stories or major feature articles alleging that political indoctrination was the order of the day throughout higher education. I was asked to appear on TV and radio shows to explain and defend the new curricular imperatives. Lynn Cheney, then chair of the National Endowment for the Humanities, devoted a good portion of a major address at the National Press Club to attacking my book. In the spring of 1991, President George Bush made a speech at the University of Michigan attacking what was now being called "political correctness." Suddenly ordinary citizens who had never thought very much, if at all, about higher education curriculum, were being asked to believe that changes in the field were a threat to their own lives and to the future of the nation. Ironically, all of this gained tremendous visibility for my text, ensuring that it would become one of the best-selling texts in the field.

---

*Gribben is quoted in "A Civil Rights Theme for a Writing Course," *New York Times,* March 3, 1990.

Almost ten years earlier, in 1981, when Leslie Agard-Jones and I had first begun team-teaching William Patersons's new racism/sexism course, our task had been complicated by the lack of a text that integrated rather than alternated issues of race and ethnicity, gender, class, and sexuality. During the summer of 1980, I had assumed primary responsibility for creating the syllabus for the new course, and over the next several years, I revised the course constantly as I sought and found new materials that would allow us to teach the content in ever more integrated and inclusive ways. Since I had already co-edited three college text-anthologies, and I knew there was a tremendous need for such a book, it was only natural that at a certain point I began thinking about turning the racism/sexism syllabus into a textbook. Inviting Les and J. Samuel Jordan, another African-American colleague, to co-edit the book was the obvious thing to do. They were two of my closest friends and colleagues, and our history of successful collaboration while teaching the racism/sexism course meant we already knew that we could work well together. Unfortunately, neither of them was in a position to undertake the project, and that is how this white woman came to be the sole editor of *Race, Class, and Gender in the United States.*

Of the seven publishers that received the book proposal, six turned it down flat. They said it would never sell. An editor at Random House, publisher of my two philosophy texts, wrote me a two-page letter explaining in detail why there was no market for such an anthology. Another editor called me with the same bad prognosis but tried to persuade me to do a different book for his list. The others sent form rejections. But fortunately, Michael Webber, the sociology editor at St. Martin's Press, liked the book from the start and was persuaded of its importance.

Another fortunate circumstance was that the College Division at St. Martin's was then headed by a very sharp editor, a woman named Jean Smith who would have ultimate responsibility for recommending the book for publication. Jean had defied the glass ceiling within publishing and, at that time, occupied the highest position in the field that was held by a woman. She and I had worked together years earlier when she was at McGraw-Hill and had responsibility for my women's studies text, *Feminist Frameworks*. Because of our past association, and her understanding of the importance of gender and race issues, she was favorably disposed toward the book. That turned out to be a good thing. One of the reviews that Webber commissioned as part of the press's acquisition process trashed the proposal, arguing that there was no market for the book and then criticizing the proposal itself.

When I found out who the reviewer was, I was astonished. I couldn't understand why she, a sociologist I had worked with on a number of projects and who, I believed, shared a similar concern with the issues, would critique not only my book but the very premise of the project itself. Fortunately, Webber was so committed to the anthology that he ignored her review. Imagine my surprise when one of the first books to appear to compete with my text turned out to be co-edited by the reviewer.

From the start, conservative critiques complained that the book was political because it failed "to present both sides." That was fine with me. I did not set out to create a book that would "present both sides"—in some simplistic sense of that phrase—although I was quite used to the demand. In fact, a conservative historian on the college curriculum committee at William Paterson voted against the course proposal on which the first edition of the book was based on the grounds that it began with the assumption that racism and sexism existed in the United States instead of allowing students to make up their own minds. My refusal to change that premise almost led to the course's defeat. But I was no more prepared to change that assumption than I was prepared to add a section discussing the benefits of slavery (another of his requests), even though some have indeed argued that slavery was "good" for Black people.

So yes, the perspective of the course "assumed" the existence of racism and sexism and class privilege but having done so, it proceeded to argue for its thesis. Statistics, historical information, and arguments were used in an effort to persuade readers of the book that those forces were indeed operative in the past and the present. At a time when most students, and probably most Americans, did not know that some 120,000 Japanese-Americans had been incarcerated during World War II, had no real understanding of how slavery was institutionalized within the law, did not really understand the extent to which women had been denied the rights of citizenship, and so forth, the particular challenge of the book was to find a way to incorporate enough historical information to overcome this ignorance and still leave room to do more than simply teach history. The technique I adopted was to reprint key historical documents, often excerpts from laws and court decisions, that would paint a picture of the legal status of women and people of color from the beginning of the Republic. Another strength of this approach is that the fundamental nature of the racism and sexism in our past and present would be revealed by the public record rather than through some writer's interpretation. Instead of wondering whether they were getting a distorted picture of the past, students could construct their own picture from the documents. That these documents are powerful and that reading them can literally change a person's life was something I had already discovered in high school. I continue to be amazed that every one of the book's conservative critics ignored my reliance on such public documents to tell the story.*

Over the years, I have been gratified by students' reactions to the text. I often meet young people who tell me that using the book in a course was a turning point in their lives, that it helped them understand things that had never made sense before. I remember a young white male student some years ago who had been relatively quiet during the first part of my racism/sexism course, greeting early conversations about race and gender with a degree of skepticism that bordered on hostility. And I remember the day he cried in class after reading excerpts from slave codes. He was amazed to learn a portion of his history that had been kept from him, and when he did so, he became overwhelmed by the enormity of what white people had done

---

*For a more detailed discussion of teaching about U.S. history in a diversity course, see Paula S. Rothenberg, "Teaching U.S. History as Part of Diversity Studies," *American Behavioral Scientist* 40, (1996): 134–42.

to Africans in the course of institutionalizing slavery. Then there was a young white woman, a nursing major, who talked about the fact that her nursing textbook included material on "minority" health topics, such as "Black infant mortality," but who observed that had she not been taking the racism/sexism course, she never would have understood that race mattered; consequently, she might have read those sections in her nursing text but would not have paid attention to them. And I remember a young Black woman who was in the class the first time J. Jordan and I taught together. In response to our request that students share why they had signed up for the still experimental course, she brought the class to a screeching silence by explaining that she hoped it would help her understand white people better. She said she had always wondered how it was possible for whites to carry out the atrocities committed against Black people during slavery, and she speculated that there might be something deficient in their moral sensibilities that allowed them to commit such unspeakable acts. Her question/comment was a watershed experience for me. In a couple of sentences, she had turned my "race" into the problem and made me and people with my color skin the "other," whose behavior needed to be interrogated as abnormal and then explained. As a woman, I was used to being in that position; as a white person, I had never been there before.

Traveling around the country to lecture on inclusive curriculum issues, I often meet students of color who tell me that they find the content and approach of the book personally affirming and who seem to take some comfort in the fact that a white person wrote it. I imagine that their relief is similar to that experienced by people who were sexually abused by relatives when they were children and then have their hazy memories corroborated by other family members. I also meet white students who tell me how important it was for them to study race, class, and gender issues in order to understand the context in which their relations with friends and other people of color occur. Whatever their sexual orientation, students welcome the opportunities the book provides to think about issues of sexuality and the ways in which both sexual and gender identity have been and are constructed in our society. They are grateful to have some place and space in the college curriculum to talk about issues like these, which are of such great and immediate importance to them but which rarely seem to be addressed in meaningful ways within education. The economic data and analyses in the book often make students angry. They find them disturbing and unsettling. Many tell me that before reading it, they had little understanding or awareness of the vast differences in opportunity and conditions that separate people in our society. They also tell me that before using the book, they had very unrealistic expectations about what their financial future might look like. In a society that perpetuates the illusion that we are all middle class, students need to learn about the ways race, class, and gender impact on opportunity. This information is essential to prepare them to deal with some of the realities they will encounter in life after college. Otherwise, when their lived experience fails to match their expectations, they will blame themselves, as did the women Betty Friedan profiled in *The Feminine Mystique* so many years ago. In this way, they will mistake what is in fact a social problem for a personal deficiency and blame themselves rather than engage in collective action.

But, of course, not everyone was similarly pleased with the opportunities the book created. The column by George Will was just one of many that appeared over the next six months attacking the alleged politicization of education and my book in particular. And since most were churned out as part of a carefully orchestrated right-wing attack, each repeated the same misinformation. For example, each one incorrectly referred to me as a "New Jersey sociologist" (my degrees are in political science and philosophy), and each one used "quotes" attributed to me that had only the barest resemblance to anything I had ever said. One of my favorites is included in a "guest commentary" by Leslie Carbone that popped up in a number of local newspapers around the country during the spring of 1992. Carbone, then executive director of the right-wing, and misnamed, group Accuracy in Academia, quoted me as saying, "Let's put class, race and gender in all the classes . . . that's the nirvana." While it's true that I have often talked about the need to inject issues of race, class, and gender into the curriculum, I have never been known for my pursuit of "nirvana" or any other mystical state. In addition to the articles that appeared in the popular press, a number of scathing and often bizarre attacks on my work were published in a right-wing newsletter called *Measure*, put out by the University Centers for Rational Alternatives, headquartered in California. Ironically, each issue announces on its masthead that the publication was founded by my former mentor, Sidney Hook.

As the debate about "political correctness" heated up, I found that I was being bombarded with requests to appear on television and radio shows and was frequently called by journalists from all over the country who were looking for a marketable comment. In the beginning, I welcomed interviews and naively believed that if I took the time to talk to each reporter at length, I would be able to move each past his or her misunderstandings. After a while, I stopped agreeing to interviews altogether. They took a considerable amount of time and rarely produced more than one or two mangled and misleading "quotes."

One afternoon, I spent several hours talking to Fred Siegel, who was writing an article for the *New Republic*.* Anxious for a hot quote, he kept pressing me to identify some books that I thought should be banned from the curriculum. When I refused to comply on the grounds that I didn't think education was about book banning, he reported in the article that prominent academics around the country were unable to name even a single book that was so racist and sexist that it should be excluded from the canon. He failed to make any mention of my clearly articulated position that faculty should be free to chose their own readings, a position I explained by pointing out that something that *I* might consider objectionable might be used very effectively by another teacher. My dealing with Siegel and others led me to propose a new category of veracity—one according to which something is neither exactly true nor entirely false, but definitely misleading.

---

*Fred Siegel, "The Cult of Multiculturalism," *New Republic*, February 18, 1991, pp. 34–36, 38, 40.

After several months of reading the misinformation that was being circulated about my book and the seriously warped accounts of the curricular changes allegedly being spawned by the new scholarship, I began to think about what might be the proper forum for responding to them. I was tired of having media journalists cut and paste my remarks to fit their own points of view and wanted the opportunity to respond to critics on my own terms and in my own way. I called Cheryl Fields, who was then serving as op-ed editor for the *Chronicle of Higher Education*, and proposed writing a piece for the journal. The resulting essay, which appeared on April 10, 1991, was entitled "Critics of Attempts to Democratize the Curriculum Are Waging a Campaign to Misrepresent the Work of Responsible Professors."* In the article, I argued that education had always been political in the sense that the curriculum has always privileged the interests and history of some groups over others. I repeated the feminist argument that what had previously masqueraded as a neutral voice offering timeless truths and objective knowledge was itself a fairly narrow androcentric, Eurocentric view of the past and present. It is, after all, not whether the curriculum proceeds from a perspective (how could it help but do so?), but whether that perspective is specified and interrogated, that gives knowledge a degree of credibility. After naming the perspective from which traditional education and scholarship have emanated, I went on to challenge the misrepresentations of the new curriculum that were being circulated by the right wing and pointed out the irony that the very groups that bemoaned the alleged politicization of education were doing everything they could to close the curriculum to new critical perspectives.

The article brought a flurry of letters and phone calls from academics around the country applauding my position and expressing appreciation for the way in which I had crafted my argument. Many younger scholars have told me that they felt empowered and emboldened by the article because it was simultaneously such a strong

---

*Also appears in *Debating P.C.*, ed. Paul Berman (New York: Dell, 1992), pp. 262–268.

defense and critique. Copies of the piece were circulated on numerous campuses, thereby legitimating the feminist/multicultural approach to curricular issues, leaving many younger faculty members more comfortable with continuing to teach their courses in ways that were being denounced by the right as "PC." Junior faculty who felt relatively isolated teaching in conservative departments at colleges and universities in middle America reported that the appearance of the piece actually turned the tide for them and made their work, if not wildly popular among their senior colleagues, at least acceptable.

During this period, in addition to appearing on radio and TV, I was invited to speak at many colleges and universities around the country, and I welcomed the opportunity to talk to students and faculty in person about my book and my ideas. My own children were still fairly young at the time, and during these trips, I was frequently asked who was taking care of them, a question I had not anticipated. When I said that they were with their father, people were often surprised but rarely reassured. No wonder. Although the number of men who know how to care for their children is increasing, the number who know how to procreate but not parent remains very high. I am still amazed at the attorney, stockbroker, and business exec dads in our town who are able to make babies and to make money, but who do not know how to change a diaper or quiet a crying child. No wonder people raised an eyebrow when I told them that the children were home with their dad.

In addition to worrying about who was taking care of my children, many people expressed sympathy for the fact that I had to travel. This always amused me. The fact is—I love to travel. Even after racking up thousands of frequent-flyer miles, I still love airports and they still feel like gateways to adventure. I love to visit new places and meet new people and stay in small towns whose names I am just learning, and I find it odd that so many people think this is a burden rather than a treat. I love the absolute quiet of a solitary hotel room where I can read or think whenever and for as long as I like. I even enjoy eating alone in a restaurant or coffee shop with no one but myself for company. When the children were small, I rarely traveled more than two or three times in any month, and most of those trips occurred in only six months out of the year. But when they were small, I was especially grateful for the chance to get away and feel like a person again. An added bonus was that these trips ensured that Greg would have uninterrupted parenting time without me there to offer my two cents at every turn.

Most of my lectures were followed by a question-and-answer period, and I found that one question occurred with predictable frequency. Judging by it, many of the book's readers were disturbed by my definition of racism as the subordination of people of color by white people. According to this position, which was hardly exclusive to me at that time, only white people can be racists. This is said to be true because although people of color clearly can be "prejudiced" against whites or against other people of color, in this society they do not possess the institutionalized power required to translate their attitudes into policy and practice. According to this definition, racism requires "prejudice plus power." By extension, only men can actually be identified as sexist in spite of the fact that women can certainly dislike and devalue other members of their sex.

The point here is as much about the use of language as it is about careful analysis. Our society's tendency to lump together all kinds of expressions of hate seems to me mistaken. Each form of hatred—be it ethnic prejudice, anti-Semitism, homophobia, or racism—has its own unique characteristics, and using language carefully to make these differences clear seems to me an important concern. In the text, I argued that it was necessary to distinguish between mere prejudice and prejudice that was backed by power. Like others, I recommended reserving the term "racism" to refer to the latter cases. I did so in order to underscore the point that racism is institutionalized prejudice with a compelling and brutal history. It seems to me essential that we develop a vocabulary that allows us to distinguish this form of oppression from other expressions of hate.

I think the primary reason that many white people are disturbed by this position is their fear that it excuses hate violence on the part of people of color toward whites or toward one another. This is understandable. Certain behavior strikes us as so hateful, so reprehensible, that we want to decry it in the strongest possible terms. Denying people the use of the word "racism" seems to many to deny them the ability to condemn that behavior with the full force of their moral outrage. And they mistakenly equate this denial with approval for the behavior itself. I often meet people who want to take issue with this point. For example, in 1992, I was part of a New Jersey state mission to Israel that was led by Jim Florio, then the governor of New Jersey. At the welcome reception in Jerusalem, one of the other U.S. participants, an executive of the Anti-Defamation League, began to berate me as soon as he recognized my name. He complained that African-American men he encountered in his work often used my book to "prove" that Blacks can't be racist. My assurances that I believe both Black and white people can do terrible things wasn't any comfort. He wanted to use the "r" word, and nothing short of it would do.

While I sympathize with his frustration and the frustration expressed by other whites as well, I am even more concerned about the consequences of using the term "racism" indiscriminately to cover too wide a range of attitudes and behaviors. In the first place, it leads easily to rationalizing hate by saying that in the end, we are all racists—that hating people who are "different" is part of human nature. And this, of course, absolves everyone of responsibility either for perpetuating or for ending the phenomenon. More significantly, the indiscriminate use of the word "racism" points away from the unspeakable history of slavery and the historical and contemporary policies and practices that have *institutionalized* discrimination against some members of this society. It tends to focus attention on "feelings" and away from the legal, social, economic, and cultural practices that have operated for centuries to deny people of color their humanity. Finally, using the term "racism" broadly prevents people from looking at the ways in which white-skin privilege has been woven into the fabric of this nation and turns our attention away from white responsibility. The reaction to a speech by Khalid Abdul Muhammad of the Nation of Islam, made at Kean College of New Jersey in 1993, provides a case in point.

In November 1993, Khalid Abdul Muhammad, a top aide to the Nation of Islam's leader, Louis Farrakhan, gave a speech at Kean

College of New Jersey. Although only a few dozen students were in attendance, the hatred that Muhammad unleashed had repercussions that extended well beyond that one night and that particular audience. In his talk, which simultaneously spewed forth hatred toward lesbians and gays, Catholics, whites, and Jews, Muhammed is reported to have described Jews as the "bloodsuckers of the Black nation" and to have called for the killing of whites, including white babies, in South Africa. Evidently, his remarks were warmly received by many of those in attendance. News articles that appeared after the event described serious tensions between African-American and white students on the campus as well as between Blacks and Jews. An eighteen-year-old African-American woman is quoted as saying, "Jewish people control all the money in the United States—that's true, that's not being prejudiced."* Other Black students, even those who disputed some of Muhammed's claims, are reported to have found his talk "inspirational." According to the same *New York Times* article in which the woman is quoted, "a number of [Black] students were quick to say they admired what they considered the candor and willingness to help and inspire Black youth to gain control of their communities."

As time passed, public outrage over the speech itself was overshadowed by outrage at the perceived lack of immediate and adequate response to the speech by the Kean College administration and campus community. Jewish faculty and students were especially critical of what they saw as the failure of Elsa Gomez, the president of Kean College, to denounce the bigotry in the speech. Other educators and public officials joined the fray.

On February 17, 1994, New Jersey governor Christine Todd Whitman responded to the deteriorating situation by announcing a statewide initiative aimed at teaching tolerance. Through a special arrangement with producer Steven Spielberg, the state would provide free screenings of Spielberg's film *Schindler's List* for college students beginning on February 28. (The date was chosen to coincide with a return visit to the state

---

*John Nordheimer, "Angry Echoes of Campus Speech," *New York Times*, January 26, 1994.

by Khalid Abdul Muhammad, who was scheduled to speak on that day at The College of New Jersey, then Trenton State College.) Spielberg contributed several prints of the film, and theater owners donated the use of their facilities. Special invitations were issued to college students to attend the showings, and the governor herself would lead a panel discussion at the start of the first screening. The plan included filming the panel discussion and then using it at each subsequent screening. I was out of town with my family when the call came inviting me to be part of the governor's panel, and, of course, I immediately accepted.

From the start, the Whitman administration's response, although I think well intentioned, was poorly conceived and grew out of an inadequate understanding of the problem that had to be addressed. If the agenda was to confront the tensions and divisions on New Jersey college campuses and in the state as a whole, then placing *Schindler's List* at the center of the campaign was unfortunate. It shifted the discourse away from Black–white relations in the contemporary United States to anti-Semitism in Europe some fifty years earlier. It rode roughshod over the raw feelings of anger, pain, humiliation, and despair held by many African-Americans, Latino/as, and Asians with respect to the American dream and its failure to include them. It placed white people as both victims and heroes at the center of the canvas and once again consigned people of color to the margins even when the topic, hatred and oppression, might seem to give them claim to more than bit parts.*

Both the panel discussion in February and a second panel discussion, held in March at Bloomfield College, again including myself as a speaker and again presided over by Governor Whitman, provide good illustrations of how even well-intentioned efforts to create public conversations about hate violence are consistently undermined by

---

*While some might question categorizing Jews as white, in doing so I am simply reporting the way they appear and are portrayed in the film. It seems clear to me that this film depicts Jews as white and that people of color watching it would see them in this way. For more on the question of Jewish identity and skin color, see Karen Brodkin Sack, "How Did Jews Become White Folks?" in *Race*, ed. Steven Gregory and Roger Sanjek (New Brunswick, NJ: Rutgers University Press, 1994).

white America's refusal to confront racism and its legacy. In the course of both programs, speakers decried hate speech, but the focus was clearly on anti-Semitism. At least one of the white panelists and several audience participants echoed public demands that African-Americans disavow Muhammad's remarks. When African-Americans in the audience tried to focus attention on the racism in education and employment that so many students of color face—conditions responsible, at least in part, for the sympathetic hearing that Muhammad's remarks received at Kean College—their remarks were ignored and they were challenged instead to dissociate themselves from Muhammad's talk as a prerequisite for being heard. During the weeks that followed his speech, African-Americans were repeatedly required to pass this litmus test in order to establish their credibility. Whites often spoke as though it were taken for granted that they occupied the moral high ground and had the right and the responsibility to pass judgment on their African-American colleagues. Ironically, a day or two before the Bloomfield event, a Jewish settler had opened fire on Muslims praying at a mosque in Hebron, killing many. Although it was a horrifying act of premeditated violence, no one present at the panel discussion demanded that I or other Jews denounce the act in order to establish ourselves as legitimate members of the civilized community. In the United States, it is only African-Americans and other people of color who are consistently called on to "prove" themselves—and when and if they do, the most they earn is the right to take their place as exceptions that somehow continue to prove rather than undermine the rule.

From the start, I was uncomfortable with the decision to use *Schindler's List* as a response to the problems on New Jersey college campuses for other reasons as well. In spite of Black feminist writer Audre Lorde's plea that "there is no hierarchy of oppressions," this choice of film inevitably invited comparisons between the atrocities of the Holocaust and the inhumanity of slavery in the United States. It implicitly set up a competition among groups, each of which already felt that its suffering had never been adequately acknowledged or addressed by U.S. society. Showing it seemed like rubbing more salt in old wounds. This competition, of course, would make it impossible for members of these groups to listen to each other, since each group feared that by acknowledging the other's suffering, its own suffering would be silenced and ignored. Based on past experience, this fear is not ungrounded. It is not unreasonable for some to fear that if we look at the Holocaust, then we'll forget about the enslavement of African-Americans; if we talk about African-American suffering, then we'll forget about the plight of Latino/as; if we discuss racism, then we're not acknowledging the horrors of anti-Semitism; if we focus on violence against women or violent attacks on lesbians and gays, then we'll forget about the violence against African-American men, which occurs on a daily basis on the streets of our cities—and so forth. The long-term experience of marginalized groups in this society is that mainstream culture will do anything it can to avoid addressing their legitimate grievances and their pain.

In this context, it is not surprising that it was difficult for some African-Americans to watch *Schindler's List* and feel compassion for the plight of Jews. To my mind, they correctly saw the attention paid to the film, and to the history it remembers, as a way of silencing them, of making their plight invisible. I do not believe that this was anyone's conscious intention in choosing the film, but it was an inevitable consequence of white society's tendency to define social problems in ways that deny or obfuscate white privilege and white racism and the part it plays in them.

What was "the problem" on which Muhammad's speech should have focused our attention? For starters, at Kean there was a long history of tensions between African-American and white students as well as between Black and Jewish students and faculty. At least some of the antagonism was bound up with campus politics—in particular, the role played by and the power exercised by the faculty union and the faculty senate in distributing resources and privileges. As it turned out, some of the most visible members of the faculty union at Kean were white and Jewish. These tensions were further complicated by the appointment of a Latina educator, Elsa Gomez, as president of Kean College. In fact, during the ensuing period, one faculty member wrote a letter to the *New York Times* in which he charged that the hate speech delivered by Muhammad was "being used in a politically opportunistic manner to present Dr. Gomez as falsely condoning anti-semitism." Long before the speech, Kean's campus had been riddled by antagonisms within the faculty, antagonisms that spilled over into the student body, and the uproar that erupted after Muhammad's speech needed to be understood in that context—a context that was unique to Kean College but not specific to it.

In addition, on Kean's campus and at virtually every other New Jersey state college and university, various groups within the faculty, the staff, and the student body must compete continually for funding, recognition, and perks. If women's studies receives a faculty line, perhaps the Hispanic Caucus will lose part of its funding. If Africana studies gets a full-time secretary, why does women's studies have only part-time office staff? Groups regard one another with suspicion and envy as they are forced to compete for limited resources. On each campus, certain buildings and lounges become the de facto territory of students from one ethnic group rather than another. Each campus is balkanized, and students of color must function throughout their entire college career in an environment that assumes whiteness as normative, just as women, whatever their color, learn to function in a chilly climate that pressures them to disavow the very feminist per-spective that might help them make sense of their experiences and empower them to succeed. The decision to "teach tolerance" as the "solution" to these and other realities ignores the real differences in power and opportunity that divide individuals and groups in this society and the competing histories of oppression that we carry with us. It tries to smooth over these differences with a veneer of good manners and the illusion of "One Family, Many Faces,"* instead of confronting the long-standing grievances and injustices that produce, on the one hand, hatred, violence, and despair and, on the other, dis-proportionate power, privilege, and opportunity. Hatred on the part

---

*This was the name given to the Whitman administration's campaign, which was developed in conjunction with the office of Lonna Hooks, New Jersey Secretary of State, and the highest ranking person of color in the Whitman administration.

of African-Americans and other people of color toward whites is not racism; it is the legacy of centuries of racism from which whites have profited. Who ever said that privilege comes cheap? Certainly not my mother.

As a white woman who feels a deep responsibility to talk about race, I have discovered that one very effective way of getting a hearing for any form of injustice is to ask each other's questions. When I talk about sexism, it's easy for some people to dismiss what I have to say. They are not surprised to hear a woman complaining about women's plight, and they can easily, if incorrectly, explain away my passion by assuming that some individual and very personal slight has simply made me bitter and turned me against men. In this way, they avoid thinking about male privilege by redefining sexism as a personal complaint rather than a social issue. But when I talk about racism, my remarks are harder to dismiss. People are often puzzled and intrigued to hear a critique of white privilege coming from one who benefits from it. I think this is one reason that I do not feel uncomfortable talking about issues of race. I believe that it is by asking another's questions that we can get a hearing for them. Nonetheless, I admit I was taken aback the night I was invited to do commentary on a New York metropolitan area TV newscast and was introduced as a "racism expert." The title seemed incompatible with my skin color.

It was December 1987, and my race, class, and gender text had been published a few months earlier. A year earlier, on the Friday night before Christmas, three Black men from the East New York section of Brooklyn had wandered into a pizzeria in Howard Beach, a virtually all-white neighborhood in Queens, looking for help because their car had broken down. They were attacked and beaten by a group of white teenagers who used racial epithets as well as a baseball bat in the assault. When one of the Black men, twenty-three-year-old Michael Griffith, tried to flee his attackers, he was chased onto a busy highway, where he was struck by a car and killed. The incident was disturbing on so many levels that movie director Spike Lee decided to make *Do the Right Thing* after reading about the attack and dedicated the film to Michael Griffith and to five other African-Americans who had died under suspicious circumstances around the same time while in the custody of the New York City Police Department.

And the Howard Beach attack was not an isolated event. It occurred some six months after Bernard Goetz, a white man, had been acquitted of virtually all charges stemming from an attack on four Black youths on a New York City subway and was preceded and followed by other similar seemingly random acts of violence by whites against African-Americans. Journalists and ordinary citizens alike debated the facts of each case and speculated about what they revealed about U.S. society. By the fall of 1987, attention was focused on the upcoming verdict in the Howard Beach trial. Still angered by Goetz's acquittal, which to many proved what they already knew—that there was no justice for Black people in the American justice system—African-Americans and others staged marches and protests to focus attention on the trial and its outcome.

When the jury began its deliberations, a New York metropolitan area television station contacted me and asked me to stand by to comment on the verdict as soon as it was in. Twelve days after the jury began deliberations, and after several false alarms, I received a call telling me that the verdict was imminent and asking me to come to the station in time to appear on *The News at Ten*, the first area evening news program that would break the story. I washed my hair, jumped in my car, and drove to the TV studio in Secaucus, New Jersey.

By the time I got to the station, it was dark and cold and the parking lot was almost full. Feeling somewhat apprehensive because the area was unfamiliar and the lot appeared to be deserted, I circled a few times hoping for a parking space near the building entrance. That none was available became more of a cause for concern when I noticed a large black car with two suspicious-looking Black men in it, circling as well. After a while, I gave up looking, parked the car a distance from the door, and made my way quickly through the unlit parking area to the entrance. Once inside, I met the newscasters, went through the preliminaries, and met the other commentators, a white male law professor from Rutgers who was a former chair of the Essex County Bar Association and Newark mayor Sharp James, who, to my embarrassment, I immediately recognized as one of the Black men in the car that had caused me concern.

Although a jury of seven men and five women found three of the four white youths guilty in the attack on Michael Griffith, the most significant charge of which they were convicted was manslaughter—not murder in the second degree. Griffith's mother, who had feared an acquittal, was relieved, but other Blacks were outraged. At the same time, whites in Howard Beach considered the verdict overly harsh, and those interviewed by the press consistently denied that racism had played a part in the attack. The youths and their attorneys claimed that they were being used as scapegoats and adopted what seemed to me a peculiar defense by maintaining that the attack had been nothing more than an ordinary fight. Much of the news footage aired on the newscast focused exclusively on the defense's claim that the white youths were the victims in the case.

When it was my turn to go before the cameras, I denounced the verdicts and tried to provide enough background to contextualize the original incident for viewers. From the very beginning of the Republic, large areas of this country's cities and towns have been off limits to African-Americans. As early as 1712, South Carolina passed "An Act for the Better Ordering and Governing of Negroes and Slaves," legislation that then served as a model for slave codes in the South during the colonial and national periods. The act stipulates that "negroes and slaves" not be allowed off the plantations where they labor and mandates whippings and other punishments for those found to be on the streets of Charleston improperly. What happened in Howard Beach in 1986 was simply one more in a long line of incidents reinforcing white control of white neighborhoods and making them off limits for people of color.

At the time of the incident, many white students protested that what had happened to the Black men who found themselves in Howard Beach was only what would have happened to them if they had wandered into all-Black areas. This was meant to excuse the white attackers on the grounds that they were simply "protecting" their neighborhood, which is implicitly understood to be a "good" and "natural" thing, I suppose, based on the idea, popular then, that men, like other animals, have a sense of territorial imperative. It is also somewhat reminiscent of the claim that everybody is racist insofar as it suggests that if given the chance Blacks will attack whites and whites will attack Blacks—so what's the big deal. And, finally, it fails to recognize the reality that given the location of most employment opportunities and cultural and other resources, it is much more likely that people of color will be forced to enter "white neighborhoods" on a regular basis than that whites will have to visit "Black" ones.

A few days after appearing on the newscast, I started to receive hate mail at the college. One communication, handwritten on an index card, purported to be concerned about my well-being: "You should not swallow the cum when you suck Black dicks. It's getting to your brains." Another began, "PU You Stink. Commie Jew Swine— You subhuman (nagger) animal f——cker. Ugly, and I mean ugly kike. Dog, saw you on TV crying for nagger ape pig. Hey Jew bastard, why weren't you demonstrating in front of the Soviet Embassy for Russian Jews instead of bewailing the fate of a drug crazed, filthy nagger ape like Griffith. I hate niggers with a passion, but I hate ugly liberal Jew masochists worse." It went on for some time in a similar vein and, interestingly, echoed the first piece of mail's concern when it asked, "Tell us Rothenshit, how many nagger organs have you swallowed? How many nagger tucheses have you licked." It ended with the assurance that "90% of whites want acquittals. We want apartheid. We want a nagger free America. Niggers cause crime, disease and ruin the quality of life of everyplace they inhabit. Masochistic dogs such as yourself are lower than the lowest coon." And with some more helpful advice: "Rothenshit, the best thing that you can do is commit suicide and rid the world of your repulsive presence." It was signed "WHITE AND PROUD."

This letter is notable because it is simultaneously horrifically racist, anti-Semitic, and sexist. Like much of the genre, it posits oral sex between a white woman and a Black man—perhaps the writer's ultimate fantasy and ultimate fear. In his eyes, the woman both degrades herself and is degraded by this act. The white woman, the Black man, and the act itself are all understood to reflect a base animal nature. In the writer's mind, there is a direct connection between her "liberal" views and what he considers unorthodox and unrestrained (unbridled!) sexuality. In this way, the hate mail simply reflects white America's on-going interest in Black men's genitals and continues the persistent stereotype in white society according to which Black men are portrayed as being oversexed, as possessing unusually large genitalia, and as lusting after white women. There is also the related assumption and fear that white women secretly lust after Black men. The irony, of course, is that throughout the history of slavery, it was *white* men who repeatedly, brutally, and wantonly raped and impregnated African-American women.

But, of course, the worst thing in that letter was the writer's disparaging remarks about my appearance—because, as everyone knows (smile), the worst thing a man call tell a woman is that she is unattractive. In fact, like the writer of this letter, many men seem to consider an ugly woman a personal affront. For example, I still remember the day I heard a popular radio announcer introduce Janis Ian singing "At Seventeen," with the suggestion that she sing with a paper bag over her head. In an instant, my happy anticipation of the song was replaced by an icy chill. The cruelty of his remark extended beyond its object and went straight to my heart because there was no doubt that he would use these words against me and against any other woman who stepped out of line. It's interesting to conjecture about why he made the comment in the first place, why he felt entitled to make the comment, and why he assumed that his audience would be charmed by his cleverness—and this was years *before* Ian came out as a lesbian. One can only imagine what he might say *now*.

Accepting responsibility for her own sexuality continues to be a radical and revolutionary act on the part of a woman. This is one reason that society feels so threatened by out-lesbians, entertainers like Madonna and Cher, women in interracial relationships, and others who violate society's taboos by taking control of their bodies and their sexuality and by choosing how they will use it. This is one reason that I am not married. I have always believed that who I slept with was

no one's business but my own. And once you believe that and live
your life that way, you rob society of tremendous power over you.
The same is true when you stop wanting to look like Barbie.

For me, one of the enormous benefits of the women's liberation
movement during the late 1960s and into the mid-1970s was that it
gave women permission to stop trying to conform to traditional standards of feminine beauty. What a relief it was to stop curling and
straightening some of our hair and plucking and shaving the rest it.
How nice it felt to wear comfortably baggy clothes without bras, gar-
ter belts, and girdles to keep us in our place. Amazing not to have to
worry whether our makeup was smudging or running or streaking
or turning color—because we weren't wearing any. And how revolutionary to stop dieting and start feeling healthy and strong. But it
didn't last long. Today, 80 percent of girls in the fourth grade are on
diets.* I watch my beautiful seventeen-year-old daughter and her
beautiful friends agonize over the size and shape of their bodies and
subject every body part to the most unforgiving critical scrutiny. These
smart, sassy, creative young women spend hours each week hating
themselves because no matter how hard they try, they are never thin
enough. Their thighs are always too big, and their abs are never
flat. Even being size 6 isn't good enough. This preoccupation with
being thin and conforming to unrealistic and unrealizable socially
constructed images of feminine beauty continues to give society a
stranglehold over girls and women. It keeps us from claiming our lives
and demanding control of public space by ensuring that we will never
feel good enough about ourselves to do so. Go back and read early
radical feminist Shulamith Firestone on love and the culture of romance, and tell me she didn't get it right.†

Still, as soon as it became clear that I was about to become a public
person, I started to think more about my appearance and got my hair
permed. I thought of it as wash-and-wear hair. I needed hair that could
keep on giving even after a long plane ride, hair that could go from

---

*See http://www.sirius.com/~sfnow/volunteeer/girlempow.htm.
†Shulamith Firestone, *The Dialectic of Sex* (New York: Bantam Books, 1970).

airport to podium and back without much fuss. And I bought some professional-looking suits. Up until this time, I would describe my style as moderately disheveled and definitely informal. But at a certain point, I realized that in order to be taken seriously, I would have to adopt a more professional style. This was especially true because so much of my public speaking involved asking audiences to think about, or think differently about, difficult topics. I wanted my appearance to enhance, not undermine, my credibility. But I was very conflicted about the politics of "dressing for success" until the day in 1985 when I went to Newark Airport to pick up two consultants whom we had invited to work with the race and gender faculty group at William Paterson.

Johnella Butler, at that time on the faculty of Smith College, and Margo Culley, who was at the University of Massachusetts, were co-directors of a curriculum integration project funded by the Fund for the Improvement of Post-Secondary Education (FIPSE) and called "Black Studies, Women's Studies: An Over-Due Partnership." I had invited them to speak and consult at William Paterson College as part of a curriculum transformation project I was directing. Both women stepped off the plane looking, to my mind, more like business executives than women who made a career of interrogating the politics of the curriculum. At first, I was disappointed that their appearance didn't reflect what I knew to be their politics, but as I watched them move through the day, I realized how much more effective they were in communicating with each of the different constituencies on the campus than they would have been had they been dressed less professionally. Over the next few months, I began to notice that, in particular, women of color in academia were dressing up, while many of us white girls were still in our post-hippie dress stage. And I had heard Black women friends ask rhetorically why middle-class white women worked so hard at dressing as though they were poor when so many in the rest of the world were trying hard to move beyond poverty. Since I continued to be concerned about the politics of appearance issues raised by the women's movement, I thought a lot about how to dress more professionally without feeling compromised. In my case, this was complicated by the fact that I had had a mastectomy in November 1984 and, since that time, had chosen not to wear a prosthesis.

It is quite likely that the women's movement literally saved my life. Because of it, I understood how important it was to be actively involved in caring for my own health. I found my breast cancer in the course of self-examination, and I was considerably more aggressive and focused in obtaining treatment for my cancer than I would have been without the prevailing feminist critique of the medical system. But even I wasn't prepared for the conversation I had the day after my surgery when a young male resident came to check my incision. When I asked him how it looked, he answered: "Don't worry. You'll still be able to wear a bikini." I was incredulous at his response—the mother of a six-year-old son and a four-year-old daughter, I was not thinking about bikinis, but about whether I would live or die. In the absence of a visit from my surgeon, what I wanted from the resident was his assurance that the surgery had gone well and my body was healing, not a fashion consult.

Things got worse when, only a few hours later, a woman from the American Cancer Society stopped by to give me a complimentary fake breast. Like the young resident, she seemed to think that looking as though I still had two breasts was my paramount concern. In fact, the prospect of wearing a prosthesis became increasingly unappealing as it became clear that the doctors, nurses, and everyone else involved had an almost desperate need for me to do so. People kept assuming that my one fear was that I would no longer be attractive to men, and so they kept assuring me, even though I never asked, that once I had a well-fitted prosthesis no one would be able to tell the difference.

To be honest, it never occurred to me to worry about whether Greg would miss my breast. To this day, I have a hard time understanding women who postpone having breast irregularities diagnosed because they fear their husbands will not be able to tolerate such a loss or, worse yet but true, because their husbands refuse to allow them to have their breasts examined at all. And it's still difficult for me to forgive my own mother, who chose to die rather than undergo chemotherapy for her lung cancer because, as she told me, she would not be able to face looking in the mirror if she lost her hair.

Nonetheless, and in spite of my antipathy, a few weeks after my surgery, I did get fitted for a breast. I was trying to keep an open mind and to explore all my options. The form was surprisingly lifelike to the touch and had a nice bounce to it when I walked. My children thought it was a neat toy and enjoyed tossing it back and forth like a bean bag. On the other hand, it was heavy and uncomfortable—probably all the more so because I hadn't worn a bra in years. I tried wearing it a couple of times when I went out at night but put it away for good after four-year-old Andrea saw me dress without it one night and came running after me shouting, "Mommy, you forgot your breast." It seemed really important that I model for her in the most dramatic way possible what it means to love and accept your body the way it is without feeling compelled to conform to socially defined norms. And it felt dishonest to pretend to be something I was not—a two-breasted woman. I fantasized how the world would look if all post-mastectomy women walked around in an Amazon-like, one-breasted display, and I thought how liberating that would be for all women. I also thought it might do something to increase funding for breast cancer research, which at that time was still abysmally underfunded. And so for years, I worked at dressing professionally for public talks and TV appearances with the added challenge of not wearing a bra or an artificial breast. For the most part, I doubt anyone noticed.

Ironically, sometime after I turned fifty, I finally started wearing the prosthesis on a fairly regular basis. As my body slumped into middle age, I got tired of how oddly clothes fit my increasingly lop-sided torso. Breast forms became lighter and more comfortable, and by then I knew that no one, least of all myself, might accuse me of wearing the prosthesis so that I would be attractive to men. I guess you could say that I started wearing it when I could finally choose to do so for my own reasons and not because I felt compelled to do so by society's. Like my permed hair, it was more like a convenience than a subterfuge.

Several years ago, I heard Carolyn Heilbrun talk about what a relief it was to be getting older, not just because of the alternative, but because of how liberating it is to age. And by and large, I agree. There is something wonderful about having a body with a mind of its own that once and for all overcomes all your efforts to mold and cajole it into society's fantasy of a woman. I look around the town in which I live and see women who ten or twelve years ago still looked embarrassingly like cheerleaders now sliding gracefully (or perhaps being dragged kicking and screaming) into middle age. Their hips are finally wider than their chests, they have nice rounded bellies and crinkle lines around their eyes, and, if they're lucky, their hair is an interesting salt-and-pepper mix, not some chemically induced shade of bottle brown. And I think they look terrific.

6

Our Town

❖ ❖ ❖ ❖ ❖ ❖ ❖ ❖ ❖ ❖ ❖ ❖ ❖ ❖

Montclair is a town of gracious homes and tree-lined streets approximately twelve miles from Manhattan. Once home to the Leni-Lenape Indians, a branch of the Algonquin, who hunted and traded in the hills of northern New Jersey, Montclair has a population of approximately 38,000. It distinguishes itself from other Jersey suburbs by the age and grandeur of many of its homes, the diversity of its population, and the wide range of cultural activities it nurtures, including theater companies, art galleries, dance studios, concert series, an art museum, numerous restaurants, and craft shops. My mother was amazed the first time we drove around town together. It looked just like the kind of place *she* would have chosen to live.

I chose Montclair because of its reputation as an unusually diverse suburb with a rich history of making integration work. Even before moving to town, I had heard stories from older Black acquaintances who had grown up in neighboring Newark and knew Montclair well. They reminisced about walking all the way to Montclair as teenagers in order to have access to some of the only integrated social and cultural activities in the area. The trip, in those days, was not without its pitfalls. It required walking through Glen Ridge, a lily-white community that welcomed neither Blacks nor Jews. The challenge for those who made the trip on foot from Newark was to get through Glen Ridge without being stopped and harassed by the police. They rarely succeeded.

To this day, Glen Ridge continues as an all-white, all-American, community—home to many of those dirty little secrets that are woven into the fabric of our lives. In 1989, it gained national attention as the site of a vicious sexual assault by three white high-school athletes on a mildly retarded, young white woman. Having used the promise of friendship to lure her to a basement, the three boys proceeded to use a broom handle, a baseball bat, and a stick to sexually assault her while an audience of ten friends looked on. An investigation into the incident revealed a community with a history of tolerating out-of-control behavior on the part of its young male athletes. When the 1989 case came to light, a survey of attitudes in the town revealed considerable resistance to prosecuting the boys on the grounds that, after all, "boys will be boys."*

For as long as I have been teaching in New Jersey, I have heard stories from my African-American students about their experiences while driving through such all-American, white communities. The names of the towns change, but the experiences are always similar. On their way to work or school, Blacks, particularly Black men, are likely to have their cars stopped for no reason other than their skin color. (In 1998, a bill to limit this kind of harassment, informally referred to as "guilty of driving by race," was introduced in Congress. In 1999, New Jersey state troopers were accused of "racial profiling" based on the wildly disproportionate number of African-Americans who are stopped by troopers on the New Jersey Turnpike.) To this day, the presence of a dark-skinned person on an ordinary suburban street is in itself reason enough for a frightened homeowner to call the police to report a suspicious presence and reason enough for the police to respond. When I read about the murder of Yoshihiro Hatori, a sixteen-year-old Japanese exchange student, shot to death in 1993 in

---

*For a complete account of the assault and a history of the events leading up to and surrounding it, see Bernard Lefkowitz, *Our Guys: The Glen Ridge Rape and the Secret Life of the Perfect Suburb* (Berkeley: University of California Press, 1997).

a suburb of Baton Rouge, Louisiana, because a white couple saw him coming up their front walk and were frightened, I was not surprised.

On the surface, Montclair looked different. It seemed to be the kind of place where people from different ethnic and economic backgrounds might really manage to create a community together. In the 1960s, when Newark erupted along with Detroit and other cities, Blacks and whites formed a human chain across Bloomfield Avenue, the main local artery, which runs from Newark through Bloomfield to Montclair and then on through the northern suburbs, to prevent the violence from spreading. Several generations of African-Americans and Euro-Americans have grown up together in this town, which can trace its substantial and stable Black population to the mid-nineteenth century. Originally brought to the area to work as servants in the large homes that served as summer residences for wealthy, white, city families, many Blacks stayed to buy property and settle here. Since that time, the African-American population of the town has remained at approximately 30 percent.

Montclair's success with school integration was another reason to be optimistic about the town. The schools in Montclair managed to achieve a roughly 50–50 racial mix by creating a system of magnet schools and voluntary busing. This meant that although the town itself clearly had separate white and Black neighborhoods, the judicious placement of so-called gifted and talented magnet schools in Black areas ensured that children from every part of town would grow up together—or so it seemed.

My search for a home in the suburbs began while I was still married and before I had children. My then husband and I had settled on Montclair after briefly considering houses in Teaneck and Englewood Cliffs, two other New Jersey towns that also had reputations as integrated communities. Looking for a house in each of these towns followed the same pattern. Each time we were shown a photograph of an available house, we asked whether it was in an integrated neighborhood and each time we were assured that it was not. It took a while for us to realize that the real-estate brokers thought we would be pleased by their answer. Once we began making our requirement of an integrated neighborhood clear at the start, we found ourselves listening to carefully worded lectures on the folly of our ways. Some realtors assured us that they shared our values but went on to offer friendly advice about what a mistake it would be to move into one of *"those* neighborhoods." Others were even more crudely racist. In 1972, the practice of red-lining was standard and pervasive, and people were dissuaded or prevented from crossing the line in either direction.

In November 1972, we moved into a fifty-year-old Dutch colonial in Montclair, located in a mixed neighborhood that was literally a few blocks from the other side of the tracks. Being on the wrong side of town, and so close to a neighborhood that some considered "marginal," probably saved us a few thousand dollars. At the time, we laughed over this inadvertent way of benefiting from racism.

Although we had no money saved for a down payment, we were able to draw on our privilege to buy a house. Had we not had family who could make it possible for us to become homeowners, we would have spent the next ten years saving for a down payment instead of acquiring equity in a home. We would have been paying rent instead of paying off a mortgage. But my father-in-law was a Miami Beach surgeon with a substantial practice, and he was delighted to be able to provide us with the down payment—not as a loan, but as a gift. In addition, because our combined teaching salaries totaled more than $18,000, considered a respectable family income in those days, we were able to qualify for a special mortgage that required that we put down only 10 percent of the cost of the house. Drawing twice on our class privilege, we were able to buy a four-bedroom house for $4,000 cash and obtain a twenty-five-year mortgage. However, gender almost got in the way.

The very first realtor who took us around explained that the bank would not take my salary into account when calculating our eligibility for a mortgage because the bank knew that I would get pregnant and quit my job. Evidently, these bankers had brothers on medical school admissions committees who had passed along this information. But the agent did a complete about-face when he learned that I was a college professor. Once again, class compensated for gender. Evidently, the bank was confident that a college professor would be able to use birth control to prevent an unwanted pregnancy and would be serious enough about her career to do so. We got our mortgage based on two incomes.

The bankers were correct about one thing. I did know how to use birth control to prevent an unwanted pregnancy. I had to. I grew up at a time when abortion was illegal and women tried hard not to make any mistakes. I knew girls who had sought abortions from ersatz doctors wearing ski masks or stockings over their faces, girls whose only anesthesia was a piece of wood jammed between clenched teeth to keep them from screaming. I had friends who could afford to fly to Puerto Rico, where several well-run clinics provided reasonably safe abortions under hygienic conditions, and friends who had traveled to Pennsylvania, where a compassionate doctor was well known for his willingness to help women terminate their pregnancies. Even in the days when abortion was completely illegal, people with money could pick and choose. But the prospect of an abortion and the financial, emotional, and family complications it involved meant that, like most of my friends, I worried about getting pregnant all the time and took great care to avoid it. I was twenty-nine and childless at the time we bought our house, and the bank had every reason to have confidence in my ability to plan a pregnancy carefully if I chose to have a child.

Within days of moving to Montclair, we were greeted by visits from neighbors who came bearing gifts of zucchini bread and walnut cake. The single Jewish family down the block expressed relief that another Jewish family had finally moved in, and a neighbor who lived several doors down stopped by to welcome us and say how relieved she was to hear that white people had bought the house. This is not ancient history. Ten years later, a neighbor whose house was up for sale complained after Ted, a Black neighbor who lived a few doors away, came over to borrow a lawn tool just when a real-estate agent drove up with a white family that was interested in buying his house. My white neighbor, a self-described liberal, told me after they left that he couldn't believe that Ted would have the poor taste to show himself at such an inauspicious moment and perhaps jeopardize the sale.

Twenty years later, in 1994, the widowed neighbor who still hadn't learned to drive sold her house to take an apartment in the center of town. When I met her on the street after she had moved, she told me proudly that although a "colored" family had been interested in buying her house, she had prevented them from doing so. She said that she couldn't do that to her neighbors and seemed to expect my gratitude. Today one of the white faculty members who regularly teaches the race, class, and gender course at William Paterson lives in one of the "restricted" lake communities so popular in northern New Jersey and sees no contradiction. If you were to go to visit her, you would find her community marked with a sign reminding all that "Membership is a Right and a Privilege."

Within weeks of moving to Montclair, I got a taste of the more sophisticated political community that seemed to coexist in town and in the surrounding area along with the traditional suburban set. One Sunday morning in 1972, I found myself attending a pancake breakfast in one of the Oranges where Gus Hall, chairman of the Communist Party USA, was flipping pancakes. I was invited to pot-luck suppers, Sunday brunches, and evening meetings for a broad spectrum of grassroots political causes and was pleased to find that life in a New Jersey suburb could have such a rich and varied political content. Some years later, the unique nature of political life in Montclair was reaffirmed for me when noted civil rights attorney Arthur Kinoy ran for political office and his old friend Pete Seeger came out to do a benefit concert for him in the high-school auditorium.

Living on the wrong end of town had many benefits, among them the existence of a strip of small stores just two blocks from the house that resembled the stores I had shopped in when I lived on Sullivan Street in New York City. Having lived in Little Italy for six years, it was wonderful to find I could still take a short walk to an Italian deli—one that made its own fresh mozzarella daily—and to a candy store/smoke shop that happily looked like it belonged in a rundown neighborhood on the Upper West Side. A bakery, dry cleaner, laundromat, and pharmacy—yes, even here, I was still buying my tampons in pharmacies, not drugstores—were sandwiched in among the other stores, creating the physical terrain where the races met and mixed. Otherwise, the streets of most of the town, including my own, looked overwhelmingly white.

White people move to our town because it is racially/ethnically diverse, or so they say. This does not necessarily mean, however, that they expect their children to go to public school or, if they do, to attend classes that are actually integrated. Many have moved here from the Upper West Side of Manhattan, often after having a second child and realizing that for less than the cost of private school tuition for two children, they can make mortgage payments on a four-bedroom, two-and-half-bath, Victorian charmer. They plunge into this picture-perfect, turn-of-the-century town with great gusto, enroll their children in "swim and gym" classes at the Y, become active in the PTA, attend craft fairs and carnivals, coach soccer and Little League, and celebrate New Year's by participating in First Night. After that, as the children get older, they begin to have their doubts. As one parent said at a recent board of education meeting on detracking a course at the high school: "I moved to Montclair because it was an integrated community, but this is going too far."

By the time they are forced to confront the long-term consequences of race and class privilege as they play themselves out in tensions at the high school, they are earning enough at their law firms or brokerage houses to send their kids back to private school for the last four years—the years that count. Everyone knows that these are the years that count, just as they know that the whole point of going to high school is to gain admission to one of five or six prestigious colleges in the country. For this, they are willing to sacrifice their own and everyone else's children.

Current statistics indicate that approximately 10 percent of Montclair's school-age children attend private school, which is twice the average in the state. In addition to two parochial schools, Montclair is home to the Montclair Kimberley Academy (MKA), an elite private school where tuition amounts to $15,600 annually and books are extra. Several times a year, Montclair High and MKA compete in one sport or another, and the rivalry is intense. At a recent game, the public school kids began to chant, "We go to school for free," to which the Montclair Kimberly students gleefully responded, "But you're gonna work for me."

I like our town best early on weekday mornings when yellow school buses crisscross the neighborhoods picking up children while the children's aunts and uncles, parents and grandparents, and other caretakers cluster on corners waiting to send them on their way. I like the mix of these clusters. At least at our end of Grove Street, the corners are punctuated by random assortments of three-piece suits and jogging suits, beards and bald heads, hair curlers and bandannas, Reeboks and high heels. There are stay-at-home men and off-to-work women of different colors sending a rainbow of children onto their buses. But by 10:30 the corners are empty, and the streets of the town belong to dark-skinned women from the Caribbean who push white babies in imported strollers aimlessly up and down the block. When I see them, I often think of a story told to me by a white colleague who moved to the States years ago from a small town in England, where she had been raising her two young children. She settled in New York, and the first time she took the children to play in Central Park her younger son wanted to know why so many Black women in America had white babies.

With three large town swimming pools, an indoor ice-skating rink, art museum, numerous parks, and a surprising number of tennis courts, Montclair seems to offer its residents the best of life in the suburbs. Some might say that having three town pools instead of just one, as do the neighboring towns with more homogeneous populations, allows residents of different neighborhoods to have easy access to a pool on a hot summer day. Others will tell you that three pools were built to enforce rather than overcome the de facto segregation of the town by neighborhood. And when the pools need repair or renovation, it always seems like the one in Upper Montclair, where property values are the highest and the streets are the whitest, gets preference.

Of course, many people in town don't use the public pools; they prefer to spend their summers at one of the two local swim clubs, or perhaps at one of the two country clubs close by. After my marriage ended and Greg and I started living together and then had children, we considered joining one of the swim clubs. Unlike the town pools, which did not offer a seating area, refreshment stand, or even shade, the swim clubs seemed like good places to spend long hot summer days with two small children. But our summer plans came to an abrupt halt when we found out that both clubs were segregated. Of course, some white people will tell you that this isn't really true and will accuse me of using deliberately inflammatory language. Reflecting the kind of denial I have come to associate with so many well-intentioned liberals, they will insist that the swim clubs aren't actually segregated, they simply didn't have any members who aren't white. And they will believe it.

When I first began inquiring about the clubs in the mid-1980s, it never occurred to me that they might be restricted, because so many of their members were people with public roles in the community. Some of the best white teachers who taught our children at the elementary school belonged to them, and, naively, I did not believe that they would join a club that excluded Blacks. After hearing rumors about the clubs' exclusionary policies, I began to make inquiries. To my surprise, each of the people I asked acknowledged the clubs' policy but assured me that they disagreed with it—as though their lack of approval excused them of culpability. Some of the members even assured me that they, along with others, had been trying to change the policy for years. Since the policy was clearly in violation of the law, it seemed to me that getting it changed wouldn't be very difficult. All someone would have to do was file charges, publicize the policy, or, simply, resign in public protest of it. But that would have put their own privilege at risk. Almost twenty years later, at the start of the twenty-first century, the policy remains the same and the clubs continue to be virtually white—our dirty little secret.

In the end, Greg and I wrote a letter to the town paper expressing our outrage. It resulted in a couple of letters to our house expressing agreement but little else. We weren't allowed to include the name of the swim club in our letter because newspaper policy prevented it. The newspaper never followed up with some investigative reporting, as one might have hoped, probably because it was spending so much time doing stories about real-estate agents in town who had become eligible for their company's million-dollar-sales club. And no town officials ever called us or showed any interest.

As disturbing to me as the policy itself was the complicity of so many white people who should have known better. What allowed those public school teachers to spend their summers at swim clubs that excluded half the children in their classrooms because of the color of their skin? Why didn't they see a problem with doing so? These were teachers who led the Pledge of Allegiance each morning of the school year and who were charged with providing all the town's children with an equal and equitable educational experience. What does their failure to take a stand personally say about the way in which issues of race and racism have been constructed in our society? Why didn't they see any personal or professional contradiction in being members of a segregated club? In the end, this is one of the puzzles that prompted me to write this book. As a white person, I feel both anger and shame when I think about the role that so many well-meaning white liberals play in maintaining the color line, and I need to understand what allows them to live this way.

As they play themselves out in our lives and in the lives of those we love, the dynamics of race, class, and gender are always complicated and often painful, and even the best of intentions will not see us through. Having grown up attending segregated private schools in the 1940s and 1950s, I resolved that things would be different for my own children. I promised myself that I would try hard in the course of my life to live my beliefs instead of merely spouting them. Like many other well-intentioned whites, I naively thought that sending my children to integrated public schools would be enough to ensure that they grew up as part of a multicultural community predicated on equality and mutual respect. For this reason, I understand some of the frustration of the white liberal parents who start out committed to public education and in the end seek the privileges of a private school for their teenagers. They tried, in their own way, to do what they thought was right and are understandably confused by the charges of racism that are leveled at them as they become part of white flight. They are filled with nostalgia for their children's second- and third-grade birthday parties when rainbow children played and sang in their backyards.

My own experience in Montclair is not atypical. In the early years, things seemed to go well as far as race was concerned. Both of our children had friends of many colors and teachers who were African-American, Latina, and Asian, as well as white. Gender difference was the real issue in those early days as we watched the schools and community replicate the sex-role stereotyping of the past even as they paid lip service to the new nonsexist education of the present. Zealous in their efforts to create nonsexist bulletin board displays, in the early grades teachers routinely praised my daughter for what she was wearing while greeting my son and other boys with questions about their opinions, interests, and expectations. On occasion, they still threatened the disruptive second- or third-grade boy with the punishment of having to sit at the girls' table if he didn't behave, and each spring the class plays encouraged far too many girls to be cheerleaders and princesses to the boys' football players and kings. But, at least on the surface, race looked better.

Early on, out schools adopted something of a multiculturally inclusive curriculum, and clumsy as it sometimes was, it was heartening, at least to this white parent, that the past was no longer completely whitewashed in the kids' social studies books. Most birthday parties were conspicuously integrated in the earliest grades, and the kids' school friends were as likely to be named Malik and Sharif as Jennifer and Brian. And then a strange thing began to happen. The birthday parties began to be increasingly homogeneous. Over the years, the number of kids who were not white decreased until there were none. Over the years, the invitations to celebrate birthdays with Black classmates diminished and then disappeared entirely. The children's playmates all began to look very much alike, reflecting an economic and ethnic homogeneity that calls into question the very premise of a town like Montclair.

Perhaps it will be instructive to tell the story of the friendship between my daughter, Andrea, who is white and her onetime friend, Jewel, who is Black. Although it is simply the story of two little girls who managed to be best friends for a very brief time and is highly specific to them, it sheds light on the complex nature of relations across race/ethnicity and class in the suburbs.

Jewel and Andrea met in kindergarten and were kindred spirits from the start. Both were smart and spunky, and both loved to be silly. The girls wanted to play together after school, but that was easier said than done. They managed to trade phone numbers, but whenever I called Jewel's house her grandmother answered and said that Jewel's parents were not available and she was not able to make arrangements for a play date in their absence.

After several weeks of fruitless calls, persistence finally paid off; one day, Jewel's mother, Carol, called back. Yes, Jewel could play at our house after school as long as I didn't mind keeping her until after dinner. Her mother worked late and wouldn't be able to come by until 7:30 or so. Since that was no problem, I picked up both girls at school the very next day. What I remember about the visit was Jewel's amazement as she explored our house for the first time and discovered that we had more than one bathroom.

After a series of other play dates and several conversations over coffee, Carol told me what I suspected. It was so difficult to reach her and so hard to coordinate play dates for the girls because Carol and her husband did not live in Montclair and Jewel managed to go to the Montclair public schools by claiming her grandmother's house as her residence.

This practice is not uncommon. Taxes in Montclair are very high, and many African-Americans who were raised in town and whose parents still live here can't afford either the price of a house or the taxes they would have to pay as residents. A common solution is to live in East Orange or some other surrounding community in a neighborhood where the schools are inferior but the taxes and property values are much lower and use a parent's or relative's address to claim residency and gain access to the Montclair school system.

Obviously people react to this subterfuge in different ways, depending largely on their race and their class. Many whites in town are angered by the fact that some children, mostly Black, who don't actually live in town attend the public schools, thereby raising their tax burden, while many Blacks see nothing very wrong with the practice. They question why education should be funded by local property taxes in the first place instead of on a statewide basis, which could ensure equal education for all children. Besides, having grown up here, they think of themselves as part of the town—quite apart from the technicality of their legal residence. While many of the white homeowner/tax payers are recent arrivals to Montclair, many of the African-Americans who resort to the subterfuge are members of families that have lived in the town for several generations. In many cases, they attended the same schools that their children now attend. What seems like a gross violation of law and justice to some of the whites, who focus on whether the parents of the children actually live in town, hardly seems that way to many of the African-Americans whose sense of family is much more inclusive. Children and grandchildren, cousins and nieces are understood to be part of the extended family of the relatives who are Montclair residents and taxpayers. These relatives care for the children at their homes on a regular basis, often having the children spend nights as well as days with them. The children's parents and other family members see the house itself as part of their extended residence, frequently eating and socializing with one another there, dropping in to use the phone or to help with home repairs. Legal residency often seems like a procedural technicality rather than an accurate indicator of who is part of town life. In fact, according to some criteria, these Black Montclairions, whose roots are firmly planted in the town, have more claim to being part of it than the newly arrived white professionals who simply sleep here, commuting to work in New York each day and spending their weekends playing golf at the country club in Glen Ridge.

When Carol finally gave me the family's address and phone number in another town, it was a real sign of trust. The first priority in her life was keeping Jewel in a good school system, arranging afternoon play dates with a white classmate was low on the list. But as the girls' friendship blossomed, Carol, like me, was eager to let them enjoy time together.

And then the inevitable happened. During one of the periodic efforts that the town officials make to track down children who are attending public school illegally, Jewel's illegal status was discovered. Carol never asked whether I had provided the school officials with the information—of course, I had not—but it's difficult to imagine that the idea didn't cross her mind. How could she ever be sure? Through some special arrangement, Jewel was allowed to finish up the school year, which was almost over. During the summer, her family moved out of their apartment and into a small house on the outskirts of Newark, about twenty minutes away. The following September, Jewel began attending parochial school. For her family, as for others like them, parochial school provided the only viable alternative to the inferior and dangerous public school near their home.

Jewel attended Andrea's birthday party that September, as she had in the past, and in January, Carol called to invite Andrea to Jewel's birthday party a week later. Andrea was thrilled with the prospect of seeing Jewel again and of visiting Jewel's house for the first time. She could talk of nothing else.

Jewel's new house was located in a fairly rundown Black neighborhood of small, single-family, urban-style homes. In spite of its appearance, I knew that it would be classified as a middle-class neighborhood by other Black families, since definitions of what counts as "middle class" are themselves race specific, and it is informal residential segregation that often determines how neighborhoods are defined and who gets to live in them. The front door of the house opened into a tiny living room that, in turn, opened into a larger, but still small, dining alcove. Sitting around a large wood table, filling all the space in the room, was a gaggle of aunts and uncles, grandparents and cousins. Apart from Jewel's young cousins, Andrea was the only child present, and she and I were the only white people. Conversation among the adults was friendly, if labored, with everyone trying hard to make us feel welcome. I tried hard not to cramp their good time.

But Andrea was very uncomfortable. Many of the social cues that she counted on to negotiate such events were missing, and she had not had the opportunity to learn the ones that were in place. People talked to each other in unfamiliar ways, and, at times, what I recognized as affectionate teasing must have sounded to her like sharp criticism or argument. She was frightened by how dark the house was and couldn't understand why only one lightbulb was burning on such a dark day. Coming from a world where people have enough money to use lighting as much for decoration as to be functional, she couldn't know that for most of the world, electric lights are a luxury or at least a carefully conserved resource.

A special point of pride for Jewel was the second toilet—literally a water closet—her dad had rigged up in the basement of the house to supplement the full bath upstairs. It consisted of a four-sided wooden cabinet set on a platform in the middle of a dark basement. The cabinet itself had no electric light, but some open space had been left between the ceiling and one side of the cabinet to allow light to enter. Jewel's pride was my daughter's terror. She went to the bathroom only after it was clear that one more postponement would have dire consequences, and she could use the bathroom at all only because I stayed in the cabinet with her.

As we drove home, I knew it was unlikely that the girls would continue their friendship. And in fact, they did not. It was just too difficult. Although Carol and I had tried to help the girls be friends, perhaps because we wanted the possibility of friendship for ourselves as well, the odds against it were too overwhelming and the differences separating the girls were just too great to bridge. In the end, personal relations occur within social contexts, and, in this case, it was unreasonable to expect two eight-year-old girls to be able to negotiate each other's worlds.

Different people will make different things out of this story. Some will see class as the villain here and argue, along with William Julius

Wilson and others, that it is class, not race, that separates whites and Blacks today. This I think is an oversimplification. Jewel and Andrea carried with them the combined history of three hundred years of race, class, and gender oppression and privilege, and the differences created by them were just too great to overcome. For example, why was I able to live in the town and have legitimate access to the schools for my children while Jewel's mother, who had grown up there, could no longer claim access to her own community? Both Jewel's mother and I worked full time, but my job as a college teacher allowed me flexible hours with good pay. Carol worked in the accounting department of a large supermarket corporation in a job that often required her to stay until 11 P.M. Although both she and her husband worked full time, as did Andrea's father and I, their combined income was a fraction of ours. This was not surprising, since statistics indicate that in 1996 annual income for the typical Black family was about half of the $47,000 a year enjoyed by white families. In fact, according to a report issued by the White House's Council of Economic Advisers, Black and Hispanic family incomes are farther behind those of whites today than they were twenty years ago.* For so many years, while I was fortunate enough to be paying off a mortgage on a home I obtained because my in-laws could afford to provide a down payment, Carol and her husband were paying rent and working overtime to save up for a house. Their down payment ultimately bought them a poorly constructed home in a marginal urban neighborhood with inadequate schools, dirty streets, and food stores that overcharge. Some little white girl, a mirror image of my long-ago self, drives through those streets today, and her parents caution her to roll up her window and lock her door. They shake their heads over the way some people choose to live when nothing more than hard work and ability are required to earn us all a piece of the American dream. They do not know that for Jewel's family, this *is* their piece of the American dream and they have had to work very hard to achieve it. They do not understand that those of us who have more have drawn on the privileges of our race, our class,

---

New York Times, February 17, 1998, A18.

our gender, or some combination of them and have done so at the expense of the very people we denigrate.

Although in Montclair, many of us pride ourselves on the 50–50 racial balance within each school, these figures tell only half the story. By the time the town's children arrive at the high school, they have been sorted into tracks that will ensure that some go to selective four-year colleges, others will attend state schools, and some will head for community colleges or dead-end jobs. The top classes are identified as advanced placement, the next level down is honors, and the lowest track is identified with simply the number 2.

When I first arrived in Montclair, I liked the idea that the town designated one of its magnet schools the "gifted and talented magnet" because, unlike programs for so-called gifted and talented children in New York City, our public school program was open to any child. I used to think that calling it a "gifted and talented magnet" and opening it to everyone was a way of debunking elitism. Now I'm not so sure. Perhaps the name simply tells us that some people will participate in a system only if it allows them to obtain the designation "gifted and talented" for their children. Perhaps instead of reflecting efforts to dismantle hierarchy and elitism, this name reflects a pandering to it. Why else would a school system use the designation "honors course" for those taught at the standard grade level, leaving the numerical designation 2 for everyone else's kids?

Before the magnet school system was introduced at the start of the 1977/1978 school year, residential segregation in Montclair had created schools that were dramatically segregated by race right through junior high. When Blacks first moved to Montclair in the middle of the nineteenth century, they settled in the southeastern corner of town, joining the Italian immigrants who worked in a nearby mill. They chose this neighborhood both because the housing was relatively cheap and because white homeowners and realtors barred them from other parts of town. Between 1887 and 1896, two elementary schools were built in this area: the Cedar Street School, later renamed Nishuane, and the Maple Street School, later renamed Glenfield. The board of education went on to reinforce this segregation by drawing the boundaries of school districts to correspond to the division of neighborhoods by race and ethnicity. A corollary practice, typical of northern segregation, created an "optional area" system that allowed the few white middle-class families whose homes fell outside a white middle-class school district to send their children to schools in other parts of town.*

By the late 1940s, most of the Italians had moved away from the southeastern corner, leaving the area almost completely Black. School records indicate that in 1961, Glenfield's student body was approximately 90 percent Black. In May 1961, the first public challenge to Montclair's pervasive school segregation by race was made by several of the Glenfield school parents at a board of education meeting. Harris Davis, a former Glenfield PTA president, was disturbed to find that although his daughter Lydia had been a straight-A student while at Glenfield, she began receiving Ds in her classes once she graduated and went on to the town's high school. Believing that his daughter's performance might reflect inferior educational practices at Glenfield, he organized a group of other Glenfield parents who brought their concerns about unequal education in the schools to the board of education. The ensuing investigation revealed that Montclair, like countless other "separate but equal" school systems, offered very different educational opportunities to its children based on the color of their skin. The predominantly white schools, such as Mt. Hebron, Northeast, and Bradford, had newer textbooks, better supplies, more rigorous curricula, better facilities, newer furniture, and more experienced teachers than Glenfield and Nishuane, which were situated in Black neighborhoods. Unlike the white schools, which had new science laboratories, extensive libraries, and well-equipped gyms and cafeterias, Glenfield had exposed and leaky pipes, broken toilets, and a run-down gym that doubled as a cafeteria at lunchtime.

---

*My discussion of the history of segregation in the Montclair public school system relies heavily on Jane Manners, "Repackaging Segregation? A History of the Magnet School System in Montclair, New Jersey," *Race Traitor* 8 (1998): 51–98. Manners, a graduate of the Montclair public schools, wrote this article as a senior honors thesis at Harvard.

Between 1961 and 1975, and in response to continuing pressure from the town's Black population, Montclair explored a number of strategies designed to alter the racial balance and improve conditions in the town's schools without provoking white flight. By 1977, the school board and then superintendent Walter Marks had fashioned and begun to implement a magnet school system plan that was quickly hailed as a model for desegregating suburban schools around the country.

Although the magnet plan did succeed in creating a racial balance within each of the town's eight elementary and three middle schools, these figures tell only half the story. While the schools are integrated, the classes are not. A disturbing practice of employing ability groupings within electives starting in the earliest grades creates a two-track system in the schools that places white students on a fast and largely white track. Informal work groups within each class also cluster children according to perceived ability in math and reading, and, unsurprisingly, the lowest groups tend to be almost exclusively Black. As schools continue to increase their use of ability groupings in response to the demands of white parents who make such teaching strategies the price for their continued support of the public schools, the promise of desegregation held out by the magnet school system is increasingly empty. Furthermore, like those in countless other school districts around the nation, Black students in Montclair schools are placed in special education and basic skills classes in disproportionate numbers. Were I a Black parent, I would have a great deal of difficulty allowing those well-meaning white teachers who spend their summers at virtually lily-white swim clubs to decide where my son or daughter should be placed—not because I doubt their good intentions but because their good intentions will make it more, not less, difficult for them to interrogate their own racial blinders.

By the time Montclair children attend the high school, the distribution of children among the levels breaks down according to race and class, which suggests a rigid system of tracking that perpetuates the prevailing race and class hierarchy in our society. For example, in 1993, when the English department at Montclair High

School proposed doing away with tracking in ninth-grade English by offering the experimental and heterogeneously grouped "World Literature" course as the single course offering for that grade, the following reality prevailed:

NINTH-GRADE ENGLISH AT MONTCLAIR HIGH SCHOOL

	Whites	Blacks
Level 1A (advanced placement)	63	13
Level 1 (honors/average)	47	32
Level 2 (lowest level)	7	72

Only the experimental "World Literature" class was evenly divided, with twenty-five blacks and twenty-six whites.

This modest proposal, to remove tracking and introduce heterogeneous grouping for only one course and in only one grade at the high school during the entire four-year sequence, provoked a surprisingly strong response. Outraged white parents threatened to remove their children from the school if the proposal was adopted; some even vowed to move out of the town. After months of heated debate and through the efforts of an unprecedented and heterogeneous coalition of parents, teachers, students, and concerned residents, the proposal was adopted. The heterogeneously grouped course was offered on an experimental and tentative basis subject to review, but not before some white parents had made good on their threat and removed their children from the public school system.

Montclair's segregated classrooms are not very different from classrooms in public schools all over the country. A report released by the National School Board Association in 1993 showed that up to 70 percent of African-American and Hispanic students study in classrooms that are predominantly made up of so-called minority students.* Each year, surveys report that the schools in New Jersey are among the most

---

*Gary Orfield, with the assistance of Sara Schley, Diane Glass, and Sean Reardon, *The Growth of Segregation in American Schools: Changing Patterns of Separation and Poverty Since 1968*, a Report of the Harvard Project on Desegregation to the National School Boards Association, Alexandria, VA; National School Boards Association Council of Urban Boards of Education, December 1993.

segregated in the nation. The tragedy, of course, is that in Montclair things should have turned out differently.

So where does the problem begin? Many of the privileged white parents argue that all the kids in town start out with the same opportunity in the early grades, so the distribution of children by race that exists by the time they get to the high school must be the result of factors other than racism. They speculate that it is parental indifference, laziness, a lack of ability, dysfunctional families, economic deprivation, or some combination of them—not racism—that is at fault.

But how is it possible to separate the impact of race, class, and gender on individual lives, and why do some people think it desirable to do so? Perhaps there is a strong desire to deny the impact of racism because recognizing it might demand that we talk about white responsibility, white complicity, white privilege. Many are more comfortable looking at economic inequality because in their mind it fails to imply such clear responsibility. If racism is the issue, then white people will have to ask how they have, perhaps inadvertently, benefited from it. If economic inequities are at fault, then many whites can point to their own humble origins as children or grandchildren of poor immigrants as proof that anyone who works hard can succeed. In this way, they fail to understand the difference between the ethnic or religious prejudice that their families fought to overcome and the racism that pervades our society.

Many white people continue to believe that racism and sexism, like ethnic prejudice, are simply hateful attitudes toward people. They look inside themselves and cannot find either the feelings or the beliefs they associate with prejudice and so conclude that they are *not* prejudiced. Because they are *committed* to treating people fairly, they believe they do so. They teach their children not to judge others by the color of their skin, and they contribute to various charities that address issues of equity and civil rights. Because they have never been taught the difference between simple "prejudice" and the more complex and recalcitrant forms of oppression signified by the words "racism" and "sexism," they cannot understand why some people want to talk about "racism" all the time instead of individual initiative. They do not understand that racism and sexism are perpetuated every day by nice people who are carrying on business as usual. They do not recognize that what passes as "business as usual" already institutionalizes white skin, male, and class privilege. They honestly believe that what separates them from Jewel and her family are intelligence and hard work.

But, as I have tried to illustrate in these pages, neither our good intentions nor our ignorance prevents us from being the beneficiaries of privilege. The reality is that many of us benefit from some form or combination of privilege all the time without any particular action or intent of our own. This was brought home to me in a very personal way when I was diagnosed with breast cancer in 1984 at the age of forty-one. At that time, statistics indicated that, as a white woman, I had a 47 percent greater likelihood of being alive five years after my surgery than did an African-American woman diagnosed on the same day. Clearly, this was not because I wished any other woman harm. However, quite apart from my own intentions or design, this cruel statistic testifies to the race and class privilege I enjoy. This does not make me a racist but does make clear that I am, inadvertently, a beneficiary of racism. It is a consequence of a history of racism in our society that has resulted in different access to nutrition and health care, to information and housing, and to a host of other services for people of different races and classes. It includes the long-term consequences of dangers like environmental pollution, the result of urban and suburban policies that historically have situated incinerators and garbage dumps in neighborhoods where poor and nonwhite people live. In turn, the reality that both my African-American sister and I did not enjoy higher odds of survival in 1984 reflected, among other things, the long history of gender bias in medicine and medical research that, until recently, has significantly underfunded research in the field of women's health.

Privilege is an elusive thing. It is woven into the fabric of people's lives and, in this way, becomes invisible. The fact that my children see a doctor when they are sick, do not go to bed hungry or cold, wear Gap jeans and J. Crew T-shirts, went to camp each summer while they were growing up, travel outside the country on a regular basis, and had access to piano, voice, and dance lessons and to a private tutor if their grades began to slip are all part of the privileges that their father and I have secured for them using privileges of our own. Because we take them for granted, because so many of us are ignorant of the lives of families who must do without, they cease to be privileges in our minds. The reality that some children have parents who can tell them how to use the more difficult words on their spelling lists in sentences when they do their homework is the result of past privilege, too. How many children can use a word like "fealty" in a sentence without some help, and how many parents are in a position to provide it? Even a good dictionary is no substitute for an educated parent.

In elementary school, all our children are assigned projects that involve building models of the solar system or the ocean floor, but some kids must do these projects with little help from their overtaxed working parents, who do not have the energy or the skill to create Disneyesque fantasies and who cannot get home from work in time to drive to a crafts store to buy materials. Other children bring in projects that were done not by themselves but by their stay-at-home moms, who, looking for outlets for their own creativity and energy, throw themselves into this work with a passion. In our town, these women call on friends who are interior decorators and set designers to supply ideas and materials that produce extravagant results. What does it feel like to be a seven- or eight-year-child whose model of the solar system reflects her own hard work rather than the exceptional talents of a professional designer? Why don't some parents consider the long-term consequences of their own self-indulgence and their need to have their children "excel"? When I was a little girl of five or six spending the summer in a rented house near the beach in Belle Harbor, my mother set up an art studio in the garage and hired my school art teacher, a moderately well known sculptor named Charlotte Haupt, to come to Long Island one day each week and do art projects with me. Those summer days are part of the race, class, and gender privilege I carry with me and on which my own children draw.

In some ways, the roads in Montclair, as in so many other suburban towns, are paved with good intentions, and they lead to dead ends. Because so many of us have never been taught to identify racism, sexism, or class privilege, because we live in a society that never demands that we take them seriously, and because we are encouraged to think about diversity and tolerance rather than racism and privilege, it is easy for many of us who are white to take comfort in our good intentions. Because we know we mean well, because in our hearts we really do believe in the rhetoric of equality, we don't understand that our own behavior can perpetuate the oppression of others. For example, the white parents who cannot understand why there might be racial animosity among students at the high school may be the ones who inadvertently sowed the seeds of discontent when they served on the elementary-school PTA.

In our town, as in so many others, the active PTAs or PTSOs enrich the quality of the educational experience at our schools immeasurably. They provide class parents, help with programming in the arts, enlist volunteers to serve as tutors in reading and writing workshops, help with Project Graduation, and provide expertise and resources in many different areas. The mothers, and the few fathers, who spearhead these activities, who are largely white and privileged, also gain special access to the schools. Because they are in a position to volunteer their time and because they carry with them the sense of entitlement that their experiences in general have created, they are able to reap benefits that other families do not enjoy. They are on a first-name basis with the principal, the teachers, even the school superintendent. Their children, who are used to seeing their own mothers and the mothers of their friends at the school, quickly acquire a special sense of empowerment from their presence. It is clear to them that they themselves belong. They are more likely to be greeted by name in the hallway by the principal and other staff. Their friends, too, most often children from the same background, enjoy the comfortable feeling that comes from seeing Lisa's mom in the hall or getting a tissue from David's mother when she helps out in the library. In this way, from an early age the learning environment is different for different children—more welcoming for some. The complexion and class composition of the teaching staff and administrators, the contents of the curriculum, the pedagogical styles employed, as well as the presence of certain people's parents and neighbors in the building all provide subtle messages from day one about who really belongs.

Even before the most recent round of cuts in state aid to education, PTAs and PTSOs have seen fundraising as one of their primary objectives. Because of the volunteer efforts of many parents, schools in our town have computers, video equipment, library books, and funding for special science, social studies, and arts programs that they would not ordinarily have. As a result, magazine drives and sales of T-shirts, candy, wrapping paper, books, plants, and crafts seem to come along at a dizzying pace. The children who sell the most magazines or wrapping paper are widely petted and feted, and they receive flashy prizes like TV sets and boom boxes. In some years, these children bring in sales worth $200 or $300, the result of a quick trip to mom or dad's office where employees are pleased to buy gift wrap and magazines from the boss's daughter or son. Sometimes the children don't even make the trip. Mom or dad brings in the order sheet and has her or his secretary circulate it throughout the day. I wonder what it feels like to be one of the children in those classes at age seven or eight or nine or ten, whose order form is empty.

Some schools and teachers try to direct attention from the efforts of individual children and award prizes to the class that brings in the largest sum. What does it feel like to be one of the children who is unable to contribute any dollars to the group effort? Some people will find my question irritating. After all, anyone can sell a few magazines or a couple of rolls of gift wrap if they try—can't they?

One year, a particularly enthusiastic team of PTA fundraisers developed a project that offered parents the opportunity to buy flashy satin zippered jackets for their elementary-school children. These jackets, designed to be worn by children between the ages of four and eight, came in two versions, the more expensive of which had both the school name and the school logo emblazoned on it. These jackets cost something like $40—and that was in 1990. Since many parents had two or even three children in the school, this fundraiser assumed that the average parent had between $40 and $120 of discretionary income available to purchase a novelty jacket for a very young child who would more than likely outgrow it after one season. Fundraisers like these drive wedges between our children. They reflect an astonishing ignorance about the financial realities within which most families operate. They are part of an unending stream of trivial experiences that construct privilege and define disempowerment. No one or two of them matters very much, but taken together they separate our children into a race and class hierarchy that creates the problems we try so hard to solve.

Like that in so many schools, the K–12 curriculum in Montclair continues to reflect old ways of thinking about race, culture, and difference even as we learn to use the new rhetoric of gender equity and multiculturalism. In spite of so many good intentions, the tacos and egg-rolls approach to multiculturalism tends to predominate. It begins in the early grades when Chinese dragons parade through the hall each January to celebrate the Chinese New Year, but where any serious attention to Chinese history, literature and culture remains absent from the core curriculum. For the most part, children will have to wait until the ninth-grade world literature course before they are exposed to any Chinese creation myths and longer still, probably until college and then only if they choose wisely, to learn very much more about this ancient civilization and contemporary world power.

Although the elementary-school curriculum on occasion allows some children to enroll in an enrichment class about Chinese culture, the core of the curriculum remains firmly white and European, with attention to "others" added on for flavor. Its position in the curriculum makes it clear that the Chinese culture course is about "them," not "us." Students are left with the belief that history and civilization began in Europe and have no understanding that highly developed and sophisticated civilizations predate our own. Teaching a multicultural world curriculum from the very start of schooling would help contextualize the development of European civilization in a way that might move us beyond a narrow Eurocentrism, but this simply doesn't happen.

One reason it doesn't happen is that the teachers who develop the curriculum are often as poorly educated about gender equity and multicultural history and literature as the children they seek to educate. Because they are the products of a Eurocentric curriculum that has left them ignorant about most of the world, they often hear the demand for a more inclusive curriculum as a demand to make non-white, non-Western children "feel good," a kind of curricular charity work, rather than a demand to improve the quality of education for all children. The best they can do is add tacos and egg rolls because they have never been taught to identify the race, class, gender, and cultural biases that pervade the traditional curriculum, let alone address them. If they have never been taught to value and respect "other" cultures and history, how can they help their students do so? Because they are so rightly convinced of their own good intentions and so well protected from an awareness of their own ignorance, they do not understand that they are perpetuating a distorted worldview that devalues or marginalizes what is not white. They would be shocked to realize that they are part of an experience that perpetuates feelings of white superiority and nonwhite marginalization that will lead to racial antagonisms and tracking in high school and ultimately to very different life chances for students of different races, classes, and genders, even though this is not their intention.

At the gifted and talented magnet elementary school, children begin to enjoy "electives" in the earliest grades. At the age of four or five, they can choose to take a creative-writing class, study a foreign language, or select other special classes from among a list that includes "Fizzy Formulas," "Creepy Creatures," and "Dinosaur Land." But even at such a young age, the girls understand that "Dinosaur Land" and "Creepy Creatures" are for the boys and that the sewing classes are for the girls, and the school doesn't do very much to move them beyond these gender stereotypes.

An international perspective is provided by classes like "Cookbook to Culture" and "Café International," in which children spend one day cooking foods from foreign lands and another learning a little bit about the customs there. I remember well my own children's delight each week when they returned home on Tuesday afternoons to announce what country they were studying and what food they would be cooking. They moved from Mexican tacos to Scottish shortbread to Chinese noodles. Then one week they announced that they would be making a snack that schoolchildren eat in Africa. Since Africa rarely received any notice at the school, I was delighted and asked which country in Africa they would be studying. They looked at me blankly. No one had told them that Africa was a continent, not a country.

Ironically, the well-meaning white teacher who had gone to the trouble of finding a recipe for an African dish that the children could make was nonetheless perpetuating a Eurocentric worldview even as her lesson plans became more inclusive. She had reduced the many nations of Africa to a single country. Left out were the names Mali, Chad, Zambia, Angola, Libya, Cameroon, Zambia, and so many others, along with the possibility of studying the histories and cultural practices of each nation. How will my children ever hear the music in those names? How will they ever know that an after-school snack would be different in Morocco and in Tanzania—and why that is the case? How will they ever come to respect and learn from the traditions and literature of each culture if all those differences are subsumed under the name of a continent masquerading as a country?

This is not meant as a cranky criticism of a well-meaning teacher but as another sobering reminder that our good intentions are not always enough to protect us from mistakes and worse. It's wonderful that some of our schools offer courses in Chinese culture and teach about "Africa"; it's even wonderful to have a Chinese dragon parade through the halls. But the problem is that, in the end, a tacos and eggs-rolls approach to multiculturalism continues to perpetuate the hierarchical worldview that lies at the heart of so many of our problems. Well-meaning white people will continue to think that in this way we have done enough for "them" without realizing that these efforts are only a small first step toward a genuinely inclusive curriculum for all of us.

The well-meaning but Eurocentric approach to thinking about Africa reflected in "Cookbook to Culture" pervades the entire system of education. If it did not, the previous story wouldn't be worth telling. For example, I remember visiting a second-grade classroom for a parent–teacher conference one year, only to have my attention distracted by a peculiar world map that was hanging on the wall. From a distance I could see the outlines of the continents and could make out that some portions of the map were blank, while other areas seemed to have a lot of writing printed on them. As I came closer, I saw that while none of the continents were divided into countries, all of Europe was covered with the names of cities. The entire continent of Africa was bare except for the names of a handful of cities along part of a coastline and the name Johannesburg printed down near the bottom of what I knew to be South Africa.

When I asked the teacher about the map, she explained that the children were too young to learn about countries and that only the important city names had been listed. "Important to whom?" I wondered. What worldview is reflected in the criterion for "importance" that presents all of Europe as alive with activity and the entire continent of Africa as blank? What are children learning about who counts and who doesn't from such a map? What kind of world hierarchy does it create or reinforce? Apparently, Africa's interest and value were exhausted once the cartographer had identified the names of several major ports at which our ships might dock and from which they would depart.

But perhaps this was an old map, I speculated out loud, soon to be replaced by a more accurate depiction of the world. No, the teacher assured me; in fact, the map was new that year and had been ordered for all the classrooms in the building. The teacher, who patiently explained all this to me and who did not share my concern, was herself of African descent. But this story is not about her; it is about the picture of the world that is implicit in the curriculum we teach and the classrooms we create and who and what is marginalized and devalued by it and where this devaluing ultimately leads.

Every February, our children read books about African-Americans and learn about their accomplishments, but the number of Black heroes mentioned remains disturbingly small and predictable. As a result, when they were quite young, each of my children somehow acquired the belief that Rosa Parks was the wife of Martin Luther King, Jr. In some years, the children receive lists of famous Black Americans from which to choose their subjects; in other years, they are on their own. For five or six years in a row, my son, Alexi, alternated between writing about Harriet Tubman and about Jackie Robinson. The assignment has become a ritual that all parents have come to expect and many white parents have come to resent. Sometimes their resentment seems justified. I remember the year my seven-year-old daughter came home and announced that she had been assigned to write about Paul Laurence Dunbar. She had no idea, and had not been told, who Dunbar was, but at least I knew enough to identify him as a poet. Born in Ohio in 1872, Dunbar may be an interesting minor American poet who is worth reclaiming for the canon, but he is not an especially good read for a second grader. His is best known for writing lyric poetry in a dense southern dialect, and much of his verse would be formidable even for teachers of English.

A quick check of books in the house revealed, unsurprisingly, that Dunbar had not been included in the anthology of seven centuries of English and American verse that I had read at the University of Chicago or in the treasuries of modern American and English poetry that I had used in high school and at NYU. Nor was he mentioned in the several other voluminous anthologies of modern American poetry that rounded out my collection. After considerable searching, we did manage to find some of his poetry at the public library, but the few poems we could locate were all in dialect and were thoroughly undecipherable for a seven year old. Instead of the very powerful "Sympathy," from which Maya Angelou took the title of the first volume of her autobiography, *I Know Why the Caged Bird Sings*, which I have since discovered, all that we could find at the time were poems like "Death Song," which begins

> Lay me down beneaf de willers in de grass.
> Whah de branch'll go a-singin' as it pass,
> An' w'en I's a-layin' low,
> I kin hyeah it as it go
> Singin', "Sleep, my honey, tek yo' res' at 'as.'"

In addition, as it turned out, the only books that contained brief biographies of Dunbar, which my daughter needed to complete her assignment, were equally formidable since it was probably wisely assumed that few seven year olds would be reading them. In spite of my own attempts at positive intervention, the assignment had little value for my daughter. I tried to imagine how a less sympathetic parent might have reacted and what the long-term consequences of asking some other seven- or eight-year-old child to write about Paul Laurence Dunbar would be for race relations in our town. It is understandable why many parents, Black as well as white, might have found the assignment ridiculous. No wonder so many white parents are hostile toward the idea of a multicultural curriculum.

But the real problem is, of course, our failure to integrate this material into the core curriculum, relegating it instead to a few weeks during the year sandwiched between the compulsory Martin Luther King project and the soon to be announced Women's History Month essay. Black women can be covered in either February or March and, for this reason, often fall between the cracks (with the exception of Harriet Tubman, of course). By now, both white and nonwhite students understand that many of these assignments are a sham undertaken to placate, not educate.

Another year, the fourth- or fifth-grade students were asked to study Black scientists and inventors during February. My daughter was assigned to do a report on Jan Ernst Matzliger, who invented the shoe-lasting machine. Matzliger was a fascinating man whose story is certainly worth telling, for there is much that all children have to learn from it. Born in 1852 in Suriname, which was then known as Dutch Guiana, Matzliger came to the United States around 1873 and settled in Lynn, Massachusetts, where he worked as a shoe-machine mechanic while working on his invention. My daughter's assignment was to write about Matzliger's life and his invention and to illustrate her report with a poster depicting the four most significant events in his life. The first event she chose to illustrate was his birth, however, the picture she painted was less a reflection of multicultural awareness than of ignorance. Over the caption "born in 1852," she painted a picture of a log cabin surrounded by pine trees. The only paradigm for rags-to-riches success that she had been taught led her to place

Matzliger in an Abe Lincoln–style log cabin, complete with smoke coming out of the chimney. And nobody told her that Suriname looked different from Kentucky. Did her teacher even notice? Perhaps there was no need. Coke and Pepsi signs line the streets leading to and from the airports in every major city, and Pizza Huts, McDonalds, Roy Rogers, and other fast-food chains hawk their wares on the streets of cities all over the globe. Why do I think it matters that my daughter believes that people in Suriname in mid-nineteenth-century lived in log cabins?

Teaching about other countries as though they were simply poor imitations of our own eliminates the very awareness of differences that multicultural education is supposed to bring about; talking and teaching about "women" one month and "African-Americans" another constructs the majority of people in our society as "minorities" and "other." It implies that they have not earned the right to a place in the "real" curriculum and can enter only by means of a kind of curricular affirmative action that sets aside certain places for them. This is both true and false.

In fact, we continue to need this kind of curricular affirmative action precisely because before it existed, these authors, this content, these peoples, were simply left out. We need these focus months because their existence has generated funding and interest for subjects and materials previously ignored or unavailable. Recently, I visited the public library and discovered that the Children's Collection now includes several biographies of Paul Laurence Dunbar. They are written in an accessible style and include appropriate excerpts from his work. Without a Black History Month, it is unlikely that even one such book would have been published. Eliminating Black History Month or Women's History Month now would be premature. But continuing to teach their content as we do can only subvert their intent.

There is another way. We can start teaching from a curriculum that acknowledges the race, gender, and class differences that have shaped every aspect of the world we live in today. We can teach our students to identify their impact and to understand that eliminating their pernicious effects is in *everyone's* interest. We can stop apologizing for our efforts to create a more inclusive curriculum, and we can start helping parents, teachers, and students understand why we need to do so. Young white boys in fifth grade who angrily mouth their parents' objections in school by asking when they will have *white* history month or a *men's* history month need to be told that education, like society at large, has been racist and sexist and that these special focus months are attempts to redress *everyone's* ignorance. Owning the past can only enhance the future. Failing to acknowledge our past leaves the present confused and confusing. Naming injustice for the sole purpose of assigning blame will divide us; identifying injustice in order to address it has the potential to move us toward a society that values both diversity and community.

EPILOGUE

There are just a few peas left now. She mashes them without determination, almost unaware, against the back of the fork. The water from
the peas finds its way to the remains of the whipped potatoes, and
this now congealed mass of indistinguishable flavors and textures is
pressed on his unwilling mouth. He tries to say that he wants a little
soup, but his lips are too dry, and besides, even if he could make the
effort, she would not hear. She brings the fork to his mouth, but he
shakes his head. The fork remains suspended in midair, not because
she yields to his unspoken request but because her mind is in another
part of the city, inventorying her tiny kitchen and wondering what
she will give the children to eat tonight. Forty-five minutes until she
can take off the soiled pink nurse's aide coat and slip her feet into the
cracked black vinyl shoes that wait in her locker in the basement. The
fork sways back and forth in the air until a sound in the corridor re-
calls her attention. Impatiently she pushes the fork toward his mouth.
Will he never be done?

Eyeing the food, he is filled with revulsion. His eyes are drawn to
the half-filled soup bowl. He thinks of a Shabbos meal long ago when
soup was served steaming hot, rich, and thick, and he sat at the head
of the table surrounded by his family. Losing all patience and catch-
ing him unaware, she forces the food into his mouth. He gags. She
reaches for the soup and shovels two heaping spoonfuls into his mouth
with fast, determined movements. She is too quick for him. Some of
the soup trickles down his chin. He wishes that she would wipe him
clean, but she does not notice. He thinks that he will not be able to
stand it if she forces more of the clotted remains of his dinner upon
him.

Mercifully, she abandons the dinner plate and sets upon the Jello. Thirty-five minutes more, and she will be walking to the subway. A cube of strawberry Jello falls onto his thigh. He notices with regret that it contains a scrap of banana. The Jello is sticky sweet. It has begun to melt. It will leave a red stain on his white hospital gown, and he will be scolded for not keeping himself clean.

A nurse sticks her head in the door. She chides Maria for her slowness. There are other patients to be prepared for bed, and only the Jamaican orderly has shown up tonight. Maria puts down the spoon abruptly and pulls the napkin-bib from around my father's neck, brusquely wiping his chin. His face burns, but a sticky wetness still coats the corner of his mouth. As Maria leaves the room, his hand feels for the terry-cloth towel that usually hangs on the arm of his chair. But it has fallen to the floor, and he cannot retrieve it.

By the time my father died at the age of eighty-two, he had lived for twelve years at the Daughters of Rebecca Geriatric Center in the Bronx. At the end, it was difficult to believe that the man who greeted me on my halfhearted visits to the home was in fact my father. For one thing, my father always wore a blue suit, but the man at the home wore an improbable assortment of browns and greens; no blues were allowed. Was it possible that the daddy of my childhood, who once charged pounds of corned beef and lox with a wave of his hand, had turned into this rag and bone, slightly rancid, man sitting in a vinyl-covered chair and looking out a window? Could it be that the same hands that now clutched a soiled terry-cloth slop towel once offered me Little Lulu and Archie and Veronica? Did those matchstick arms once hold me and give me comfort? Did I really hide in the doorway as he said his prayers, afraid to incur his displeasure?

From the time he first went to live in the home, I was ambivalent about my visits. Sometimes I thought they made it worse, reminded him of who he no longer was, of the world that continued beyond that building but that he would never enter again. I brought food. I brought him cheese danish and apple turnovers, halvah, packages of M&Ms and Juby Fruits, which he gobbled up greedily and stuffed into his broken mouth. His hunger was enormous.

After a while, they began to pull his teeth. Each time I visited, there was some new sunken place on his jaw testifying to some recent oral surgery. I tried to find out why so many teeth had to be pulled, but no one seemed to know. When I asked him if he was in pain, he usually was so dazed by the latest assault on his being that he could not reply. I remembered a time years before when my father came home early from the office because he had had a tooth extracted. My mother made pudding and applesauce, and there were fresh pillowcases on the bed. A pot of chicken soup simmered on the stove in case he felt up to eating, and the "girl" rushed back and forth replenishing the ice in his ice bag. But at the home, the brown and Black nurse's aides and orderlies have too many patients to care for and troubles of their own, and no one comes to ask how he is or to provide comfort.

For the most part, the administrative staff of this expensive old-age home is made up of white, middle-class, Jewish professionals with college degrees and MSWs. They treat the Puerto Rican janitors, Jamaican orderlies, and West Indian nurses with a mixture of condescending familiarity and professional distance. Only dark-skinned people empty bed pans at the Daughters of Rebecca. Even the doctors are from India.

When he first entered the home, my father continued to read the daily papers and showed some interest in television news shows. But after a while, the comings and goings of the outside world no longer interested him, and the names in the business section were unrecognizable. Even the obituaries held no charm. Once he went to physical therapy. They showed him how to make a hot plate out of bits of tiles. It sits on the shelf in his room and mocks him.

In the corridor, I am no longer my father's daughter. Each time I visited, I wondered whether the middle-aged Puerto Rican janitor would be at his post pushing a mop and an oversized trash can up and down the hallway. He never takes his eyes off me as I walk the length of the building to my father's room, and he makes soft sucking noises with his mouth when I come near him. I am a thirty-eight-year-old woman, college professor, mother, and writer, but none of this can silence the noises or force him to look away. Daddy, daddy if you only knew.

Several times a year, even after my father had been in the home for what seemed like a lifetime, my mother assured me that he was better off there, that he had better care, better meals, felt more secure. In reality, her assurances were questions, and I responded to them as such, answering that she had no choice, which was of course what she wanted to hear.

The hardest part came at the beginning. On one particular morning, he woke up for the last time in a familiar bed surrounded by the effects of his life. Perhaps he felt for his slippers at the edge of the bed and then awkwardly or firmly, unaided, made his way to the bathroom. Perhaps he was unable to raise himself from the mattress, and my mother helped him. By the time I arrived, he was sitting at the dining room table drinking the last cup of morning coffee he will ever have in his home. It has been sweetened with sugar and softened by a touch of cream. For the last time, someone has prepared his coffee with the thought of pleasing him. But he has drunk his coffee like this for years and even now takes it for granted, does not realize that it too is a fragile comfort. He drinks from a small cup that feels familiar to his lips and eats cereal and toast from the same English china that he has used every day of his married life. He remembers, or perhaps does not remember, his young bride showing off her choice and asking if he is pleased.

After breakfast, while they are waiting for the car to arrive, he sits for the last time in a room with long muted floral-print drapes the color of fall; his feet rest on an old and worn but richly colored Oriental rug. This is the home he has labored to build for his family, the proof that he has been a good husband and father. This home represents all the years of his life. Had he known long ago as a young boy that he would live in such a home, he would not have believed it possible. Perhaps it was never possible, was never more than a dream, for were it really his, how could it be snatched away from him now?

He is frightened. He can hardly move his body. Someone, several people, are helping him, half carrying, half supporting, half pushing him into the waiting car. Soon it will be over. His last memory will be the respectful tip of the doorman's cap when he shuts the door.

After my father went into the nursing home, my mother moved down the hall and into a studio apartment to save money on the rent. She managed to take the Oriental rug with her as well as a few of the other good pieces, but the drapes had to go. I tried to tell her that she might be able to afford a comfortable one-bedroom apartment by moving back to the West Side. But when asked to choose between a bedroom and a doorman, she unhesitatingly chose the latter.

She got a job working in the gift shop at the Metropolitan Museum of Art, where along with others of her class and gender she might pretend that paid labor was just an extension of the volunteer work that she had performed all her life. Once a week, sometimes twice, she ordered a car from the Jerusalem cab company and made the trip to the Bronx to visit my father.

A few months before my father died, my mother was diagnosed with lung cancer. She arranged his funeral as she prepared for her own. She did not consider undergoing any treatment for her condition, assuring me that, as many women but few men have believed, losing her hair to chemotherapy would be worse than dying. Instead, she set about making the best of whatever time remained and began to put her affairs in order. Always a trim and fashionable woman, she tried to gain pounds at the beginning of her illness, knowing they might buy her extra time at the end.

When it was clear that she could no longer care for herself, she arranged with an agency for a succession of nurse's aides to provide her with home care. In the beginning, they came to spend the day with her, helping her dress, taking her for a walk, bringing in some groceries, keeping her company while she watched the endless stream of daytime TV shows that had long been her companions and now were theirs as well.

These women traveled early in the morning and late at night from faraway neighborhoods in Queens and Brooklyn, where they kept house for their grown sons or brothers or occasionally their own small children. They varied in age from women in their thirties who were recent arrivals from the Caribbean to older women who had lived here for many years and were themselves moving slowly toward the ends of their own lives. They worked twelve-hour shifts, arriving at eight in the morning and leaving at eight at night. My mother's relationship with them was something like the one she had had with Verlene, who had traveled from Harlem several times a week to clean the large apartment so many years before—part servant, part confidante, occasional friend. As her condition worsened and it became impossible for her to stay alone, she arranged for them to stay for two shifts, and she handwrote a note that she taped to the wall by the phone giving instructions that she was not to be moved to a hospital or to be resuscitated under any conditions.

During my telephone calls and visits, she carefully praised the care she was receiving, flattering and cajoling whichever dark-skinned woman was on duty at that time. She tipped them generously and sent them home with the leftovers of the meals that her illness made it impossible for her to enjoy or with an article of clothing she would never wear again. When I arrived, she packed them off to do errands or to take a walk and then worried out loud about whether they were stealing things from her. She complained about the woman who never came on time and always left early, about the ones who ate up all her food and bought from the market only items that they enjoyed. Toward the end, my mother's refrigerator and cupboard were filled with an unusual array of Goya food products that would have been unrecognizable to her and with cuts of meat she would not have known how to prepare or name.

Until she could no longer do so, she kept careful records of who had worked each day and how many hours they had been there so she could check her monthly bill from the service. In an engagement book from the Metropolitan Museum filled with pictures of artwork depicting the flowers and gardens of ancient China, my mother recorded the hours worked by Zelda and Patrice and Bernadette and Hilda.

In contrast to the previous year's book, which was filled with lunch appointments and an occasional dinner and trip, this book's entries are reduced to the bare bones of an invalid's life. There are occasional visits from Anne Marie, a young neighborhood beautician who came to the apartment now and then to wash and set my mother's hair. There is one mention of a meeting with a neighborhood rabbi who would conduct her funeral and another with her attorney. In contrast to the notations of birthdays of friends and family carefully recorded in ink in my mother's meticulous hand, which must have been entered all at once when she first purchased the book, the writing from January to May grows more and more out of control until it ends abruptly with almost unreadable entries scrawled in pencil as the cancer attacked her brain.

By then, the women who came from the agency were new. Not having known my real mother, they took little interest in caring for the disoriented and frail woman she had become who could no longer charm or bribe them. Once I found her sprawled on the Oriental rug next to her chair while an attendant I had never met watched TV close by.

The doctor she had visited so regularly and pointlessly for two years in the hope that her visits and the fees she paid for them would buy her home visits when she was housebound declined to come to her apartment even when the tumor from her lung began to grow out through the back of her shoulder, creating a painful and sore protrusion that made it difficult for her to sit or lie down comfortably.

On the last day of my mother's life, the aide called me early in the morning to say that she thought the end was coming. My brother and I drove to the city together to watch her die. When we arrived at the apartment, the aide was already dressed to leave. She led me into the tiny studio kitchen and pointed to a pair of cheap wooden salt and pepper shakers and a napkin holder and asked if she could have them. If I ever see my mother again, this is the first thing she will say to me: "My body wasn't even cold, and you were giving away my things. Couldn't you wait until I was dead to pick over the remains?" Of course, she will be right. But then, so was I. What my mother had, even at the end, still looked like so very much—who could blame the aide for wanting to carry a piece of it away with her, and who would begrudge it to her? Some would say that she had earned it.